Lecture Notes in Computer Science 14618

The series Lecture Notes in Computer Science (LNCS), including its subseries Lecture Notes in Artificial Intelligence (LNAI) and Lecture Notes in Bioinformatics (LNBI), has established itself as a medium for the publication of new developments in computer science and information technology research, teaching, and education.

LNCS enjoys close cooperation with the computer science R & D community, the series counts many renowned academics among its volume editors and paper authors, and collaborates with prestigious societies. Its mission is to serve this international community by providing an invaluable service, mainly focused on the publication of conference and workshop proceedings and postproceedings. LNCS commenced publication in 1973.

Giovanna Broccia · Antonio Cerone
Editors

From Data to Models and Back

11th International Symposium, DataMod 2023
Eindhoven, The Netherlands, November 6–7, 2023
Revised Selected Papers

Springer

Editors
Giovanna Broccia
ISTI - CNR
Pisa, Italy

Antonio Cerone
Nazarbayev University
Astana, Kazakhstan

ISSN 0302-9743 ISSN 1611-3349 (electronic)
Lecture Notes in Computer Science
ISBN 978-3-031-87216-7 ISBN 978-3-031-87217-4 (eBook)
https://doi.org/10.1007/978-3-031-87217-4

This Springer imprint is published by the registered company Springer Nature Switzerland AG
The registered company address is: Gewerbestrasse 11, 6330 Cham, Switzerland

Preface

From Data to Models and Back (DataMod) is an annual, international symposium which aims to bring together practitioners and researchers from academia, industry and research institutions interested in the combined application of computational modelling methods with data-driven techniques from the areas of knowledge management, data mining and machine learning. The present proceedings marks the 11th edition of the symposium.

Over the last decade, DataMod has covered a wide range of themes and topics. The modelling and analysis methodologies covered in the DataMod series include: *Agent-based Methodologies*, *Automata-based Methodologies*, *Big Data Analytics*, *Cellular Automata*, *Classification, Clustering, Segmentation and Profiling*, *Conformance Analysis*, *Constraint Programming*, *Data Mining*, *Differential Equations*, *Game Theory*,*Membrane Systems*, *Network Theory and Analysis*, *Ontologies*, *Optimization Modelling*, *Petri Nets*, *Process Calculi*, *Process Mining*, *Rewriting Systems*, *Spatio-temporal Data Analysis/Mining*, *Statistical Model Checking*, *Text Mining* and *Topological Data Analysis*.

The symposium welcomes applications of the above listed methodologies in a multitude of domains, such as: *Biology*, *Brain Data and Simulation*, *Business Process Management*, *Climate Change*, *Cybersecurity*, *Ecology*, *Education*, *Environmental Risk Assessment and Management*, *Enterprise Architectures*, *Epidemiology*, *Genetics and Genomics*, *Governance*, *HCI and Human Behaviour*, *Open Source Software Development and Communities*, *Pharmacology*, *Resilience Engineering*, *Safety and Security Risk Assessment*, *Social Good*, *Social Software Engineering*, *Social Systems*, *Sustainable Development*, *Threat Modelling and Analysis*, *Urban Ecology*, *Smart Cities and Smart Lands*.

Synergistic approaches may include:

1. the use of modelling methods and notations in a knowledge management and discovery context,
2. the development and use of common modelling and knowledge management/discovery frameworks to explore and understand complex systems from the application domains of interest.

The 11th edition of DataMod (DataMod 2023) was held as a two-day event co-located with the 21st International Conference on Software Engineering and Formal Methods (SEFM 2023).

All contributions in the form of regular papers were reviewed by at least three Program Committee members using single-blind peer review, and were evaluated on the basis of originality, contribution to the field, technical and presentation quality, and relevance to the symposium. EasyChair was used as an online system for both submission and review, including a discussion among Program Committee members to finalise the acceptance/rejection decisions.

From 8 regular paper submissions, a total of 6 papers were accepted for presentation at the symposium and inclusion in this volume. Additionally, 2 presentation reports were submitted. Presentation reports concern recent or ongoing work on relevant topics and ideas, for timely discussion and feedback at the workshop, based on a paper which recently appeared (or which is going to appear) in the proceedings of another recognised conference, or which has not yet been submitted. The 2 presentation reports submitted to DataMod 2023 concerned works that had not been submitted to other conferences. After a lightweight review to establish their relevance for DataMod, they were accepted for presentation at the symposium. After the symposium, the two presentation reports were extended to regular papers and were reviewed by three experts in computer science and computational modelling. They were accepted for publication and appear in this volume.

DataMod 2023 had two invited speakers. The first invited presentation was given by Carmen Bratosin (TNO — Netherlands Organization for Applied Scientific Research, The Netherlands) on "Formal Methods and Domain Models in the Age of Large Language Models: An Industrial Perspective". The talk explored the role of domain models in the engineering domain, emphasising their indispensable contribution alongside data science and AI techniques. While AI models enhance applications and efficiency, Bratosin argued that domain models, rooted in precise syntax and semantics, remain fundamental to the success of AI in industry. The second invited presentation was given by Natalia Sidorova (Eindhoven University of Technology, The Netherlands) on "Navigating the Complexity: From data to models of weakly-structured processes". The talk addressed the challenges of analysing complex, weakly-structured processes by mining models from process execution data and performing conformance checking using a decompositional approach. It illustrated methods for extracting meaningful events from unstructured text data, tailored to weakly-structured processes, with case studies from the healthcare industry highlighting real-world applications.

November 2024

Giovanna Broccia
Antonio Cerone

Organization

Program Committee Chairs

Giovanna Broccia	ISTI-CNR, Italy
Antonio Cerone	Nazarbayev University, Kazakhstan

Steering Committee

Oana Andrei	University of Glasgow, UK
Antonio Cerone	Nazarbayev University, Kazakhstan
Vashti Galpin	University of Edinburgh, UK
Riccardo Guidotti	University of Pisa, Italy
Marijn Janssen	Delft University of Technology, The Netherlands
Stan Matwin	University of Ottawa, Canada
Paolo Milazzo	University of Pisa, Italy
Anna Monreale	University of Pisa, Italy

Program Committee

Oana Andrei	University of Glasgow, UK
Juliana Bowles	University of St Andrews, UK
Giovanna Broccia (Co-chair)	ISTI-CNR, Italy
Antonio Cerone (Co-chair)	Nazarbayev University, Kazakhstan
Ricardo Czekster	Aston University, UK
Flavio Ferrarotti	SCCH, Austria
Vashti Galpin	University of Edinburgh, UK
Riccardo Guidotti	University of Pisa, Italy
Lars Kotthoff	University of Wyoming, USA
Livia Lestingi	Politecnico di Milano, Italy
Sotiris Moschoyiannis	University of Surrey, UK
Paolo Milazzo	University of Pisa, Italy
Anna Monreale	University of Pisa, Italy
Reshma Munbodh	Brown University, USA
Mirco Nanni	ISTI-CNR, Italy

Lucia Nasti	GSSI, Italy
Michela Quadrini	Università di Camerino, Italy
Paolo Zuliani	Università di Roma "La Sapienza", Italy

External Reviewers

Davide Basile
Laura Bussi
Marta Marchiori Manerba

Contents

Natural Language Processing

Domain-specific Modeling and Analysis

Integrated Data Representation and Formal Analysis for Human and In Silico Experimentation in Cognitive Psychology

Antonio Cerone[1(✉)] and Graham Pluck[2]

[1] Department of Computer Science, School of Engineering and Digital Sciences, Nazarbayev University, Astana, Kazakhstan
antonio.cerone@nu.edu.kz
[2] Faculty of Psychology, Chulalongkorn University, Bangkok, Thailand
graham.ch@chula.ac.th

Abstract. This paper presents a novel framework aimed at enhancing the experimental methodology within cognitive psychology, integrating both informal and formal components to accommodate varied reasoning approaches. The framework supports the design and performing of experiments, and the structured storage of the information on outcomes in a way that is independent of specific interpretations and findings. This facilitates the replication and reproduction of the experiments and their interpretation under alternative theories. Moreover, the formal components of the information stored can be used for in silico simulation as well as within rigorous analytical approaches, such as formal methods and process mining.

Keywords: Cognitive psychology · Experiment builder · In silico simulation · Data storage · Experimental variables · Formal methods · BRDL · Real-Time Maude · Process mining

1 Introduction

Cognitive psychology research is mostly based on experimental methods to investigate the intricacies of human thought and reasoning and how these affect human behavior. In fact, around 97% of published research in cognitive psychology reports on experiments [28]. Key points of these research methods are the *interpretation*, normally based on a specific, commonly-accepted theory, and the *reproducibility* of the experiments. Reproduction refers to repeating analyses on the original data set to see if the same interpretation is reached. This is in

Work partly funded by Project "K-RSL4P—Kazakh-Russian Sign Language Processing: Data, Tools and Interaction", Nazarbayev University, Kazakhstan (Award number: 11022021FD2902).

G. Broccia and A. Cerone (Eds.): DataMod 2023, LNCS 14618, pp. 3–23, 2025.
https://doi.org/10.1007/978-3-031-87217-4_1

contrast to replication, which involves using the same experimental methods to collect a new data set and see if the same interpretation is reached [22]. The theory on which the experiments are based provides the assumptions on which the researcher builds the interpretation. However, such assumptions also tend to drive the way data are preserved for possible reproduction of the experiments. This may results in a biased selection of the 'relevant' data, which potentially excludes some aspects of the data that could be helpful for exploring alternative interpretations of the experiment outcomes.

In the literature, we can find a number of frameworks and computer applications that aim at facilitating the design and performing of experiments in behavioral science, including psychology, neuroscience and linguistics [4,19,21]. However, some of these tools (e.g., PEBL [19] and PsychoPy2 [21]) may be applied to many psychological or even behavioural science disciplines, and such a generality conflicts with the possibility of defining a standard set of controls, stimuli and reactions to be preserved in the data storage process. Other tools, on the other hand, have a very restricted focus, such as the comparison of computer applications in a human-computer interaction context (e.g., CogTool [4]). Moreover, these tools often fall short in offering a cohesive structure that marries informal reasoning with formal, executable models.

In this paper, we define a framework that focuses on experiments conducted within the area of cognitive psychology and define a general experimental design model that integrates informal and formal aspects as well as a way to provide a structured description of experimental data.

In Sect. 2, we informally describe how experiments with human subjects are conducted in cognitive psychology and we introduce some terminology. In particular, we focus on experiments aiming to understand how human memory works and how its logical components interact with each other and support various aspects of human reasoning and behaviour. Two categories of classical experiments are introduced in order to provide illustrative examples through the paper. In Sect. 3, we define our experimental design model. In Sect. 4, we show how our framework can be used to perform in silico experiments and apply formal methods, specifically model checking, in order to compare and validate alternative cognitive models. We also suggest how to carry out process mining to explore the outcomes of experiments with human subjects in order to discover anomalous behaviour, enhance the in silico model and analyse its conformance with the reality. In Sect. 5, we draw conclusions and explore possible future work.

2 Experiments in Cognitive Psychology

A typical experiment in cognitive psychology consists of two main parts:

presentation in which some *stimuli* are presented to the subject aiming at a certain *target*;

reaction in which the subject has to react to the stimuli by providing a *response*, which may or may not be required to equal the target.

These two parts may occur sequentially as two separate phases, whereby all the stimuli are provided first and then the subject provides the responses, or be interleaved, whereby the subject provides a response after each stimulus.

A *stimulus* may be of several kinds:

numerical such as a digit of a number or any number or anything with a numerical semantics (for example, a number of dots denoting a number);
character-based such as any utterable character in a written language or any sequence of such characters, in any case with no explicit semantics associated with it (e.g. meaningless words);
semantics-based such as a meaningful word, statement or question;
symbolic such as a simple symbol or icon, which the subject can associate with a precise semantics either conventionally or intuitively;
visual such as a detailed drawing or photo or other forms of images, whose richness and multiplicity of information stimulates complex analysis rather than immediate associations.

Such a categorisation of stimuli covers all possible variants we normally find in experiments conducted within the area of cognitive psychology. However, in this paper, we will limit our illustrative examples to meaningless but utterable sequences of letters (*character-based stimuli*), and words and sentences (*semantics-based stimuli*).

A *target* may be one of the following:

- identical to the stimulus,
  - either to be recalled by the subject (*recall experiment*),
  - or to be recognised among a number of presented alternatives (*recognition experiment*);
- matching the stimulus, with respect to some relation between the two (*matching experiment*), where
  - either a *unique matching* is correct,
  - or *alternative matchings* are possible and any of them may be the single outcome of the response,
  - or *multiple matchings* have all to be captured as the outcome of the response.

In a recognition experiment, the wrong alternatives associated with the target are called *foils* or *distractors*. If the stimulus is semantics-based, various kinds of matching experiment are possible. For example, if the stimulus is a meaningful word, various forms of association may be investigated (the target may be another word or even an image); if the stimulus is a statement, the subject may be asked to assess its validity (the target is either 'true' or 'false' and the foils have the opposite truth value); if the stimulus is a question, the subject may be asked to answer (the target is the correct answer).

The purpose of an experiment is expressed in terms of research statements, called *hypotheses*, that make a prediction on its outcome. The experiment either *confirms* or *rejects* the hypotheses. It is important to note that a hypothesis can only be confirmed but never be proved to be true, whereas rejecting a hypothesis means to prove that it is false.

In general, a stimulus may have a large set of possible values, even an infinite set. For example, meaningful words of a language are normally of the order of hundreds of thousands, and the number of meaningful sentences is potentially infinite. However, the hypotheses normally identify aspects of stimuli that are apt to manipulation as well as the effect of such a manipulation. Such aspects are called *independent variables* (IVs). The manipulation consists in assigning different values to the IV, which we call *levels*. For example, we might consider the number of syllables of a meaningful or meaningless word as an IV; the levels are the possible values of this number.

The effect of the manipulation is captured by *dependent variables* (DVs), which are usually directly identified by the hypotheses. In fact, a hypothesis is normally stated in terms of the difference in the DV that is supposed to be caused by distinct levels of the IVs. A hypothesis is normally conceived as a general statement in natural language, but is then made more formal once the IVs and DVs are identified. For example, if our general hypothesis is that it is easier to remember meaningful rather than meaningless words, then we need to use two kinds of stimuli, character-based for meaningless words and semantics-based for meaningful words. Then the IV could just be a boolean, with two possible levels, meaningful and meaningless, and the DV would be the percentage of words remembered. Therefore, the hypothesis can be stated more formally as 'the percentage of meaningful words remembered is higher than the percentage of meaningless words remembered.'

Distinct ways of manipulating IVs are called *conditions*. When there is only one IV with only two levels, which describe the presence and absence of a condition, then we talk about *experimental condition* and *control condition*, respectively. With reference to the example above, the condition is the presence of meaning in the word, thus meaningful words are the experimental condition and meaningless words are the control condition. When we have more than one IV and/or one or more IVs that can have more than two values, then we may have alternative experimental conditions

At the other end of the spectrum, an extreme case in cognitive psychology experiments is when we have a single condition aiming at defining the profile of an experimental subject. For example, we might want to determine the level of knowledge of word meanings of a subject who is going to take part in the experiment described previously, since the same word might be meaningful for a subject with a high level of knowledge and meaningless for a subject with a low level of knowledge.

Research hypotheses are normally based on an existing theory and the corresponding experiments aim at validating or extending such a theory. Therefore, the theory or some of its aspects define the assumptions under which the experiments are carried out. Some of these assumptions are *essential* while others are just *preferred*. For example, in the memory experiment discussed above, an essential assumption is that memorisation is facilitated by linking what we try to memorise (e.g. a specific word) with what we already know (the meaning of the word). Moreover, a preferred assumption could be that, whenever possible, we try to associate the word with some form of visualisation driven by its meaning.

In order to illustrate this terminology, in the following two sections we consider two classical categories of experiments, which will be our ongoing case studies throughout the paper. In general, an essential assumption defines a theoretical framework underlying the hypothesis that the experiment aims to validate, while preferred assumptions are compatible with such a framework, but cannot be confirmed by the experiment.

2.1 Collins and Quillian's Experiments on Semantic Memory (SM)

In the 1960s Ross Quillian produced a computer program to model a semantic network of about 850 words [24]. Within the data representation, all properties were linked to each other within interconnected hierarchies. This model used multiple kinds of inter-connections between properties to produce an in silico representation that sat somewhere between natural language and symbolic logic, and aimed to efficiently represent meaning in terms of English-language dictionary definitions. Initially the efficiency of the semantic network was tested by comparing how well intersections of meaning could be calculated. However, as the network was biologically-inspired, based on a model of how a human semantic network within long-term memory might be organised, later studies examined experimentally how people responded to requests, using response time as indicator of processing efficiency. These experimental studies on human cognition (SM) aimed to test whether human performance was consistent with the semantic network previously modelled in silico, or on the other hand, it was consistent with a model in which attributes of concepts were stored repetitively locally. For example, whether the concept of living thing was associated with each entry for different types of animal, or whether it was associated with the higher-order concept of animal, and inherited by all subtypes of animal.

We consider experiments belonging to the category of unique matching that were conducted by Collins and Quillian [14]. The general hypothesis was that if the previously modelled semantic network were true for human long-term memory stores, response times would increase as greater distance across the network was needed to verify statements. A typical semantics-based experiment involved presentation of statements in text on a computer screen [14]. For the presentation phase each sentence was shown for two seconds, and the experimental subject, sat in front of the screen, gave their reaction by pressing a switch with one index finger to indicate true, or with their other index finger to indicate false. This was repeated over multiple trials to build up a set of response times for different statement types. In the classical SM experiments by Collins and Quillian [14] stimuli are statements in the English language. At the most basic level, there were two types of statements, those in which the correct response would be 'true' (e.g., 'An elm is a plant') or those in which the correct response would be 'false' (e.g., 'A poplar has thorns'). In fact, the target can be either value 'true' (e.g., for 'An elm is a plant') or value 'false' (e.g., for 'A poplar has thorns'). The former of these, verifications of the truth of statements, are of primary interest. Obviously, it is necessary to include an equal number of trials with statements which are not true, randomly assorted with the trials containing true statements, otherwise the subject would be able to accurately respond 'true' on each trial without processing the meaning.

At a finer level, statements could be either property (P-statement) or superset (S-statement). A P-statement refers to a statement that can be verified by moving with n steps through the hierarchy to reach a property that affirms the statement. For example, given the hierarchy 'canary $\rightarrow$ bird $\rightarrow$ animal', the 'is yellow' attribute could be a property of 'canary'. In contrast, when n steps through the hierarchy are required to verify a statement that occurs by encountering the superset, this is called an S-statement. As an example, to decide that a canary is a bird, one has to move one step up the hierarchy from the word 'canary' to the word 'bird'. In this notation, we can also add the number of steps taken, thus an Sn-statement is the superset statement and a Pn-statement is a property statement, for which we have to move n levels up in the hierarchy to verify truth. For example, 'a canary is yellow' is a P0-statement, 'a canary is a canary' is an S0-statement, 'a canary can fly' is a P1-statement, assuming that 'can fly' is an attribute of 'bird', and 'a canary is an animal' is an S2-statement.

Collins and Quillian [14] in their experiments assumed that

1. both directly retrieving a property at a specific level and moving up a level in a hierarchy take time;
2. the times for these two processes are additive in the two cases of
   - moving up more than one level, and
   - retrieving a property after moving up

   (in accordance with Donders' assumption of additivity [26]);
3. the time to retrieve a property is independent of the level of the hierarchy;
4. searching for properties at a specific level and moving up a level my occur in parallel.

They considered assumptions 1–3 essential and assumption 4 preferred. They investigated human performance of classifying true and false for P0, P1, and P2 statements, as well as S0, S1 and S2-statements. In the context of their experimental setting, if RT denotes the reaction time, their general hypothesis can be refined into the following two hypotheses:

SM-H1 If $n > m$ then the RT of an Sn-statement is greater than the RT of an Sm-statement

SM-H2 If $n > m$ then the RT of a Pn-statement is greater than the RT of a Pm-statement

Such hypotheses were confirmed by the results of the experiments, consistent with their theory, previously developed in silico, that human semantic memory may consist of hierarchies of connected items and properties.

The hierarchical nature of the semantic network was later deemphasised in favour of a spreading activation mechanism [13]. Indeed, many aspects of the network originally proposed have been questioned. Nevertheless, as a classic study in cognitive science, Quillian's work modelling semantic networks remains pertinent to understanding the organisation of concepts and provides the foundations for more recent semantic network theories [16]. In particular, the overall effect of time taken to respond reflecting organisation of the semantic system is still well recognised in experimental cognitive psychology [3]. Furthermore, the sentence verification task has been adapted directly from the original network models of Collins and Quillian, and is still used in applied tools to gauge efficiency of semantic memory in clinical and psychoeducational contexts [17].

2.2 Experiments on Memory Decay and Rehearsal (DR)

A fundamental distinction is made in cognitive psychology between memory that is stored for immediate use, over a matter of seconds, usually called short-term memory (STM), and for memory traces that are robust for periods over several minutes to several years, usually called long-term memory (LTM) [1].

The evidence for dual, relativity independent stores comes from classic psychology experiments involving free recall (DR). As an example, Glanzer and Cunitz [15] used a slide projector to display a sequence of 15 words to research participants. All the words were semantic-based stimuli in the forms of simple English nouns consisting of the same number of letters. Each stimulus was presented for 1 000 milliseconds, with a 2 000 milliseconds inter-stimulus interval (presentation phase). After all stimuli were presented, the subject was asked to free recall all of the words that they are able to (reaction phase). Each subject performed these presentation-then-reaction phases several times, each time with new stimulus words. The experimenters found that free recall accuracy depended on the serial position within the list. There was a bimodal distribution producing a U shape graph, such that words early in the list were well recalled (*primacy effect*), and words late in the list were also well recalled (*recency effect*), words towards the middle were recalled relatively less frequently [15].

The experimenters, Glanzer and Cunitz, argued that this data is best explained by recall from distinct memory stores, early words from LTM, and later words from STM [15]. This distinction is still very widely accepted today and forms a cornerstone of human memory research, in both cognitive psychology and neuroscience. It is, for example, integral for the recent versions of the Multistore Working Memory Model [2], the most widely accepted cognitive interpretation of human memory. In fact, the STM store, particularly that which is targeted in the semantic-based experiments described here, is functionally equivalent to the phonological loop component of the Multistore Working Memory Model [9].

Glanzer and Cunitz's classic experiments also showed that different experimental manipulations could selectively affect the primacy and recency effects, providing further support for their functional differentiation. Firstly, the effect of lack of opportunity for rehearsal of information in the period between the presentation and reaction phases differently affects the STM-based recency effect, leaving the LTM-based primacy effect intact. Rehearsal is the process of looping the target words within STM storage (i.e., silently repeating them to yourself).

That strategy potentially holds information as long as it can be rehearsed for, negating the rapid decay which usually limits duration of STM traces to a few seconds. This is why STM is often nowadays interpreted as a phonological loop [2]. In fact, if rehearsal is blocked, phonological memory traces in STM appear to have a duration of no more than 10 s, and probably somewhat less [18].

In the original Glanzer and Cunitz experiments, they had some of the free recalls occur immediately after the last stimuli word was presented. As expected, there was a pronounced recency effect. However, in some trials there was a completion delay inserted between stimuli presentation of either 10 or 30 s, in which the subject had to wait until attempting the free recall. This effectively removed the recency effect, leaving the primacy effect unattenuated. Importantly, attenuation of the recency effect only occurred if the delay was filled with an activity that requires STM storage, such as counting out loud [15]. This is because the additional activity prevents rehearsal looping which could otherwise be used to maintain the STM trace across the completion delay. Experimental manipulation of completion delays is therefore an important factor that can be used to isolate different components of human memory storage. The second notable experimental manipulation used by Glanzer and Cunitz was presentation rate. In that way, they were able to show that slowing presentation rate enhances the LTM-based primacy effect, but not the STM-based recency effect. This is opposite to the influence of a completion delay, and likely, occurs because slow presentation of stimuli allows for greater rehearsal of items during the actual presentation phase. The ability to control the rate that stimuli are presented is therefore also an important experimental manipulation in cognitive psychology.

2.3 What Historical Data to Preserve

It is fundamental to keep a history of all instances of the experiment, including the apparatus and technology used for the setting, the interpretations used, the analysis carried out and the presentation of the findings. Such a history can be used to evaluate the impact that the apparatus and technology have on findings and to compare the outcomes of replications with those of previous experiments. This may contribute to identify pitfalls in previous interpretations and define more appropriate interpretations, replicate the experiment procedure and/or the analysis process with the support of advanced technologies which were unavailable at the time of a previous instance of the experiment, and improve the representation and presentation of the findings.

For the SM experiments, Fig. 1(a) illustrates some original outcomes. For each knowledge domain the three level of statements, Sn for supersets and Pn for properties, in the hierarchy (1, 2 and 3) are mapped onto the corresponding mean reaction time RT. According to the two hypotheses, **SM-H1** and **SM-H2**, and the essential assumptions 1–3, the resultant RT curves for the Sn and Pn should be parallel straight lines. Considering the hierarchy 'canary → bird → animal', there is an anomaly for S0 point, which corresponds to statement 'A canary is a canary' in the knowledge domain of animals. Collins and Quillian's interpretation of this anomaly is that the subjects use pattern matching on the two occurrences of the word 'canary' rather than thinking about the meaning of the statement, as documented by spontaneous reports from several subjects, thus reducing the RT with respect to the expected retrieval time. We can observe that the use of pattern matching was possible because true S0 statements, such as 'A bird is a bird' were coupled, with false S0 statement, such as 'A canary is a fish', thus enabling the subject's strategy to classify S0 statements as true by using pattern matching and as false based on their semantics. We could then replicate the experiment by replacing 'A canary is a fish' by 'A fish is not a fish', thus preventing the subject from discriminating between the two S0 statements using pattern matching, provided that we also include true S0 statements, such as 'An insect is not a mammal', to prevent pattern matching on the word 'not'. It would be interesting to see whether this change would remove the anomaly.

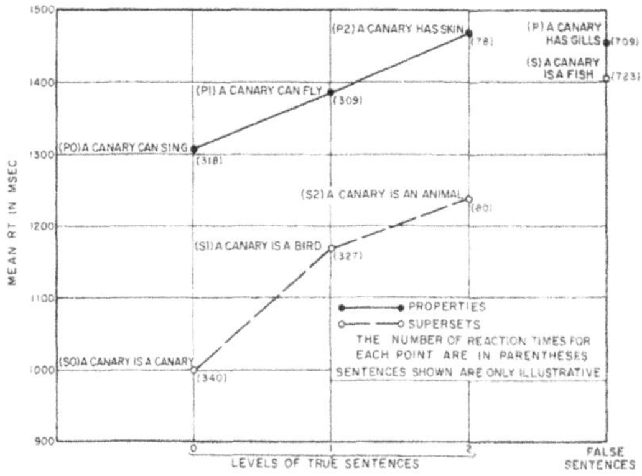

(a)

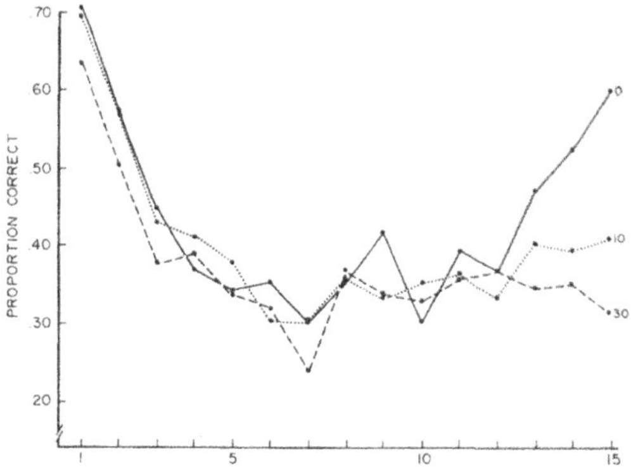

(b)

Fig. 1. (a) Average reaction times for different types of sentences in Collins and Quillian experiments (SM) [14]. (b) Serial position curve for 0, 10 and 30 sec. delay in Glanzer and Cunitz' experiments (DR) [15].

For the DR experiments, the serial position curve in Fig. 1(b) highlights the primacy and recency effects. In terms of experimental setting, it would be interesting to see how the frequency of words affects the curve. The experiment could be replicated by selecting words with a frequency within a given range, thus reducing the effect of frequency, or by using easily utterable but meaningless sequences of letters, thus ruling out the issue of frequency. In terms of interpretation and analysis, it would be interesting to understand whether the order of recall effects the outcome. In order to enable this sort of reinterpretation and alternative analysis, it is important that the order of recall is not lost while storing the dataset, although we are considering a free-recall experiment. In fact, we could speculate that if the subject tried to first recall early presented words, the time involved in the process might result in the decay of the late presented words, which have not been rehearsed, and, as a consequence, in a reduction of the recency effect. On the contrary, if the subject tried to first recall late presented words, the recency effect would be maximised and there would be no substantial impact on the primacy effect, since early words have been rehearsed.

Returning to discussion of the SM experiments, rather than using statements the experiment might have been conducted using questions (e.g., either 'Are elms plants?' and 'Do poplars have thorns?' or 'Is an elm a plant?' and 'Does a poplar have thorns?') as stimuli with a 'yes'/'no' answer as a response. Although Collins and Quillian do not discuss these possible alternatives, we can observe that the use of statements instead of questions as stimuli is more appropriate for the purpose of the experiment, that is, measuring the response time. In fact, deciding the validity of a statement is likely to better reflect the mental process of information retrieval from semantic memory and is more immediate than first decoding a question and then accessing the corresponding information stored in semantic memory.

Linguists distinguish between the structures of sentences that we speak and hear, called *surface structure* or *s-structure*, and their basic structure, called *deep structure* or *d-structure*, which is believed to be more similar to our mental representation of their meanings. When we speak and hear we apply transformational rules respectively from d-structure to s-structure and vice versa [12,23]. As a result, the additional time required for transforming the *s-structure* of a question into the *d-structure* of the corresponding statement might be greater than the actual retrieval time from semantic memory. Consequently, this could produce substantial and variable differences in response times for different questions, obscuring the actual difference between distinct retrieval times. This is especially true for the English language, in which the transformation process is quite complex due to the use of either inversion (e.g., 'Are elm plants?' and 'Is an elm a plant?') or the interrogative auxiliaries 'do', 'does' and 'did' (e.g., 'Do poplars have thorns?' and 'Does a poplar have thorns?'). Therefore, it is important that all original stimuli and responses, as well as their time- and context-related aspects, are preserved in the storage of the experiment data. This is essential not only for reproducing the experiments but also for interpreting its results.

3 Design and Dataset Description Framework

Outcomes of experiments are normally recorded in an unstructured way or, when structured, the imposed structure and information to store are usually driven by the goals of the experiments, especially in terms of the kind of planned analysis, or they might even be effected by subjective biases. Such a recording and organisation of data often determines a loss of information and, after an interpretation of the results is chosen, further information may be removed because it is considered irrelevant. If in the DR experiments the order of recall is not recorded, since it is irrelevant in a free-recall experiment, then some of the hypotheses discussed in Sect. 2.3 cannot be validated. Therefore, in this section, we provide a methodology for structuring experiment outcomes in a general way that is not affected by the goals of the experiments and is neither driven by the planned analysis nor affected by the chosen interpretations. Moreover, we provide definitions that can be used for both human and in silico experimentation.

We start considering the kind of stimulus we need to use. We can observe that a numerical or character-based stimulus is a *basic stimulus*, whose properties are *internal*, in the sense that they can always be inferred from its syntactical representation, though sometimes through complex algorithms. For example, possible properties of an integral number are being odd, even or prime, and possible properties of a meaningless, but utterable sequence of characters are its length or the number of syllables comprising it. Instead, a meaningful word has a number of *external* properties that are related to its usage and semantics rather than its syntax. It is the case of the word frequency and the word meaning. Therefore, this sort of stimulus, which we call *complex stimulus*, has to be stored in a database that associates a set of external properties with it. In the case of external properties of words or sentences, there are a number of linguistic databases to refer to. For the English language we refer to the web-based interface to the British National Corpus[1] (BNCweb). A corpus is a large and structured set of texts from speech transcription and/or written language usage, which includes annotations that identify the roles of words within sentences and extracts properties of words such as their frequencies. In addition, dictionaries, such as the Cambridge English Dictionary,[2] can be sources for the word semantics.

Therefore, complex stimuli are defined together with their properties within a database. A stimulus entry in the database is formally defined as follow.

Definition 1. *A* **stimulus entry** *consists of*

a key *for accessing the stimulus;*
a type *which can be a* text *or a* reference*;*
a representation *which is an ascii sequence if the type is text or a link to another database if the type is reference;*
external properties *whose number and quality depends on the nature of the stimulus and may be restricted depending on the nature of the experiment.*

[1] http://bncweb.lancs.ac.uk.
[2] https://dictionary.cambridge.org/dictionary/english.

A word would be of type text and would normally have its key identical to its representation. External properties associated with the nature of the word are syntactic category (e.g., noun, verb, etc.), grammatical category (e.g., for nouns: gender, number, etc.), semantic category (e.g., for nouns: concrete or abstract.), meaning definitions, frequency and dispersion.[3] Internal properties, such as length and number of syllables, do not need to be included in the entry since they are explicit in the representation.

A statement would also be of type text and its key might or might not be the same as its representation, depending on the requirements of the experiment. A meaningful code associated with the level of the statement may be more useful an access key than the statement representation. For the SM experiments, a key could encode statement type (S = superset or P = property), level in the hierarchy (0,1,2), source point in the hierarchy, truth value (0 or 1) and target point in the hierarchy. For example, statement 'An elm is a plant' would have 'S2elm1plant' as the key (true 2-level superset hierarchy: elm $\subseteq$ tree $\subseteq$ plant).

For the DR experiments, relevant external properties of words are syntactic, grammatical and semantic categories, frequency, frequency rank and dispersion, whereas a meaning definition is too fine-grain a property to be relevant. In fact, it is important to use words that are familiar (high frequency and dispersion close to 1) and can be easily visualised (concrete nouns with singular gender).

There is no rule of thumb to decide which restrictions should be imposed by the nature of the experiment. Common sense should be used here. For example, for the DR experiments, meaning definitions may not be considered relevant, since the human subject is not expected to retrieve a formal definition of the word from semantic memory, but just to read the word. Thus the only relevant semantic aspect of the word is the fact of being a singular concrete noun.

3.1 Experimental Design Model

Information on the experimental design needs to be stored in a detailed way in order to enable reproducibility and support the interpretation process. Experimental design is a very creative process and involves several interconnected aspects, which cannot be captured within a formal process but require a rigorous, though informal description, normally in natural language. As we discussed in Sect. 2.3 it is also important to keep a history of all instances of the experiment as a reference for future replication and variants of the experiment.

Definition 2. *An* **experimental design** *consists of the following components:*

experiment identifier *which is unique for each experiment;*
design version *which is a sequential number greater than 0;*
condition identifier *which is a sequential number greater than or equal to 0, with 0 denoting a* control condition, *and a positive number denoting an* experimental condition*;*

[3] Dispersion measures the distribution of a word over different parts of the corpus. A value close to 1.00 indicates that a word is perfectly spread all over the corpus.

experiment type *which can be one of the following:* recall, recognition, unique matching, alternative matchings *and* multiple matching;

experiment instructions *in textual form, to appear at the beginning of the presentation;*

research hypotheses *as a list in which each research hypothesis consists of an* identifier *and a* textual description;

set of independent variables (IVs) *with each IV consisting of an* identifier *and a* textual description;

set of dependent variables (DVs) *with each DV consisting of an* identifier *and a* textual description;

set of stimulus presentations *with each stimulus presentation associated with*

- *a* stimulus key, *which is the key in the stimulus entry,*
- *a* sequential position *which is a sequential number greater than 0,*
- *a* presentation duration *in ms (milliseconds),*
- *a* presentation location *which may be* centre, top, bottom, left *or* right,
- *a* presentation size *which may be* small, normal *or* large,
- *an* interstimulus interval, *which is the time in ms between the end of the current stimulus and the start of the next stimulus in the sequence, randomly selected between* min *and* max *time or fixed if* min = max,
- *a* pre-response delay, *which is the minimum time in ms after the start of the stimulus when a response can be recorded, with 0 denoting that the subject's response may already occur at the start of the stimulus,*
- *a* completion delay, *which is the maximum time in ms after the start of the stimulus when a response can be recorded, with 0 denoting that there is no limit to the delay of the response;*
- *an* IV mapping, *which maps each IV identifier into a value;*
- *a set of* targets;
- *a possibly empty set of* foils;

assumptions *as a list in which each assumption consists of an* identifier, *a* significance, *which may be either* essential *or* preferred, *and a* textual description;

The experiment identifier is common to all instances of the experiments, which may be carried out with different design versions.

Collins and Quillian [14] ran three different variants of the SM experiment. In our formal definition, the experiment identifier would be the same for all three variants, say SM. Each of the three variants would have a distinct sequential number as design version, that is, 1, 2 and 3. In the first experiment (design version 1) each subject reads 128 two-level sentences followed by 96 three-level-sentences. The statements are grouped in runs of 32, with a rest period of 1 min between runs. The statement appears for 2 s in normal format in the centre of the screen followed by a blank screen for 2 s before the next statement appears. The subject's response can occur any time within the 4 s between the start of the consecutive stimuli. Therefore:

- the presentation duration is 2 000 ms;
- the presentation location *centre*,
- the presentation size *normal*;
- the interstimulus interval is min = max = 2 000 ms, except for the last statement of each run for which it is min = max = 60 000 ms.
- the pre-response delay is 0 ms.
- the completion delay is 4 000 ms.

The two research hypotheses and the four assumptions have been presented in Sect. 2.1. Each presented statement is characterised by the following three IVs:

1. $k \in \{S, P\}$, the kind of statement, either S-statement or P-statement;
2. $h \in \{0, 1, 2\}$, the number of level in the hierarchy we have to move up to decide the truth value of the statement, which may be 0, 1 or 2;
3. $v \in \{0, 1\}$, the truth value of the statement, with 0 representing $false$ and 1 representing $true$.

The set of DV is $\{RT\}$. The hypotheses predict that RT is different for different levels of h. Thus, as an example, for the statement 'An elm is a plant':

- the IV mapping to values is $k = S$, $h = 2$ and $v = 1$, which are reflected in the stimulus key 'S2elm1plant'
- the set of targets is $\{1\}$, which represent the truth value $true$;
- the set of *foils* is $\{0\}$, which represent the truth value $false$.

3.2 Structured Description of Experiment Data

We see an instance of a given experiment as a sequence of structured *experimental events*. Each of them is a record of information, which includes a number of fixed components but can be extended with further components, whenever needed.

Definition 3. *An* **experimental event** *(or simply* **event***) consists of*

event identifier *to identify the event;*
experiment identifier *to identify the experiment;*
design version *to identify the design version;*
case *to specify the specific instance of an experiment with a specific subject;*
instance type *to denote the purpose of the instance of the experiment among:*

exploration *to discover information aiming at defining the human subject's profile,*
profiling *to extract subject's information aiming at defining the human subject's profile,*
learning *to deliberately carry out transfer of learning to the subject,*
practice *in which the subject gets familiar with the experiment,*
trial *in which the experiment is used to test its suitability,*
performance *in which the experiment is used with human subjects for its planned purpose,*

- **simulation** *in which a model simulates the human behaviour,*
- **event type** *which can be either* presentation *or* response*;*
- **subject identifier** *to identify a specific human or model as the subject;*
- **value** *which is either the key of the presented stimulus or the response value,*
- **timestamp** *which is the start time of the event.*

The access to the experimental design through the experiment identifier and the design version equips an experimental event of all relevant information.

The timestamp, together with the temporal parameters defined in the experiment design, fully provides the temporal characterisation of the event and its sequential position within the case. A further benefit of storing events with timestamps, is that it allows for greater detail of analysis of the data. Traditionally, cognitive science has emphasised the importance of temporally dense data on human performance in experiments [25]. Such temporally dense data potentially allows for a microscopic analysis of processes underlying performance, and how they may be active at different time points.

When an instance of an experiment is created, the experiment identifier and the design version are selected among the available designs of experiments defined in the database, by the experimenter, who also chooses an instance type. For example, the experimenter may select design version 1 among SM experiments (SM identifier). The *profiling* instance type can be used to evaluate the response time of the subject to a purely visual stimulus separately for the right and left hand. This test can be implemented by asking the subject to push specifically one of the two buttons as soon as any sentence appears on the screen. The *learning* instance type can be used to analyse how learning occurs in using pattern matching rather than semantic meaning. The *practice* instance type allows subject to practice with the experimental procedure and apparatus before taking the actual experiment. The *trial* instance type is for testing the experiment. Obviously, the *performance* instance type should not be used with the same human subjects who serve in the same experiment with an incompatible instance type. For example, those who test the experiment cannot take part in the actual experiment. In fact, perfomance is incompatible with exploration, learning and trial, but it is compatible with profiling and practice. The *simulation* instance type is for in silico experiments, in which subject identifiers identify models of human behaviour rather than real humans.

The instance type is chosen by the experimenter and, depending on it, the subject identifier is either assigned by the experimenter or automatically assigned by the system. Table 1 shows the first eight events for the first SM experiment. For example, the first event (with identifier 1) is the presentation of the statement 'An elm is a plant' to subject with identifier 'H001'. The timestamp is the seconds since the epoch provided by any Python interpreter and rounded to the milliseconds. The second event (with identifier 2) is the response of the subject. The timestamp shows that it occurs 146 milliseconds ($146 = 907 - 761$) after the start of the presentation. This is the value of the dependent variable RT.

Table 1. Example of event log of the first eight events for the first SM experiment: 'An elm is a plant', 'A canary can eat', 'A pine is barley', 'A birch has seeds'.

Case	Ev	Exp	Vers	Instance Type	Subj	Ev Type	Value	Timestamp
1	1	*SM*	1	performance	H001	presentation	S2elm1plant	1716378651.761
1	2	*SM*	1	performance	H001	response	*true*	1716378651.907
1	3	*SM*	1	performance	H001	presentation	P2pine0barley	1716378655.761
1	4	*SM*	1	performance	H001	response	*false*	1716378656.099
1	5	*SM*	1	performance	H001	presentation	P2canary1eat	1716378659.761
1	5	*SM*	1	performance	H001	response	*true*	1716378660.103
1	7	*SM*	1	performance	H001	presentation	P2birch1seeds	1716378663.761
1	8	*SM*	1	performance	H001	response	*true*	1716378664.081

4 Human Versus In Silico Experiments

Experiments with human subjects and in silico experiments may be compared according to three perspectives:

global perspective in which the global result of the experiment (for example, the serial position curve in DR) for human subjects is compared against in silico models;
local perspective in which the result of the experiment (for example, the serial position curve in DR) for each category of human subjects with a given profile is compared with the result for the in silico model for that category.
unitary perspective in which each result of the experiment on a single human subject (for example, the serial positions of the recalled words in DR) is compared with the result for the in silico model of that subject.

Although the global perspective already gives a rough idea of how the model reflects the reality, it does not directly provide an explanation about why this happens. For example, the global serial position curve in DR does not show that the primacy effect is due to rehearsal. This interpretation is the result of the analyst's intuition and reasoning in linking the outcomes of the experiments to an existing model or theory from cognitive psychology. In the case of DR, the outcomes are linked to the Multistore Working Memory Model. However, the link may be the actual result of the analyst's belief or even bias and cannot be validated using a conceptual, nonexecutable model.

If the conceptual model is implemented into an executable model, as in our previous work [8,9,11], validation is instead possible. The local perspective has the purpose to facilitate such a form of validation. Categories of subjects may be defined using various forms of data collections: interviews/questionnaires, observations or experiments. These three forms of data collection can be captured by our notion of experimental event with profiling instance type. In fact, questionnaires can be designed using a matching experiment with some empty components (e.g., research hypotheses and sets of variables) and closed questions defined as stimulus presentations. Observations may be emulated using interactive tasks augmented with instrumented code that records reaction times, habits and other patterns of behaviour. Profiling data is then stored in the database, where it is accessed by experimental events through the subject identifier field.

For example, in the case of DR, we can validate the hypothesis that the number of words in the primacy effect may be affected by a number of parameters: the actual STM capacity, which limits the number of words that may be rehearsed simultaneously, the language used in the mental phonological rehearsal process (e.g., Welsh number words are slower to pronounce than English words, leading to an average digit span of 5.8 versus 6.6 items), which affect the measured STM capacity, the chunking ability, which increases the amount of information stored in STM as a single item, and the STM decay time, which affects the number of words we are able to rehearse. These characteristics of the human subject can be measured through preliminary profiling experiments and associated with the human subject entry in the database. Then, for each identified category of human subjects, a distinct in silico experiment is carried out with a different combination of the considered parameters: STM capacity, word processing time, chunking factor and decay time. This allows us to analyse each of the parameters in isolation as well as in various combination by running multiple instances of the in silico experiment. The comparison of each in silico experiment with an experiment with human subjects belonging to a compatible category highlights which parameters affect the primacy effect and to which extent they do so.

The profiling data can also be used singularly to define a specific model for each human subject. The resultant population of human models can be used to emulate an experimentation on the entire population of the human subjects in the database, independently of whether or not those human subjects participated in the actual experiment. The result of the emulation may be compared with actual experiments, limited to the specific models that correspond to experiment participants, using the three perspectives above. In particular, the unitary perspective allows us to carry out a fine-grained validation of the model and identify anomalous outcomes which may need further investigation. Such an investigation may lead to refinement or change of the implemented cognitive model. This approach also provides a continuous validation by predicting the outcome of future experiments with the subject in the database and by running a new single model emulation for each new human subject added to the database and a full population emulation every time the model is modified.

Our approach in modelling in silico experiments [8,9,11] also features model-checking analysis using Real-Time Maude [20]. Using the local perspective, model checking allows us to prove interesting properties concerning a specific category of human subjects. For example, we could limit the parameters considered above in the subject's profile and prove that the number of words in the primacy effect cannot exceed a given threshold that has been observed in reality. This would verify the in silico model by proving that it accurately reflects the reality.

A final usage of our framework is through process mining [27]. Process mining combines model-oriented and data-oriented approaches to analyse processes.

The central idea is to discover, monitor and improve real processes by extracting knowledge from event logs generated by observed instances of such processes. This leads to three kinds of analysis: *discovery* of a process model, its visualisation and, possibly, the identification of pitfalls; *conformance*, that is, the comparison of an existing process model with an event log; *enhancement*, by extending or improving an existing process model using information recorded in some event log. In our case, the existing process model is the one produced through in silico experiments. Event logs are a structured representation of data for which one of the fields, called *case*, characterises a specific instance of the process. As seen in Def. 3, in our experimental events, the case identifies a specific instance of an experiment with a specific subject.

The *discovery* use of process mining on experiments with human subjects can be used to analyse the dynamic of the experiment and discover and analyse pitfalls aiming at improvements in the way the experiment is designed and administered. In the DR experiments, we could find that a specific word has an anomalous behaviour, for example being recalled less often than the others, independently of its position in the sequence. We then check the word frequency and find out that it is considerably lower than the frequencies of other words.

The *enhancement* use of process mining can identify some characteristics of the human subject that are not addressed by the in silico model. For example, in the DR experiments, if the in silico model generates recalls in a random order, among the words still present in STM at the moment of recall, then event logs of experiments with human being would show a different order. Now, if this order shows a pattern, then it is necessary to enhance the in silico model to somehow consider aspects of the words stored in STM that could reflect the order observed in reality. The characteristics of the human subjects associated with a specific ordering pattern could provide important parameters to be incorporated in the in silico model to generate the order of recall.

Finally, *conformance* analysis is based on defined metrics that measure the kind and severity of the deviations in the in silico process with respect to the event logs from experiments with human beings. This measures how the behaviour of the in silico model deviates from the reality.

5 Conclusion and Future Work

In this paper we have proposed a framework to design experiments in cognitive psychology and record data on the design itself as well as the performing and outcomes of the experiments. Data is stored in a hybrid informal and formal format in order to support both informal reasoning and rigorous analysis using in silico simulation, model checking and process mining.

We are currently implementing the framework in a toolset that supports the forms of analysis described in Sect. 4. The toolset will feature the translation of event logs from experiments with human subjects into the representation of human perceptions and human actions in the Behaviour and Reasoning Description Language (BRDL) [5,6] thus supporting in silico simulation and model checking through its implementation in Real-Time Maude [8,9,11].

The toolset will build on a previous web-based tool and portal (ColMASC) for the collaborative modelling and analysis of human cognition, behaviour, and interactive systems [7]. The new toolset will also be based on a web portal and will target researchers in human-computer interaction and cognitive science by supporting collaboration in the design, performance and replication of experiments, both with human subjects and in silico, and will be equipped with tools for their comparison according to the three perspectives introduced in Sect. 4.

The toolset will include a simulation tool to be used not only for in silico experiments, but also for emulating the interaction between computer/physical components and human components. BRDL will be the modelling language for the human components while the use of various modelling languages will be possible for the computer/physical components: variants and extensions of labelled transition systems and Petri nets as well as Real-Time Maude. Additionally, domain oriented modelling and visualisation interfaces will ease the modelling process, making it accessible to cognitive scientists, psychologists and usability experts. The output of the simulation will be converted into various presentation formats, including domain-oriented visual representations, possibly animated, and natural language description according to different linguistic codes to address a variety of experts from computer science, interaction design, usability analysis, psychology, sociology, linguistics and neuroscience. Moreover, the conversion to appropriate exchange formats will provide the interface to external tools, such as process mining tools.

The toolset will also include an analysis tool, which will exploit the Real-Time Maude model-checker to carry out formal verification of interactive systems and to validate theories in cognitive psychology and neuroscience. This tool will also aim at addressing domain experts by making use of visual interfaces that support high-level definition of properties and visual representations of the outcome of the analysis process.

The collaborative aspects of the toolset will be provided through the web portal and will include:

- collaborative design of experiments and interactive systems;
- synergetic collaboration between computer system designers on one side and domain expert involved in experiments aiming at studying various aspect of the human-system interaction;
- comparison of experiments conducted by distinct teams;
- replication and reproduction of the experiments;
- reinterpretation of previous experiments;
- online testing of system protoypes;
- online access to a large number of experimental subjects and users for an extensive period of time and creation of rich subject and user profiles;
- sharing, comparison and reuse of data from subjects/user profiles and experiment outcomes.

Obviously, the toolset will be built incrementally, by incorporating existing modules developed in previous work [7–10] as well as developing the new modules. Finally, the development will proceed through three phases:

1. functionalities for design, simulation and analysis and their use through a command-line interface;
2. definition of the domain-oriented interfaces for design and the visual representations, natural language description and animations for simulation;
3. definition of the domain-oriented interfaces for property specification and the visual representations for the analysis and comparison processes.

Orthogonally to these three phases, the toolset will be applied to a number of case studies of interactive systems and experiments in cognitive psychology, neuroscience and linguistics and will be deployed on a public website.

References

1. Atkinson, R.C., Shiffrin, R.M.: Human memory: a proposed system and its control processes. In: Spense, K.W. (ed.) The psychology of learning and motivation: Advances in research and theory II, pp. 89–195. Academic Press (1968)
2. Baddeley, A.: The episodic buffer: a new component of working memory? Trends Cogn. Sci. **4**(11), 417–423 (2000)
3. Beckage, N.M., Colunga, E.: Language networks as models of cognition: understanding cognition through language. In: Mehler, A., Lücking, A., Banisch, S., Blanchard, P., Job, B. (eds.) Towards a Theoretical Framework for Analyzing Complex Linguistic Networks. UCS, pp. 3–28. Springer, Heidelberg (2016). https://doi.org/10.1007/978-3-662-47238-5_1
4. Bellamy, R., John, B., Richards, J., Thomas, J.: Share on using CogTool to model programming tasks. In: Proceedings of PLATEAU 2010. ACM (2010)
5. Cerone, A.: Behaviour and reasoning description language (BRDL). In: SEFM 2019 Collocated Workshops (CIFMA), LNCS, vol. 12226, pp. 137–153. Springer (2020). https://doi.org/10.1007/978-3-030-57506-9_11
6. Cerone, A.: Modelling and analysing cognition and interaction. In: Formal Methods for an Informal World — ICTAC 2021 Summer School, LNCS, vol. 13490, pp. 30–72. Springer (2023). https://doi.org/10.1007/978-3-031-43678-9_2
7. Cerone, A., Mengdigali, A., Nabiyeva, N., Nurbay, T.: A web-based tool for collaborative modelling and analysis in human-computer interaction and cognitive science. In: Proceedings of DataMod 2021. LNCS, Springer (2022). https://doi.org/10.1007/978-3-031-16011-0_12
8. Cerone, A., Murzagaliyeva, D.: Information retrieval from semantic memory: BRDL-based knowledge representation and maude-based computer emulation. In: Cleophas, L., Massink, M. (eds.) SEFM 2020. LNCS, vol. 12524, pp. 159–175. Springer, Cham (2021). https://doi.org/10.1007/978-3-030-67220-1_13
9. Cerone, A., Murzagaliyeva, D., Tyler, B., Pluck, G.: In silico simulations and analysis of human phonological working memory maintenance and learning mechanisms with behavior and reasoning description language (BRDL). In: SEFM 2021 Collocated Workshops (CIFMA). LNCS, Springer (2022). https://doi.org/10.1007/978-3-031-12429-7_3
10. Cerone, A., Ölveczky, P.C.: Modelling human reasoning in practical behavioural contexts using real-time maude. In: Sekerinski, E., et al. (eds.) FM 2019. LNCS, vol. 12232, pp. 424–442. Springer, Cham (2020). https://doi.org/10.1007/978-3-030-54994-7_32

11. Cerone, A., Pluck, G.: A formal model for emulating the generation of human knowledge in semantic memory. In: Bowles, J., Broccia, G., Nanni, M. (eds.) DataMod 2020. LNCS, vol. 12611, pp. 104–122. Springer, Cham (2021). https://doi.org/10.1007/978-3-030-70650-0_7
12. Chomsky, N.: Language and Mind. Cambridge University Press (2006)
13. Collins, A.M., Loftus, E.F.: A spreading-activation theory of semantic processing. Psychol. Rev. **82**, 407–428 (1975)
14. Collins, A.M., Quillian, M.R.: Retrieval time from semantic memory. J. Verbal Learn. Verbal Behav. **8**, 240–247 (1969)
15. Glanzer, M., Cunitz, A.R.: Two storage mechanisms in free recall. J. Verbal Learn. Verbal Behav. **5**(4), 351–360 (1966)
16. Jones, M.N., Willits, J., Dennis, S.: Models of semantic memory. In: Oxford Handbook of Mathematical and Computational Psychology, vol. 1, pp. 232–254. Oxford University Press (2015)
17. May, J., Alcock, K.J., Robinson, L., Mwita, C.: A computerized test of speed of language comprehension unconfounded by literacy. Appl. Cogn. Psychol. **15**(4), 433–443 (2001)
18. Mueller, S.T., Krawitz, A.: Reconsidering the two-second decay hypothesis in verbal working memory. J. Math. Psychol. **53**(1), 14–25 (2009)
19. Muellera, S.T., Piper, B.J.: The psychology experiment building language (PEBL) and PEBL test battery. J. Neurosci. Methods **222**, 250–259 (2014)
20. Ölveczky, P.C.: Real-Time Maude and its applications. In: Escobar, S. (ed.) WRLA 2014. LNCS, vol. 8663, pp. 42–79. Springer, Cham (2014). https://doi.org/10.1007/978-3-319-12904-4_3
21. Peirce, J., et al.: Psychopy2: experiments in behavior made easy. Behav. Res. Methods **51**, 195–203 (2019)
22. Peng, R.D.: Reproducible research in computational science. Science **334**(6060), 1226–1227 (2011)
23. Pinker, S.: The Language Instinct. William Morrow (1994)
24. Quillian, M.R.: Word concepts: a theory and simulation of some basic semantic capabilities. Behav. Sci. **12**, 410–430 (1967)
25. Simon, H.A.: Information processing models of cognition. Annu. Rev. Psychol. **30**(1), 363–396 (1979). https://doi.org/10.1146/annurev.ps.30.020179.002051
26. Smith, E.E.: Choice reaction time: an analysis of the major theoretical positions. Psychol. Bull. **69**, 77–110 (1968)
27. Aalst, W.: Data science in action. In: Process Mining, pp. 3–23. Springer, Heidelberg (2016). https://doi.org/10.1007/978-3-662-49851-4_1
28. Youyou, W., Yang, Y., Uzzi, B.: A discipline-wide investigation of the replicability of psychology papers over the past two decades. Proc. Natl. Acad. Sci. **120**(6) (2023). https://doi.org/10.1073/pnas.2208863120

Probabilistic Model Checking of Temporal Interaction Dynamics in the Supreme Court

Susmoy Das(✉) and Arpit Sharma

Department of Electrical Engineering and Computer Science, Indian Institute of Science Education and Research Bhopal, Bhopal, India
{susmoy18,arpit}@iiserb.ac.in

Abstract. The Supreme Court plays an extremely critical role in ensuring adherence to the rule of law and in strengthening the democracy. Due to this reason, modeling and analysis of small group interactions in the courtroom setting is an important task as it can help in understanding court decision-making. We apply probabilistic model checking for the modeling and analysis of temporal interaction dynamics in the context of the Supreme Court of the United States. We have used the transcripts of the oral arguments of cases from the Supreme Court for constructing a discrete-time Markov reward model (DTMRM). Next, we formulate interesting queries over interaction by using probabilistic computation tree logic (PCTL) and PCTL with rewards and verify them using a probabilistic symbolic model checker (PRISM). Our experimental results show that probabilistic model checking is very effective in identifying trends, hidden patterns, and how justices behave during the trials. These results not only provide valuable feedback to the justices but may also be used by the advocates and law students for finding better ways to present their arguments in the court.

Keywords: Interaction analysis · Markov chains · Temporal patterns · Logic · Model checking · Social sequence

1 Introduction

Supreme Courts play a key role in modern democracies as they focus on cases of the greatest public and constitutional importance. They are responsible for upholding the rule of law and for ensuring that the rights of all citizens are preserved. It is, therefore, extremely important to study, model, and analyze the temporal dynamics of interactions [10] in the courtroom setting for understanding court decision making, and how justices and advocates behave during the trials. For example, it may be used to answer the following queries: how often do justices react to each other?, does the behavior of a justice change when he/she and the rest of the bench have opposite views on the case?, how would the bench react whenever an advocate expresses negative sentiment in his/her arguments?,

G. Broccia and A. Cerone (Eds.): DataMod 2023, LNCS 14618, pp. 24–45, 2025.
https://doi.org/10.1007/978-3-031-87217-4_2

and is there a necessary critical mass of self-conscious justices which can guide the resolution of a case?. Modeling temporal interactions and detecting behavioral patterns that emerge over time is a very complex and time-consuming task.

This paper presents a novel application of probabilistic model checking for modeling and analysis of temporal interaction dynamics in the context of the Supreme Court of the United States. Probabilistic model checking [5] is an automated verification technique that is widely used for the evaluation of performance and dependability of information processing systems, e.g., randomized protocols. State-of-the-art probabilistic model checking tools such as Probabilistic Symbolic Model Checker (PRISM) [20], and Storm [12,16] have been developed to model check Probabilistic Computation Tree Logic (PCTL) [5,14] and PCTL with rewards [2] on discrete-time Markov chains (DTMCs) [5]. We have used the transcripts of the oral arguments of cases from the 'Supreme Court Oral Arguments Corpus' [8,11] for constructing a discrete-time Markov reward model capturing the interaction behavior in the courtroom scenario. A discrete-time Markov model has been used because the group interactions involving spontaneous and unscripted speech are known to follow the Markovian property [3,22]. Every case has been converted into a trace, i.e., a sequence of utterances where each utterance is represented as a state, i.e., 10-tuple of this model. In other words, states have been used to store important information about every utterance of the case, e.g., speaker name, speaker side, votes side, utterance type, and utterance sentiment. The state transition probabilities have been computed directly from the transition counts in the corpus. Next, we specify interesting properties over behavior using PCTL and PCTL with rewards and verify them on the PRISM model checker.

Our experimental results show that probabilistic model checking of courtroom behavior can be very effective in analyzing the interactions and identifying trends and hidden patterns. For example, our results demonstrate that except for one justice, all the other justices tend to participate in the trial right from the start. Similarly, it was observed that cases where a unanimous verdict was passed, were not only shorter in length than average, but the justices also had limited involvement (interventions) in these cases. In contrast, cases where the bench is divided, i.e., $5-4$ are not only longer than average but the expected number of interventions from the justices is also higher than average. Another interesting observation is that like-minded jurors tend to jointly intervene the advocates of the opposite side during the trials. Our results also show that rebuttals usually go unintervened, but for certain cases, they may result in long one-on-one conversations between a justice and an advocate. Finally, our results also empirically validate the claims made by popular newspaper articles, e.g., [9,21]. This type of analysis can be very helpful for the justices as it provides them valuable feedback to enable better coordination, information about specific issues that need to be handled, and to find out how they actually vote. Additionally, it may also be useful for the advocates and the law students as they can identify better ways to present their arguments during the trials. Courtrooms across the globe may also model their cases, and compare/correlate their results with our findings.

To the best of our knowledge, this is the first work on modeling and analysis of temporal interaction dynamics in the courtroom setting using probabilistic model checking. We believe this work would encourage researchers from different disciplines, e.g., computer science, computational social science, psychology, and linguistics to jointly focus on the problems of small group interactions [10] in the judiciary and other related domains.

Organization of the Paper. The rest of the paper is organized as follows. Section 2 briefly discusses the related work. Section 3 recalls the basic concepts of DTMCs, probabilistic logics, and also discusses the ConvoKit dataset. Section 4 discusses the procedure for building a Markovian model followed by Sect. 5 which presents the reward structures and filters. Section 6 defines the queries and analyses them. Finally, Sect. 7 concludes the paper and provides pointers for future research.

2 Related Work

In [4], authors investigate the differences in discourse styles, e.g., information density for various stakeholders involved in the Swedish court hearings. The results have been interpreted using speech accommodation theory. In [15], authors use the transcripts from the U.S. Supreme Court to explore the hypothesis that discourse markers and personal references are important features in models exhibiting the turn-taking behavior of participants. In [6], authors study and measure the pair-wise similarity between adjacent filled pauses in justice-lawyer pairs. Their results show that the mean difference between these pauses was smaller for those justice-lawyer pairs where the justice gave a favorable vote as compared to the pairs where the justice gave a non-favorable vote. In [11], authors show how variations in linguistic styles can provide information about power differences within social groups. For this study, authors have used discussions between editors on Wikipedia and oral arguments of the U.S. Supreme Court. In [13], authors demonstrate using a predictive model that justices implicitly reveal their leanings during oral arguments, even before arguments and deliberations have concluded by extracting emotional arousal using vocal pitch from audio transcripts of the proceedings of the Supreme Court of the U.S.

Unlike these research papers, we focus on end-to-end modeling of the behavior, which enables us to reason about temporal dynamics in peer interaction events in the courtroom setting. The idea of using Markov reward models for studying group dynamics was originally proposed by Murray in [22]. In this paper, a value iteration algorithm has been proposed to estimate the value of every state. Andrei et al. [3] have extended this line of research by empirically demonstrating the expressiveness of probabilistic temporal logic and model checking for the analysis of group dynamics in social meetings.

3 Preliminaries

This section recalls the basic concepts of discrete-time Markov chains (DTMCs) with finite state space and probabilistic computation tree logic (PCTL) used for specifying properties over these models.

DTMC [5,18]: A DTMC is a tuple $\mathcal{D} = (S, AP, \mathcal{P}, s_0, L)$ where: (a) S is a countable, nonempty set of states; (b) AP is the set of atomic propositions; (c) $\mathcal{P}$ is the transition probability function satisfying $\mathcal{P} : S \times S \rightarrow [0,1]$ s.t. $\forall s \in S$: $\sum_{s' \in S} \mathcal{P}(s, s') = 1$; (d) s_0 is the initial state; and (e) $L : S \rightarrow 2^{AP}$ is a labeling function.

$\mathcal{D}$ is called finite if S and AP are finite. Let $\rightarrow = \{(s, p, s') \mid \mathcal{P}(s, s') = p{>}0\}$ denote the set of all the transitions for a DTMC $\mathcal{D}$. We denote $s \xrightarrow{p} s'$ if $(s, p, s') \in \rightarrow$. A sequence of states $s_0, s_1, s_2, \ldots$ where $\mathcal{P}(s_i, s_{i+1}) > 0 \ \forall i$ is an infinite path in a DTMC. We denote a path by π. A finite path is of the form : $s_0, s_1, s_2, \ldots, s_n$ where $\mathcal{P}(s_i, s_{i+1}){>}0$ for $0 \leq i < n$. The length of a finite path, denoted by $len(\pi)$ is given by the number of transitions along that path. The length of the finite path given above is $len(\pi) = n$. For an infinite path π, we have, $len(\pi) = \infty$. We denote the n-th state along a path π by $\pi[n-1]$ ($\pi[0]$ denotes the first state from which the path starts). Let $Paths(s)$ denote the set of all infinite paths starting in s. Let $Paths_{fin}(s)$ denote the set of all finite paths starting in s.

Let $s_0, \ldots, s_k \in S$ with $\mathcal{P}(s_i, s_{i+1}) > 0$ for $0 \leq i < k$. $Cyl(s_0, \ldots, s_k)$ denotes the *cylinder set* [5,24] consisting of all paths $\pi \in Paths(s_0)$ s.t. $\pi[i] = s_i$ for $0 \leq i \leq k$. Let $\mathcal{F}(Paths(s_0))$ be the smallest σ-algebra on $Paths(s_0)$ which contains all sets $Cyl(s_0, \ldots, s_k)$ s.t. $s_0, \ldots, s_k$ is a state sequence with $\mathcal{P}(s_i, s_{i+1}) > 0$, $(0 \leq i < k)$. The probability measure Pr on $\mathcal{F}(Paths(s_0))$ is the unique measure defined by induction on k in the following way. Let $\Pr(Cyl(s_0)) = 1$ and for $k > 0 : \Pr(Cyl(s_0, \ldots, s_k, s')) = \Pr(Cyl(s_0, \ldots, s_k)) \cdot \mathcal{P}(s_k, s')$.

PCTL [5,14]: PCTL is a probabilistic branching-time temporal logic that allows one to express the probability measures of satisfaction for a temporal property by a state in a DTMC. The syntax is given by the following grammar where $\Phi, \Phi', \ldots$ range over PCTL state formulae and $\Psi, \Psi', \ldots$ range over path formulae:

- State Formulae: $\Phi ::== \textbf{true} \mid a \mid \neg\, \Phi \mid \Phi \wedge \Phi' \mid \mathcal{P}_J(\Psi)$, for some $a \in$AP
- Path Formulae : $\Psi ::== \mathbf{X}\Phi \mid \Phi\mathbf{U}\Phi'$

where $J \subseteq [0,1] \subset \mathbb{R}$ is an interval. Satisfaction of a PCTL state formula Φ by a state s or a path formula Ψ by a path π, notation, $s \models \Phi$ or $\pi \models \Psi$ is defined inductively by :

- $s \models \textbf{true}$ always;
- $s \models a$ iff $a \in L(s)$;
- $s \models \neg\Phi$ iff $s \not\models \Phi$;
- $s \models \Phi \wedge \Phi'$ iff $s \models \Phi$ and $s \models \Phi'$;
- $s \models \mathcal{P}_J(\Psi)$ iff $Pr(s \models \Psi) \in J$;
- $\pi \models \mathbf{X}\Phi$ iff $\pi[1] \models \Phi$; and
- $\pi \models \Phi\mathbf{U}\Phi'$ iff $\exists k \geq 0$, s.t. $\pi[k] \models \Phi'$ and $\forall 0 \leq i < k, \pi[i] \models \Phi$.

where $Pr(s \models \Psi) = Pr\{\pi \in Paths(s) \mid \pi \models \Psi\}$.

3.1 The Supreme Court Oral Arguments Corpus

The 'Cornell Conversational Analysis Toolkit (ConvoKit)' [8,11] contains tools that are capable of analyzing conversations and the social interactions embedded within. It provides intuitive and user-friendly abstractions that enable one to both represent and manipulate conversational data. Several interesting conversational datasets are part of this toolkit, and the 'Supreme Court Oral Arguments Corpus' [1] that we have used in our work is also part of this collection. The dataset contains a collection of cases from the Supreme Court of the United States, along with the transcripts of the oral arguments of these cases.

Dataset Details: This dataset is split into different years spanning 1955 to 2019. Each case can be identified uniquely and has the following attributes:

- Speaker-level Information: contains a unique `ID` for each speaker, `name` and `type`, which could either be a justice, an advocate, or an unknown.
- Conversation-level Information: contains a unique `ID`, the `case_ID` giving information about the case to which it belongs, an `advocates` dictionary containing the details of each advocate involved in the case and their `role`, i.e., the side which they represented and if they were *'amicus curiae'* or not, `votes_side` which is again a dictionary where each entry lists the side for which a particular justice voted in that session, and `win_side` which contains the information of the outcome of the case.
- Utterance-level Information: it contains a unique `ID`, `speaker`-information, `conversation_ID`, `case_ID`, `speaker_type` which gives the information if the speaker is a justice or an advocate, `side` the side of the speaker, the utterance `text` and other utterance related information.

We have considered 125 cases from this dataset collected over the span of two years, i.e., 2018 and 2019 as the bench of the justices was identical in both these years. For these subsets of cases, we also had the voting information available for more than half of the bench.

4 Model Construction

We pre-process the dataset to extract and keep the information that is required for modeling the behavior and discard all the other attributes which are not used in our analysis. We construct an interim 'CSV' file. For every case, we convert each utterance to a row in the CSV file which would preserve information about its parent case. Next, we consider every case as a trace, i.e., a sequence of utterances where each utterance is a row of the CSV file. In other words, we have a collection of 125 traces that were used for constructing the DTMC model. Each row has been converted into a tuple which is as follows:

1. Speakers' name: the name of the justice or 'nreq' in case of the advocates;
2. Speakers' side: 'JJ'- for a justice, 'PP'- for the petitioner, 'RR'- for the respondents, and 'SU'- side unknown;

3. AC-value: 'ACYES' if the speaker is an amicus-curiae, 'ACNO' otherwise;
4. Win-side: takes the value 0 if the case was decided in favor of the respondents, 1 if it was in favor of the petitioners;
5. Votes-side: is a 9-tuple representing the individual votes of the nine justices, where 0 at i^{th} position denote that the ith justice voted for the respondents, 1 denotes vote in favor of the petitioner and "IU" means that the information is unknown. Here, the sequence used for the justices is as follows: J_1, J_2, J_3, J_4, J_5, J_6, J_7, J_8 and J_9.
6. Utterance-type: (a) Opening: The chief justice opens the case. (b) Closing: The chief justice closes the case. (c) Conclopening: The chief justice thanks one speaker and gives a turn to the next speaker. (d) Intervening: A justice intervenes a speaker. (e) Normal: Any utterance by an advocate not during the rebuttal. (f) Rebuttal: An utterance by an advocate during the rebuttal.
7. End of Utterance-type: (a) MS- Utterance finished in the middle of a sentence. (b) SF- Utterance finished with a sentence being completed. (c) LG- Utterance finished with laughter (d) NR- Utterance finished with no response.
8. Utterance-sentiment: Sentiment associated with the utterance, i.e., positive, negative, or neutral (no-sentiment).
9. Utterance-length: the length of the utterance, long (LoU) or short (SoU).
10. Number of pauses: the number of pauses in an utterance, i.e., more (MP) or less (LP).

Here, 'Intervening' can take one of the following tags: (a) Intervening(PP/RR) refers to the side that was being intervened (b) InterveningP-PRE denotes that the petitioner is intervened during the rebuttal, (c) InterveningAC(PP/RR) is similar to (a) with the additional property that the speaker is an amicus curiae and (d) Intervening(PP/RR)JJ represents that two or more justices are intervening one after another. For example, a state tagged 'InterveningPPJJ', would require that 'Intervening', 'InterveningPP', and 'InterveningP-PJJ' are all true in that state.

These components jointly constitute the state space of our Markovian model. Furthermore, we introduce two new states: 'Initial' is the initial state of the model, which with equal probability, goes to each unique 'opening' state of a case. Similarly, all the 'closing' states reach a single 'Final' state with probability 1. The state transition probabilities have been calculated using the transition counts obtained from the dataset. For the utterance sentiment, we have used the Natural Language Toolkit (NLTK) sentiment analysis library [7] which calculates the compounded score for each statement in the utterance. Finally, we take the average over all the sentences of an utterance and determine the value of utterance-sentiment. In the case of the last two tuples, for each speaker type, we calculated the average lengths of their utterances and also the average number of pauses used in these utterances. This allows us to identify a threshold that can be used to classify an utterance as either long or short. Similarly, we can also classify an utterance as either with more pauses or with less pauses.

A typical courtroom proceeding begins with the chief justice opening the session and presenting the floor to the petitioner to present their argument. The argument is intervened by the bench of justices following which the chief justice invites the respondents side to present their argument which is also intervened by the justices. In the end, the petitioner gets a chance to present a rebuttal argument following which the chief justice closes the session and submits the case. Note that each side may have multiple arguments during a trial, but the broader framework remains the same. Additionally, there may be arguments by the amicus curiae ('friend of the court'), who is/are permitted to assist the court by offering additional information, perspective, and expertise about the case. An amicus curiae may or may not support any side.

Example 1. Consider the following state: $(J_6, JJ, ACNO, 0, 0, 1, 0, 0, 1, 0, 0, 1, 0), InterveningPP, MS, Neg, LoU, MP)$. This is a state where justice J_6 intervened the petitioner in a case where the respondents won. The utterance was long, and the sentiment was negative. The utterance ended mid-sentence and had more pauses. Here, it can be observed that justices J_2, J_5, and J_8 have voted for the petitioner, and the rest of the justices voted for the respondents.

Example 2. We show a snapshot of our Markovian model in Fig. 1. Here, the state $(NREQ, PP, ACNO, 1, (1, 1, 1, 1, 1, 1, 1, 1, 1), Normal, LG, Pos, SoU, LP)$ is an utterance by a member from the petitioner side who is not an amicus curiae and the argument is not a rebuttal argument. The utterance was small with less number of pauses that ended with laughter. This is a case where the petitioner won unanimously. This utterance was immediately followed (amongst others) by an intervention from J_6 with probability $\frac{1}{7}$, and an intervention from J_2 with probability $\frac{3}{7}$. The intervention by justice J_6 was a long utterance that ended mid-sentence, had a negative sentiment and more pauses. In contrast, the intervention by J_2 was a short utterance with a positive sentiment. The rest of the model can be interpreted in a similar fashion.

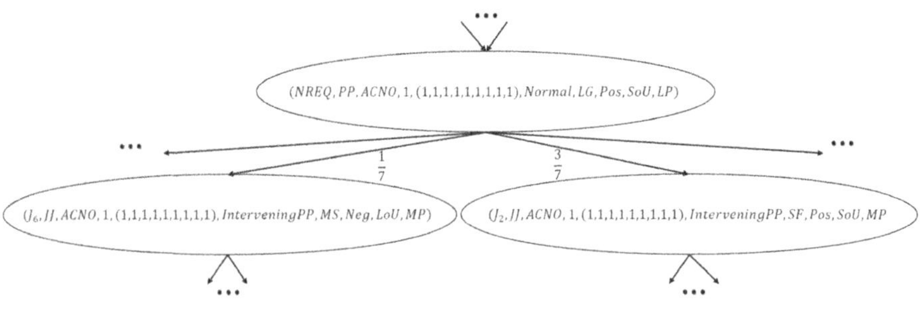

Fig. 1. Snapshot of the Model

5 Reward Structures

For the modeling and verification, we use the PRISM model checker [20], which is widely used for the design and analysis of systems that exhibit probabilistic behavior. PRISM allows us to capture the system behavior using its modeling language and specify interesting properties using PCTL logic. Additionally, PRISM also allows the operator $\mathcal{P} =?$, which computes the probability of satisfying a property.

PRISM also allows us to augment the DTMC models with rewards, which are non-negative real-valued quantities assigned to states [2,19]. The resulting models are known as discrete-time Markov reward models (DTMRMs). We can define multiple reward structures on the same model [2,17]. This enables us to specify interesting reward-based properties using PCTL with rewards, which is also supported by PRISM. Reward-based properties can be broadly classified into two groups: 1) Instantaneous properties - the expected value of the reward at some time point, 2) Cumulative properties - the expected cumulated reward over some period. For example, $R\{r\} =?[C^{\leq n}]$ computes the expected reward cumulated up to time-step n. Similarly, $R\{r\} =?[F\ \Phi]$ computes the expected reward cumulated before reaching the set of states which satisfy Φ.

PRISM uses filters to verify properties that are valid when initiated from a collection of states which meet specific conditions. In this paper, we use two distinct types of filter operators: (a) The filter $(state, \Phi, clause)$ assesses the satisfaction of a state-based formula (Φ) from a state uniquely identified by the Boolean-valued expression ($clause$). (b) The filter $(avg, \Phi, clause)$ calculates the average across all the states where the condition $clause$ holds true. We can replace avg by min or max to get the corresponding minimum and maximum values, respectively from the states where the condition $clause$ holds true.

For the sake of convenience, we introduce the following short forms:

- `jname` can be replaced with the names of any of the justices,
- `side` can be replaced with any of the speakers side,
- `type` can be replaced with any of the end of utterance-type,
- `sentiment` can be replaced with any of the sentiments, and
- `pauses` can be replaced with MP or LP.

Next, we define the following reward structures on the model:

1. `n_step` assigns a value of 1 to each state and is used to compute the number of steps (time);
2. `r_jname_intervening` assigns a value of 1 to each state where `jname` and 'Intervening' is true. It is used to calculate the number of interventions by a particular justice;
3. `r_JJ_intervening_side` assigns a value of 1 to each state where 'JJ' and 'Intervening' is true for a particular `side`. It is used to calculate the total number of interventions by all the justices towards a particular side;
4. `r_jname_intervening_side` assigns a value of 1 to each state where `jname` and 'Intervening' is true for a particular `side`. It is used to calculate the number of interventions by a particular justice `jname` towards a `side`; and

5. `r_type` assigns a value of 1 to each state where `type` is true. It calculates the number of occurrences of each utterance type during a trial.

One can suitably develop more reward structures based on the properties that need to be analyzed and verified.

6 Experimental Results and Analysis

In order to analyze the interaction, we formulate several interesting properties/queries using PCTL and PCTL with rewards, and model check these queries on the PRISM toolset. The PRISM model and all the PRISM queries (PCTL properties and PCTL with reward properties) can be found on the Zenodo repository[1]. Our PRISM model has 10099 states and 24534 transitions including a unique initial state and a unique final state. Throughout this section, we use j in the queries to denote an integer variable which can take values ranging from $0 - 10098$ (number of states in our model).

1. Queries for Validating the Model. (a) What is the expected number of steps required for the first involvement of each role during a proceeding?

```
R{"n_step"}=?[F "side"]
```

The result of this query for the justices would be 1 (as the chief justice opens the hearing), for the petitioner it is $\sim$ 3 as the chief justice offers the floor to the petitioner. For respondents, it is 105 as they participate at a later stage of the trial. The formula `R{"n\_step"}=?[F "CLOSING"]` will provide us with the expected duration of a proceeding, and the result is $\sim$ 234. This shows that the respondents are offered the floor roughly halfway through a trial, as some time also needs to be allocated for the rebuttal towards the end of the trial. This is also expected in a courtroom, where both sides should get the same amount of time for presenting their arguments.

(b) What is the average probability of an event where utterances from the advocates of opposite sides immediately follow each other?

```
filter(avg,P=?[X ("side")],"side")
```

As advocates from one side never directly interact with the advocates of the other side during the trial, it is expected that the value of this query should be 0. This is indeed the case for the following query: `filter(avg,P=?[X ("PP")],"RR")` and its counterpart.

(c) What is the average probability of an event where the model has erroneously skipped the justice name or not abstracted the name of the advocate?

```
filter(avg,P=?[F ("NREQ"&"JJ")],"INITIAL")=0.0
filter(avg,P=?[F ("NREQ"&("PP"|"RR"))],"INITIAL")=1.0
```

[1] https://doi.org/10.5281/zenodo.8166141.

These queries ensure that there are no states in the model where the name of the justice is missing or the name of an advocate has been stored.

(d) What is the probability that the current state and the next state of the model are the same?

```
filter(max,P=? [X(x=j)],(x=j))
```

The result of this query confirmed our expectations that no two utterances can have the same set of values for all the attributes. This is due to the fact that utterances are segregated at those instances where the value of some attribute changes. The filter returned no states with non-zero probabilities, which implies that the probability is 0.

(e) What is the probability that a trial ends where only one side has presented its argument? The property can be encoded in PRISM as follows:

`P=?(!("PP")U("CLOSING"))` and `P=?(!("RR")U("CLOSING"))`

As expected, the value for these queries is 0 as every proceeding must have at least one argument from both the sides.

(f) What proportion of cases went in the favor of the petitioner/respondents?

`P=?[(X("FP"))U("FP")]`=0.58 `P=?[(X("NFP"))U("NFP")]`=0.42

We augment these queries with an additional clause for validating the model. The set of queries and their values are given below:

`filter(avg,P=?[X ("FP")],"NFP")`=0
`filter(avg,P=?[X ("FP")],"NFP")`=0

From the first set of queries, it can be observed that the petitioner has a slight edge in winning the cases as compared to the respondents. The second set of queries assures us that the model does not mix states from cases having different judgments.

(g) What proportion of the judgments went in favor of the petitioner/respondent for each justice? This query can be encoded in PRISM as follows:

```
P=?[(X"jname0")U("jname0")] P=?[(X"jname1")U("jname1")]
```

As mentioned earlier, for a small number of cases, the votes for some of the justices were unknown, and therefore a small probability mass is seen missing while classifying their judgments, viz., J_6 and J_7 (1%), and J_9 (7.4%). As expected, the results of this query also followed the same trend where all the justices have a slight inclination towards giving the decision in favor of the petitioner (except J_6). We also calculated the following: what proportion of judgments were given with a unanimous verdict? The result of this query is 31% where 18% were in favor of the petitioner, and the rest was given in favor of the respondents. In order to further check the correctness of our model, we calculated if a state could be reached where a justice favors the respondent from a state where the same justice favors the petitioner. The corresponding query is as follows: `filter(avg,P=?[(X"jname0")],"jname1")` and `filter(avg,P=?[(X"jname1")],"jname0")`. As expected, the result is 0 for each justice.

(h) What are the expected occurrences of each utterance type during the course of a proceeding? This query can be formalized in PRISM as follows:

```
filter(avg,R{"r_type"}=?[F "FINAL"],"INITIAL")
```

As expected, the model has correctly captured the typical behavior of a courtroom proceeding where there will be a single instance of 'Opening' and 'Closing' (query result = 1). 'Conclopening' refers to the utterance where the chief justice thanks the advocate and moves to the next speaker. As both the sides participate in all the trials and this is followed by at least one rebuttal, the chief justice will need to thank the speakers at least twice. Hence, there has to be a minimum of 2 instances of 'Conclopening' (query result = 3), and at least one instance of 'Rebuttal' (query result = 4). The other occurrences are either 'Normal' utterances (query result = 106) or 'Intervening' (query result = 116) type utterances. The sum of each utterance type is 231.

2. Sentiment Analysis of the Environment in the Courtroom. The first set of queries refers to the long-run probabilities of being in a state of 'Positive/Negative/No-Sentiment' which can be encoded as follows:

```
S=?["Pos"] S=?["Neg"] S=?["Neu"]
```

These queries result in the following values: 0.44, 0.19 and 0.37, respectively. This indicates that the courtroom sentiment is either mostly positive or neutral, with occasional negativity. We can modify these queries to include the roles as well which will provide us with the long-run probabilities for each role with a given sentiment. The modified queries are: `S=?["role"&"sentiment"]`. From these queries, we see that justices are more likely to be neutral (0.2) or positive (0.2) than negative (0.1). The petitioners/respondents mostly express positive sentiments (0.1), followed by no sentiments (0.075) and very few instances of negative sentiments (0.025). We can conclude that the overall sentiment of the courtroom is positive, and justices tend to express neutral or positive sentiments most of the time. In order to check if the stakeholders involved in a trial try to maintain a positive outlook inside the courtroom, we look at the following set of queries and their corresponding values:

```
filter(avg,P=?[X("Pos")],"Pos")=0.51
filter(avg,P=?[X("Pos")],"Neg")=0.44
filter(avg,P=?[X("Neg")],"Neg")=0.23
filter(avg,P=?[X("Neg")],"Pos")=0.15
```

These values suggest that the stakeholders try to not get stuck in the negativity, and make efforts to get out of it. For example, if we are in a state with positive sentiment, then the chances of moving towards positivity (0.51) is much higher than negativity (0.15). Similarly, if we are in a state with negative sentiment, then the chances of coming out from it (0.44) are higher than continuing with the negativity (0.23).

3. What Is the Expected Number of Steps Before each Justice Participates During a Trial? The corresponding queries can be formalized as follows:

```
R{"n_step"}=?[F ("jname")]
```

Note that, we need to modify the query for the chief justice because otherwise, the value is always going to be 1 as he opens the session. The modified query is as follows: `R{"n\_step"}=?[F ("jname"\&!("OPENING"))]`. The average value for all the justices other than J_2 is 33. The maximum number of expected steps is 50 for J_9. This shows that all the justices get themselves involved in the case right from the start and, latest by the 50th utterance which is 20% of a trial. Justice J_2 is an exception, where the expected number of steps for the first involvement is 1134.

4. What Is the Expected Number of Interventions by Each Justice During a Trial? The above query can be translated into PRISM as follows:

```
filter(avg,R{"jname_INTERVENING"}=? [F "FINAL"],"INITIAL")
filter(avg,R{"jname_INTERVENINGside"}=?[F "FINAL"],"INITIAL")
```

We have observed that J_6 intervenes the most whereas J_3 and J_2 intervene much lesser than the average. Interestingly, for J_2, the value is ~ 0.8 which means that there are proceedings where J_2 has remained silent throughout the trial. Additionally, we have also observed that the collective share of interventions towards the petitioners and the respondents side is very even (6/7). This indicates that the judiciary is free and fair.

5. Analyzing the Behavior of a Justice in Cases where His/her Vote Was the only One in Favor of the Losing Side. This situation took place for six of the nine justices from the bench. The expected number of interventions by a justice can be seen from Table 1.

We see that justices tend to intervene less (on average it decreases by $\sim$ 65%). For example, in all the cases where only J_6 voted for the respondents, the expected number of interventions for the RR was only 3 as compared to the expected number of interventions by J_6 for all the cases which is 8. Similarly, J_8 voted for the respondents, and therefore expected number of interventions for the RR was 1 as compared to the expected number of interventions over all possible cases which is 9. Note that J_3 is an exception, where the expected number of interventions is increased by 1 when the justice has voted for the petitioner. For the top three justices in the same table, we also see a rise in the expected number of interventions for the PP (the other side) when the justices voted for the RR.

Table 1. Interventions during normal trials to those where the judgment was $8-1$.

Justices	All cases			$8-1$ Cases			Justice	Outcome	% Change
	Total	PP	RR	Total	PP	RR	vote		In favor
J_6	21	13	8	20	17	3	0	1	−62.5%
J_5	13	6	7	13	12	1	0	1	−85.7%
J_8	14	5	9	12	11	1	0	1	−88.9%
J_3	7	4	3	8	5	3	1	0	25.0%
J_4	18	8	10	4	2	2	1	0	−75.0%
J_2	0.8	0.4	0.4	0	0	0	1	0	−100%
J_2	0.8	0.4	0.4	0	0	0	0	1	−100%

6. Analyzing the Changes in the Behavior of The justice(s) for Special Cases. (a) Cases with unanimous judgment: In these experiments, we try to study the behavior of the justice(s) for cases where the bench had given a unanimous decision. We have compared the expected number of interventions for the cases where the decision is unanimous with the average over all the cases. An example PRISM query is shown below:

```
filter(avg,R{"r_INTERVENING"}=?[F "FINAL"],"OPENING"&
                    "(0,0,0,0,0,0,0,0,0)")
```

This query calculates the expected number of interventions during a trial where the judgment was unanimously favouring the respondents. Other queries can be written in a similar fashion. The detailed results are shown in Table 2. We observe that the expected number of interventions decreases for the cases where there is a unanimous decision. We also see that the share of interventions for the winning side for those cases is less than the average share. Similarly, the share of interventions for the losing side is more than the average share. The share in favour to against becomes $45-55$ approximately as compared to $49-51$ for the average over all the cases (see Table 3 (Unanimous Bench)). The decline in the total number of interventions indicates that the duration of the trials has decreased (in terms of the number of utterances). In other words, cases tend to go longer when the bench of justices differ in their opinion.

(b) Cases where the judgment was $(5-4)$: A similar study was conducted but we now shift our focus to the cases where the bench is most divided, i.e., all those cases which have been decided by a single vote. The queries can be formulated analogously. The results are also shown in Table 2 (Divided Bench). We see that such trials are longer than the average in terms of the number of utterances. Moreover, the involvement of the justices is higher than the average as they tend to intervene more often to get additional insights into the case, which would enable them to make a judgment. Interestingly, we also see a rise in the expected number of interventions for the amicus curiae, showing that justices tend to discuss these cases with the friend of the court to get more clarity on the matter

Table 2. Intervention count comparisons for two extreme scenarios

Expected Interventions	All Cases	Unanimous Bench PP Won	Unanimous Bench RR Won	Divided Bench PP Won	Divided Bench RR Won
Total	115	113	98	125	133
Petitioner	55	51	52	68	67
Respondent	60	61	45	57	65
Amicus Curiae	8	8	7	16	11

Table 3. Percentage distribution of average interventions.

All cases		Unanimous Bench		Divided Bench	
Winning side	Losing side	Winning side	Losing side	Winning side	Losing side
49%	51%	45%	55%	52%	48%

which will help them in reaching a verdict. The intervention share is $52-48$ (see Table 3 (Divided Bench)), which is close to the $50-50$ scenario and implies that both sides are equally intervened for these cases.

7. Analyzing the Behavior of a Justice to His/her favorable/unfavorable Side. In this query, we study the behavior of the justices for the cases where their viewpoint of the case did not coincide with the majority of the bench. We also compare these results for each side (PP/RR) with their corresponding expected number of interventions by the justices. The results are shown in Table 4 where N denotes the expected number of interventions, the tuple (i, j) corresponds to the vote of the justice and the outcome of the case, e.g., $(1, 0)$ means that the justice voted for the petitioner and the case was decided in favor of the respondents. We can see that for the cases where the justice voted for the petitioner and the case went against them, i.e., $(1, 0)$ the expected number of interventions for the petitioner by each justice is smaller as compared to their average interventions, i.e., N. In contrast, the expected interventions for the respondents for $(1, 0)$ cases is higher than their average interventions for the majority of the justices. A similar trend can be observed in the other direction $(0, 1)$ cases. For example, all the justices tend to intervene PP more than their average interventions for these cases. Similarly, the majority of the justices tend to intervene RR less as compared to their averages for cases where justices voted in favor of respondents. Hence, we can conclude that justices tend to intervene more than expected for the advocate who the majority of the bench is convinced with but the justice feels otherwise. Contrarily, the justices intervene less than their averages when the majority of the bench is against them and they favor the advocates.

Table 4. Interventions by justice towards his/her favourable/unfavourable side.

Justice	Intervening PP			Intervening RR		
	N	(0,1)	(1,0)	N	(0,1)	(1,0)
J_1	6.2	10.5	3.5	7.9	7.7	7.3
J_2	0.4	0.6	0.2	0.4	0.6	0.2
J_3	4.2	4.2	3.9	3.3	3.8	4.5
J_4	7.9	11.4	4.9	10.2	7.4	11.2
J_5	6.1	11.1	2.2	6.5	4.2	12.2
J_6	12.6	16.4	8.1	7.7	7.7	17.6
J_7	8.0	9.1	2.7	6.6	5.7	10.5
J_8	5.4	6.7	3.3	8.5	4.5	16.4
J_9	4.5	6.4	2.9	8.5	5.7	12.0

8. Analyzing the Effect of an Intervention by A justice on the Advocate. Next, we investigate the impact of interventions on the advocate. Our assumption is that interventions will force the advocate to change the sentiment of his/her speech. Moreover, interventions also indicate that the original argument prepared by the advocate is not going well, and therefore the advocate needs to change how he/she delivers the argument. This would imply more pauses during the argument as the nature of speech shifts from prepared to organic. We tested our hypotheses by formulating the following PRISM queries:

```
filter(avg, P=? [ (!"JJ"|"INTERVENING") U<=5 (("PP"|"RR")&"sentiment"
        &"pauses")],(("PP"|"RR")&"sentiment"&"pauses"))
```

It was observed that after the interventions, the chances of an advocate's arguments with negative sentiment and fewer pauses turning into positive sentiment with more pauses are much higher (0.48) than the other way round (0.18). If we keep the sentiments aside and modify the query to just calculate the effect of interventions on the number of pauses of an advocate, we also observe a similar trend, i.e., the average probability for the transition from fewer pauses to more pauses in 5 steps is much more (0.82) than the other way round (0.36). Additionally, we also found out that positive interventions from the justices have a higher chance (0.13) of turning an advocate's arguments with negative sentiment and fewer pauses into positive sentiment with more pauses than the other way round (0.08). This implies that the impact of a positive intervention is more profound in forcing the advocate to change the sentiment of his/her argument as compared to the negative intervention. If we keep the number of pauses aside and modify the query for just sentiments, a similar trend can be observed, i.e., the average probability for the transition from negative to positive is 0.64 as compared to 0.23 for the other way around. These queries inform us about how advocates adapt their arguments during a trial, which was also reported in [4] where authors had claimed the following: "Legal professionals routinely change their language considerably as they move from the monological phases of the trials to the rather informal dialogical phases".

9. From an Utterance, What Is the Maximum Number of Times an Advocate Is Intervened During the Next 50 Time Units? The corresponding PRISM query is as follows:

```
filter(max,R{"JJ_INTERVENINGside"}=? [C<=50],"PP"|"RR")
```

The result of this query is 28. More specifically, for the petitioner, the value is 26 and for the respondents, it is 25. We convert these queries to experiments over the entire state space of the model to identify the states with maximum values. The results for the top six states are shown in Table 5.

Table 5. Maximum number of interventions during 50 time units.

(PP,ACNO,0,(0,1,1,1,1,0,0,0,0),Normal,SF,Pos,SoU,MP)	25.9
(PP,ACNO,1,(1,1,1,1,1,0,1,1,1),Normal,MS,Neg,LoU,MP)	24.85
(RR,ACNO,0,(1,0,0,1,0,1,0,0,0),Normal,MS,Neg,SoU,LP)	24.76
(RR,ACNO,0,(0,1,0,0,1,0,0,0,0),Normal,SF,Neg,LoU,MP)	24.56
(RR,ACNO,0,(0,0,1,1,0,0,1,0,0),Normal,SF,Neg,LoU,MP)	24.47
(PP,ACNO,1,(1,1,0,1,1,0,1,1,1),Normal,SF,Pos,LoU,LP)	24.17

We observe that except one, all the other advocates went on to win the trial. This can be observed from the first index (RR/PP) and the third index (0/1) of the state. We also see that the majority of the utterances have a negative sentiment (4 out of 6) which indicates that justices tend to intervene more for arguments with a negative sentiment. We also see that none of them is amicus curiae who are considered to be the friends of the court and consulted for their expertise on the matter. Additionally, we also computed the following: Within the 60 time-steps, what is the maximum number of times a particular justice intervenes the advocates from each side. We also studied the voting pattern of the justice for that case and the outcome of the case as well. The PRISM query can be given as follows:

```
filter(max, R{"jname_INTERVENINGside"}=? [ C<=60 ], x=j)
```

The maximum values for each justice for both sides, i.e., the petitioner and the respondents are shown in Table 6.

For the respondents, we see that in all the cases they went on to win the case (see the second row for each justice). Interestingly, except J_1, J_2 and J_9, all the other justices have voted against the advocates for cases where they intervened the most in 60 steps. This shows that an attempt was made by the justices to convey his/her concerns about the argument of the advocate which otherwise has convinced the majority of the justices of the bench.

Table 6. Maximum interventions in 60 time units by each justice towards each side.

J_1	(0,(**0**,0,0,1,0,0,0,0,0),InterveningPP,Pos,LoU,MP)	11.6
	(0,(**0**,0,1,1,0,0,1,0,0),InterveningRR,Pos,LoU,MP)	9.7
J_2	(1,(1,**0**,1,1,1,1,1,0,1),InterveningPPRE,Pos,SoU,MP)	4.1
	(0,(0,**0**,1,1,0,0,1,0,0),InterveningRR,Pos,SoU,LP)	4.7
J_3	(0,(0,0,**0**,0,0,0,0,0,IU),InterveningPPRE,Neg,SoU,LP)	7.5
	(0,(0,0,**1**,0,0,0,0,1,0),InterveningRR,Neu,SoU,LP)	11.6
J_4	(1,(1,1,1,**0**,1,1,1,1,IU),InterveningACPP,Neg,LoU,MP)	15.7
	(0,(0,0,0,**1**,0,0,0,0,IU),InterveningRR,Pos,LoU,MP)	14.6
J_5	(0,(0,0,1,1,**0**,1,0,0,0),InterveningPPRE,Neu,SoU,MP)	15.4
	(0,(1,0,0,0,**1**,0,0,1,1),InterveningRR,Neg,SoU,LP)	13.2
J_6	(1,(1,1,0,0,1,**0**,1,1,1),InterveningPPRE,Neu,SoU,MP)	16.5
	(0,(0,0,0,1,0,**1**,1,1,0),InterveningRR,Pos,SoU,MP)	13.6
J_7	(0,(1,1,0,0,0,0,**0**,1,IU),InterveningPP,Neu,LoU,MP)	9.8
	(0,(0,0,1,1,0,1,**1**,0,0),InterveningACRR,Neu,LoU,MP)	10.4
J_8	(0,(1,0,0,1,1,0,0,**0**,0),InterveningPP,Neu,SoU,MP)	11.2
	(0,(1,1,0,0,1,0,0,**1**,0),InterveningRR,Pos,SoU,MP)	12.8
J_9	(0,(1,0,0,1,1,0,0,0,**0**),InterveningPP,Pos,LoU,MP)	9.2
	(0,(0,1,1,1,1,0,0,0,**0**),InterveningRR,Neu,SoU,MP)	11.9

Interestingly, we see that all the justices went on to vote against the petitioner in the states where they intervened the most (see the first row and the highlighted 0 for each justice). Collectively, in the majority of the cases, the petitioner has lost the case (15 out of 18 rows). By observing the values of both PP and RR for each justice (rightmost column), it can be concluded that no justice goes out of his/her way while intervening the advocates of either side.

10. Analyzing the Rebuttal Arguments. Rebuttal arguments are usually not intervened much by the justices. In fact, in many cases (42%) they go completely unintervened by the justices which is evident from the following PRISM query:

`P=?[(!"InterveningPPRE")U("FINAL")]`=0.42

Having said that, we see frequent interventions occurring in some of the cases. We investigate this further by identifying and analyzing the corresponding states. We run the following PRISM query: `filter(max,R{"r_INTERVENING"}r=?[F "FINAL"],"REBUTTAL"&(x=j))`. The results are shown in Table 7.

We observe that in 4 out of 5 instances, the petitioner wins the case. Since the rebuttal is the last concluding argument during a proceeding, it indicates that the bench has already made up its mind about the case and the justices would like to clarify some reservations or provide comments about the case before closing the proceeding. If we conduct a similar experiment where the role is justice,

Table 7. Analyzing the rebuttal arguments.

(PP,ACNO,1,(1,1,0,0,1,0,1,1,1),Rebuttal,MS,Pos,LoU,MP)	24.0
(PP,ACNO,0,(0,0,1,1,0,1,0,0,0),Rebuttal,SF,Pos,SoU,LP)	17.33
(PP,ACNO,1,(1,1,1,1,1,0,0,1,1),Rebuttal,MS,Neu,LoU,MP)	16.42
(PP,ACNO,1,(1,1,0,1,1,0,1,1,1),Rebuttal,SF,Neu,SoU,LP)	15.25
(PP,ACNO,1,(1,0,1,1,0,1,1,0,1),Rebuttal,SF,Pos,SoU,LP)	15.0

we can identify the states for each justice which resulted in the most interventions during the rebuttals. The corresponding PRISM query is as follows: `filter(max,R{"r\_INTERVENING"}=?[F "FINAL"],"INTERVENINGPPRE"\&(x=j))`. The results are shown in Table 8.

Table 8. Justices intervening rebuttal arguments.

(J_6,1,(1,1,0,0,1,**0**,1,1,1),SF,Neu,SoU,MP)	25.0
(J_5,0,(0,0,1,1,**0**,1,0,0,0),MS,Neu,SoU,MP)	17.33
(J_3,1,(1,1,**0**,1,1,0,1,1,1),MS,Neu,SoU,MP)	17.25
(J_6,1,(1,1,1,1,1,**0**,0,1,1),MS,Neu,SoU,MP)	16.75
(J_5,0,(0,0,1,1,**0**,1,0,0,0),MS,Neg,SD,MP)	16.67
(J_6,1,(1,0,1,1,0,**1**,1,0,1),MS,Neu,SD,MP)	15.5

We see that J_6 and J_5 are involved in majority of the instances which resulted in the most interventions during the rebuttals. We also see that for the top 5 instances, the corresponding justice's vote went against the petitioner. Interestingly, the sentiment is neutral for all the cases.

11. Analyzing Those Events that Led to The multiple Justices Jointly Intervening in an Argument. In the dataset and in our previous queries, it is rare to find instances where multiple justices jointly intervene in an argument. In this query, we try to study scenarios where justices have jointly intervened in an argument. We use the following query to calculate the expected length of an inter-jury discussion following an argument by an advocate.

```
filter(state,R{"n_step"}=?[(X("JJ"))U(X(!("JJ")))],
                    (("PP"|"RR")&(x=j)))
```

We sort the experiment results for the states in descending order, and the results are shown in Table 9.

We observe that in all the instances at least 6 out of 9 justices have voted for the same side. This indicates that scenarios, where at least 6 like-minded justices

Table 9. Advocate states leading to collective interventions.

(RR,ACNO,0,(1,0,0,1,0,1,0,0,0),MS,Neg,SoU,LP)	5.0
(RR,ACNO,0,(0,1,0,0,0,0,0,1,IU),SF,Pos,LoU,LP]	5.0
(RR,ACNO,1,(1,1,0,0,1,1,0,1,1),SF,Neu,SoU,LP)	5.0
(PP,ACNO,1,(1,1,1,1,1,0,1,1,1),SF,Pos,LoU,MP)	5.0
(PP,ACNO,0,(0,1,0,0,0,0,0,0,0),SF,Pos,SoU,MP)	4.75
(PP,ACNO,0,(0,0,0,0,0,0,0,0,0),LG,Neu,SoU,MP)	4.5

are present, are the ones where the joint intervention takes place. Next, we try to investigate this further by asking the following question: in a joint intervention scenario, are all the justices who are involved in the intervention like-minded or not? The query can be modified as follows:

```
filter(max, R{"n_step"}=? [ ("JJ"&"INTERVENING") U !("JJ") ]
            ,(("JJ"&"INTERVENING")&(x=j)))
```

The states with the maximum values and the list of all the justices involved in the intervention are shown in Table 10.

Table 10. Justices involved in collective interventions.

(J_7,0,(**0**,1,0,0,0,0,**0**,**0**,0),InterveningPP,Neu,SoU)	12.0	J_8, J_1
(J_7,1,(**1**,0,**1**,1,0,1,**1**,0,1),InterveningRR,Pos,SoU)	8.0	J_1, J_3
(J_8,1,(**1**,1,1,1,1,1,1,**1**,**1**),InterveningRR,Neu,SoU)	6.37	J_9, J_1
(J_8,0,(0,0,0,0,0,0,**0**,**0**,**0**),InterveningPP,Neg,SoU)	6.0	J_7,J_9
(J_9,1,(1,0,1,1,1,1,**1**,0,**1**),InterveningPP,Neu,SoU)	6.0	J_7

It can be observed that in all the instances/rows, justices who are involved in joint intervention are like-minded, e.g., for the first instance/row, J_7, J_8 and J_1 are involved and all these justices are like-minded (see the three highlighted 0's in the 9-tuple). Similarly, for the third instance/row, J_8, J_9, and J_1 are involved and these justices are like-minded. Additionally, we also see the trend that like-minded justices who jointly intervene, tend to intervene the advocate of the opposite side. We also see that the case outcome is also aligned with their inclinations. Finally, since these are joint interventions, they are all small utterances, i.e., SoU.

12. Analyzing the Sequences Where a Justice And an Advocate Had an Extended Dialogue. In this query, we tried to look at the states that led to an extended dialogue between a justice and an advocate. Identifying such states would provide interesting insights about the nature of the arguments by an advocate, his/her side, and the sentiment that leads to such interactions. Additionally, the justices involved in such interaction can also be identified. We use the following query to obtain the maximum expected length of dialogues between a justice and an advocate:

```
filter(max, R{"n_step"}=? [ ("RR"|"PP"|"jname") U ("JJ"&!("jname"))
                          ], ("RR"|"PP"))
```

The average maximum expected length of dialogues is 12. For justice J_1, the result is not defined in the query. This is due to the following reason: this is a reachability property on rewards, and if the probability of satisfying the query is less than 1, then the expected reward is infinite. Next, we modify this query and run an experiment to find out which states led to such scenarios. The states that led to the longest one-on-one conversations between the justice and an advocate are given in Table 11, with the names of the corresponding justices and the lengths of the dialogue.

Table 11. Longest one-on-one conversations between the justice and an advocate.

(PP,ACNO,1,(1,0,1,1,0,**1**,1,0,1),Rebuttal,SF,Pos,SoU,LP)	29.0	J_6
(PP,ACNO,0,(0,0,1,1,**0**,1,0,0,0),Rebuttal,MS,Pos,SoU,MP]	20.33	J_5
(PP,ACNO,1,(1,1,1,**1**,1,1,1,1,IU),Rebuttal,MS,Neu,SoU,MP)	19.0	J_4
(PP,ACNO,1,(1,1,1,1,1,**0**,0,1,1),Rebuttal,MS,Neu,LoU,MP)	17.14	J_6
(PP,ACNO,1,(1,0,1,1,**1**,1,0,0,1),Rebuttal,SF,Neg,LoU,MP)	15.0	J_5

Another observation is that all these conversations took place with the petitioner side, and the petitioner won in all those cases except one, i.e., the second row. Additionally, we see that the five most lengthy dialogues occurred during the rebuttals, implying that the intervention must have started in the earlier part of the rebuttal argument. Interestingly, as mentioned earlier (query 10), for 42% of the cases, rebuttals go unintervened, but the result of this query shows that for certain cases rebuttals may result in long one-on-one conversations between a justice and an advocate. A possible explanation is that although the justices have already made up their minds about these cases, they would still like to clarify some points before coming to the final conclusion.

7 Conclusion and Future Work

This paper demonstrated that probabilistic model checking can be very effective for modeling, analysis, and verification of temporal dynamics of human communication in the judiciary. We built a DTMRM using the transcripts of the oral arguments of cases from the United States Supreme Court. Interesting queries were specified using PCTL and PCTL with rewards and verified using the PRISM model checker. Our results showed that probabilistic model checking can uncover hidden patterns, identify trends, and provide valuable feedback to the justices, advocates, and other stakeholders of the judiciary. In the future, we plan to investigate the following:

- Generalize this approach so that it can be applied to all the cases from the U.S. Supreme Court. This would require applying aggressive minimization techniques to tackle the state space explosion problem.
- Add more interesting linguistic markers, e.g., 'Dialogue-Acts', and 'Discourse' etc., for constructing the Markovian model.
- We also plan to apply this approach to other group interaction datasets, e.g., [8,23].

References

1. https://convokit.cornell.edu/documentation/supreme.html
2. Andova, S., Hermanns, H., Katoen, J.-P.: Discrete-Time rewards model-checked. In: Larsen, K.G., Niebert, P. (eds.) FORMATS 2003. LNCS, vol. 2791, pp. 88–104. Springer, Heidelberg (2004). https://doi.org/10.1007/978-3-540-40903-8_8
3. Andrei, O., Murray, G.: Interpreting models of social group interactions in meetings with probabilistic model checking. In: Proceedings of the Group Interaction Frontiers in Technology Workshop, GIFT@ICMI 2018, Boulder, CO, USA, 16 October 2018, pp. 5:1–5:7 (2018)
4. Aronsson, K., Jönsson, L., Linell, P.: The courtroom hearing as a middle ground: speech accommodation by lawyers and defendants. J. Lang. Soc. Psychol. **6**, 115–99 (1987)
5. Baier, C., Katoen, J.P.: Principles of Model Checking. MIT Press (2008)
6. Benus, S., Levitan, R., Hirschberg, J.: Entrainment in spontaneous speech: the case of filled pauses in supreme court hearings. In: 2012 IEEE 3rd International Conference on Cognitive Infocommunications (CogInfoCom), pp. 793–797 (2012)
7. Bird, S., Klein, E., Loper, E.: Natural Language Processing with Python. O'Reilly (2009)
8. Chang, J.P., Chiam, C., Fu, L., Wang, A.Z., Zhang, J., Danescu-Niculescu-Mizil, C.: ConvoKit: a toolkit for the analysis of conversations. In: Proceedings of the 21th Annual Meeting of the Special Interest Group on Discourse and Dialogue, SIGdial 2020, 1st virtual meeting, 1-3 July 2020, pp. 57–60. Association for Computational Linguistics (2020)
9. Cole, D., Biskupic, J., de Vogue, A.: Clarence Thomas breaks silence on bench during supreme court's first remote oral argument (2020). https://edition.cnn.com/2020/05/04/politics/clarence-thomas-question/index.html
10. Cornwell, B.: Social Sequence Analysis: Methods and Applications. Structural Analysis in the Social Sciences, Cambridge University Press (2015)
11. Danescu-Niculescu-Mizil, C., Lee, L., Pang, B., Kleinberg, J.: Echoes of power: language effects and power differences in social interaction. In: Proceedings of WWW, pp. 699–708 (2012)
12. Dehnert, C., Junges, S., Katoen, J., Volk, M.: A storm is coming: a modern probabilistic model checker. In: CAV, pp. 592–600. LNCS 10427, Springer (2017). https://doi.org/10.1007/978-3-319-63390-9_31 probabilistic model checker. In: CAV. pp. 592–600. LNCS 10427, Springer (2017)

13. Dietrich, B.J., Enos, R.D., Sen, M.: Emotional arousal predicts voting on the U.S. supreme court. Polit. Anal. **27**(2), 237–243 (2019)
14. Hansson, H., Jonsson, B.: A logic for reasoning about time and reliability. Formal Asp. Comput. **6**(5), 512–535 (1994)
15. Hawes, T., Lin, J., Resnik, P.: Elements of a computational model for multi-party discourse: The turn-taking behavior of supreme court justices. J. Am. Soc. Inf. Sci. Technol. **60**, 1607–1615 (2009)
16. Hensel, C., Junges, S., Katoen, J., Quatmann, T., Volk, M.: The probabilistic model checker storm. Int. J. Softw. Tools Technol. Transf. **24**(4), 589–610 (2022)
17. Katoen, J., Khattri, M., Zapreev, I.S.: A Markov reward model checker. In: Second International Conference on the Quantitative Evaluaiton of Systems (QEST 2005), 19-22 September 2005, Torino, Italy, pp. 243–244. IEEE Computer Society (2005)
18. Kemeny, J.G., Snell, J.L., et al.: Finite Markov Chains, vol. 356. Van Nostrand, Princeton (1960)
19. Kwiatkowska, M.Z., Norman, G., Parker, D.: Stochastic model checking. In: Formal Methods for Performance Evaluation, 7th International School on Formal Methods for the Design of Computer, Communication, and Software Systems, SFM 2007, Bertinoro, Italy, May 28-June 2, 2007, Advanced Lectures, pp. 220–270 (2007)
20. Kwiatkowska, M., Norman, G., Parker, D.: PRISM 4.0: verification of probabilistic real-time systems. In: Gopalakrishnan, G., Qadeer, S. (eds.) CAV 2011. LNCS, vol. 6806, pp. 585–591. Springer, Heidelberg (2011). https://doi.org/10.1007/978-3-642-22110-1_47
21. Liptak, A.: Justice clarence thomas, long silent, has turned talkative (2021). https://www.nytimes.com/2021/05/03/us/politics/clarence-thomas-supreme-court.html
22. Murray, G.: Markov reward models for analyzing group interaction. In: Proceedings of the 19th ACM International Conference on Multimodal Interaction, ICMI 2017, Glasgow, United Kingdom, November 13 - 17, 2017, pp. 336–340 (2017)
23. Sanchez-Cortes, D., Aran, O., Mast, M.S., Gatica-Perez, D.: A nonverbal behavior approach to identify emergent leaders in small groups. IEEE Trans. Multimedia **14**(3), 816–832 (2012)
24. Sharma, A.: Weighted probabilistic equivalence preserves ω-regular properties. In: MMB & DFT, pp. 121–135. LNCS 7201, Springer (2012). https://doi.org/10.1007/978-3-642-28540-0_9

Extracting Cyber Threat Intelligence from Social Media with Case Studies in Twitter/𝕏 and Reddit

Dainora Jakstaite and Ricardo M. Czekster(✉)

Aston University, Birmingham B4 7ET, UK
{149121837,meloczer}@aston.ac.uk

Abstract. A substantial amount of Internet traffic pertains to social media. This virtual way of interacting among peers, friends and audiences has contributed to help users test arguments and advertise statuses whilst helping organisations reaching out prospective clients. Given its global outreach, social media users produce a massive amount of daily data that are publicly available (depending on T&C). This brings interesting challenges in Cyber Threat Intelligence (CTI) as it can employ social media datasets to investigate impending cyber-attacks or latest malicious incursions on victims. Our contributions are two-fold, firstly, it outlines how to extract CTI in a timely fashion as well as the considerations and trade-offs for cyber security officers with case studies in Twitter/𝕏 and Reddit. Secondly, it proposes a *trustability metric* for determining reputable accounts to prioritise subsequent analysis efforts.

Keywords: Cyber Threat Intelligence · Cyber security · Metrics for timely decisions · Social Networks Analysis

1 Introduction

Modern society has become increasingly dependent on social media outlets as a *de facto* communication and entertainment venue to reach out family, friends, and communities, be informed on latest events, and interact with others. Previous years have witnessed the establishment of social media in general as a conduit for letting people and organisations promote business, inform audiences, or congregate users around similar preferences and points of views. The now large community of adopters aggregated around these networks enabling researchers to tackle its inherent benefits with Social Networks Analysis (SNA) [27] as a valid alternative to analyse complex systems in social spaces. One interesting research in SNA concerns link prediction [7], i.e., inferring node's relationships, and misinformation spread [2].

Latest years have seen the development of a myriad of social media instances such as Facebook, Twitter (re-branded to 𝕏 in July/2023), YouTube, Reddit, LinkedIn, Instagram, TikTok, and more recently, Threads, to mention a few.

G. Broccia and A. Cerone (Eds.): DataMod 2023, LNCS 14618, pp. 46–65, 2025.
https://doi.org/10.1007/978-3-031-87217-4_3

Given its requirements to sustain a global outreach, there are substantial technological challenges for keeping up, update, and maintain security whilst providing a privacy preserving user experience. The sheer scale of data produced daily in social media makes it a good target for conducting timely analysis that could help managers better understand interactions and information dissemination over large networks. That is the main reason to consider social media data streams as a crucial element in analysis [11,25].

From a cyber security perspective, they may provide invaluable data to help deter cyber-attacks before they spread over networks, informing cyber security officers of most likely and recent incursions from both amateur and sophisticated threat actors. Cyber Threat Intelligence (CTI) [1,20,26] is about contextual information allowing stakeholders to make decisions as cyber-attacks progress. A known drawback in security analysis is to use simple Indicators of Attacks (IoA) or similarly Indicators of Compromise (IoC) that are easily circumvented by adversaries as their attacks increase in sophistication, determination, and creativity when corrupting systems and data. CTI bridges this technical gap by working not only with IoA/IoC to sustain their analysis, but also incorporating Tactics, Techniques, and Procedures (TTP) [23,24], i.e., the 'why' and 'how' cyber-attacks could be potentially perpetrated. Central to CTI is *timeliness* inspecting how to adequately respond to impending malicious incursions to quickly identify and confirm criminal activities before they propagate over networks.

This paper will expand on the prospects of employing social media-based data for analysis and practical use in cyber security employing SNA. We shall present two case studies, one for Twitter and another one for Reddit, showcasing features and limitations. Our idea centres on working with validated users/accounts that consistently disseminate accurate and timely information to their audiences. The approach thus collects and enumerates such accounts, devise a *trustability metric* so it establishes trust in the community, and finally, it processes and presents this timely information to subscribers of our intelligence service.

The paper is organised as follows. Section 2 will outline recent approaches in CTI and social media datasets whereas Sect. 3 discusses our approach on how to extract meaning information. We proceed to Sect. 4 on a case study for Twitter and Sect. 5 with a Reddit crawler. We end our work in Sect. 6 with final considerations and ideas moving forward.

2 Related Work

The intelligence community considers crowd-based approaches to help gathering and analysing information from different sources that are public or generated by devices. There is a distinction among types for *intelligence crowdsourcing* [22], namely Open-Source (OSINT), Human (HUMINT), Signals (SIGINT) and Measurement and Signature (MASINT) Intelligence, among a few other gathering disciplines. In the context of this work we shall direct our attention to OSINT [28], due to focusing on social media outlets. It has attracted scientific attention due to its relevance on gathering indications that could lead to both cyber-attacks and mitigation efforts trusting in the collective and collaborative nature of public social networks [21,30,31].

As mentioned, TTPs focus on 'why' and 'how' sophisticated threat actors traverse networks and systems for vulnerabilities. Organisations have proposed different frameworks for modelling TTP throughout the years, such has the Adversarial Tactics, Techniques & Common Knowledge (ATT&CK®) framework[1] [23] compiles common TTPs employed by malicious adversaries to help establishing mitigations and controls to thwart their advances.

Mavroeidis and Bromander [14] discussed taxonomies and standards for CTI. MITRE has developed interesting CTI based information under the ATT&CK framework [23] where Xiong et al. [29] have devised threat modelling for advanced security analysis. The framework is sustained by the Structured Threat Information eXpression (STIX™) format, which is a standard for creating CTI models and sharing, employed by Czekster et al. [5] in a general web-system for describing cyber-attacks generating as output STIX format models.

In terms of quantitative metrics explored in social media, we highlight the work of Gräve (2019) [8] that tried to measure the impact of social media communication. Peters et al. (2013) [17] discussed social media based metrics and the impact on subsequent evaluations. These researches point out the need for better understanding and working with metrics to enhance assessments and analysis.

CTI is used across different application domains and it is particularly useful for capturing so called on-line chatter that could substantiate security analysis [19]. In the context of smart devices, it could use STIX for leveraging CTI taking into account their functionality and interaction [4]. Specifically towards the use of Twitter, we mention Riebe et al. (2021) [18] tool called `Cysecalert` for generating alerts using OSINT, `Twitterosint` [9], a tool for automated collection, analysis, and visualisation of intelligence, and `Sonar` [13], a system for detection of cyber security events using Twitter streams. We highlight `Iocminer` [15], a tool for inspecting IoC in Twitter that combines automatic graphs and text mining for CTI. The authors explore using regular expressions to extract meaningful instances from twits meriting further inspection.

3 Extracting Information from Social Media

As mentioned, social media networks may produce a massive amount of data by numerous individuals and organisations. It is a challenge to sift through all the data and uncover relevant information concerning specific problems. Our focus here is on OSINT and actionable intelligence gathering, so we must take steps to devise an approach that quickly sorts out results and presents to users so they make timely decisions. We want to avoid situations where the tool keeps processing and communicating instead of presenting users with relevant information, so our framework should be equipped with features to inspect performance and data retrieval as it is executing.

[1] MITRE's ATT&CK Framework: https://attack.mitre.org/.

We detail next the four-step process and explain our guided user-oriented tool interaction altogether:

1. Graphical User Interface (GUI): it presents users with a simple to use, friendly interface where they assign preferences, filters, and advanced options that will focus responses to meet their expectations.
2. Identification, mapping phase: to identify validated and trustworthy accounts or data sources that disseminate useful and timely information to their respective communities.
3. Tool internal execution: internally, we will use specific Application Programming Interface (API), depending on the social media, to subscribe to any events that are published by these selected accounts. It retrieves, processes and analyses data intersecting with filters put forth by users of our tool.
4. Presentation: it visually represents all gathered intelligence to the user, ordered by time, labelling it with the corresponding social media outlet to enact faster decision making and enabling quick thwarting cyber-attacks or malicious incursions before they propagate.
   - After presenting to our user base, it collects interactions with the information (such as likes/dislikes, upvotes/downvotes, etc.) so it updates top accounts for relevancy, altering the order on which to show results.

Figure 1 showcases a general approach with the necessary steps to conduct a timely analysis for intelligence gathering over different social networks outlets.

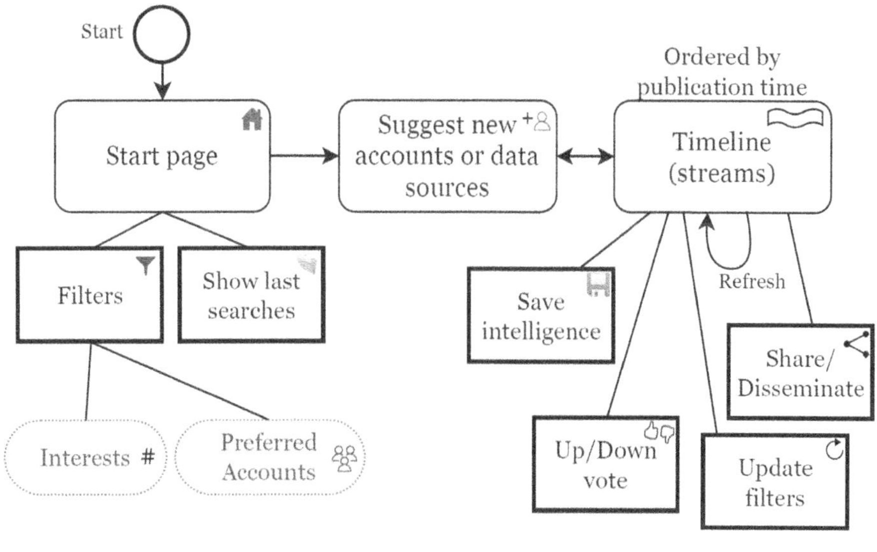

Fig. 1. General process of using social media outlets to increase analysis efforts.

A key element of our proposition is to choose reliable, trustworthy, and validated social media accounts or certified data sources. These users will vary depending on selected interests and filters as set out by our user base. Our approach will present a pre-selected number of manually inspected accounts or data sources pruned for relevance and useful content. Our users may signal different accounts to employ, and we shall take those into account and validation to present to the rest of the user base case it meets our relevance criteria.

3.1 Working on a *trustability* Metric

Given the multitude of accounts and social media networks, one interesting problem is to determine which venues to trust, which are accurate (over time), separating these selected accounts for adding to our tool's subscription mechanism. We are interested in computing a numerical value per account that indicates its level of so called *trustability*, i.e., how trustworthy such account is to be taken into consideration by our future analysis. This metric should allow new accounts to be at least visible, so as to "earn one's trust" and thus enter the selected accounts list. For these accounts, we will not consider the date on which they started operating.

There are key quantitative indices to inspect to build our trustability metric, for instance, the number of followers, number of views, quantity of reposts/share/re-tweets (each platform has its own naming), number of comments (if any) or user interactions, and a network-based property that considers how the accounts are connected altogether.

Note that there exist third-party (often paid) services that attempts to inflate the number of followers artificially has been a noticeable issue since the very beginning of social networks as they are a quality measure of content creators and their outreach over communities. Known problems plaguing social networks in general are the number of fake users, i.e., (non-validated) accounts that promotes disinformation and skew analysis efforts. This is why developing and computing a metric poses significant challenges for researchers, and the number might not represent the reality.

The idea behind many social media instances is to keep users *locked in* the platform. They do that by showing content indefinitely (e.g., infinite scrolling) as the algorithms are familiar with the things users enjoy consuming. The platforms have customised the algorithms to a point where the user simply can't leave, however, this has egregious consequences to young populace that displays symptoms similar to addiction [12].

Table 1 shows key characteristics of known social media outlets and the kind of data algorithms work to present new content to their user base. Column *Content track* indicates how one interacts with the platform, feeding it with responses in agreement, disagreement, or 'mood'. For example, "heart" (as outlined with glyph ♡) in Instagram corresponds to a positive response to the content.

A lot of social media outlets focus on providing users with a good, fun online experience, so they will not track (or show) any numerical measurement indicating any kind of stress like the number of dislikes or how many people have *unfollowed* an account over time. It is possible to infer those values, however, sometimes they are simple not available for any kind of analysis.

Table 1. Characteristics of engagement across different social media outlets.

Social Media outlet	*Linking* (naming)	Dissemination	Content track	Additional tracking
Facebook	Friend	Share, mark	Like, love, care, haha, wow, sad, angry	Comments
Instagram	Follow	Share	♡	Comments
TikTok	Follow	Share	♡	Comments
Threads	Follow	Repost, share, mention	♡	Replies, comments
Twitter/𝕏	Follow	Retweet, mention	♡	Comments
YouTube	Subscribe	Share	I like this 👍, I dislike this 👎	Views, comments

Another substantial problem is the fact that many users simply do not interact with social platforms in any way (campers/lurkers/etc.), however, this is detrimental to the social media algorithms as they should rely only on viewing content instead of actively engaging through like/dislike (or similar interaction) so it performs better (users understand that they should interact so similar content is shown in the future).

Table 2 outlines the variables we are looking for deriving a formula to compute the proposed trustability metric.

Table 2. Variables we considered to derive our trustability metric.

Characteristic	Symbol	Comments
Register date	D	Scale: days ago
Validated/verified account?	V	Possible values: 0 or 1
Date of first publication	Df	Scale: days
Last login or last seen	L	Scale: days ago
Number of followers	F	Numerical value
Total content	Tc	All produced content
Content Creation Rate	CCR	$CCR = \frac{Tc-Df+L}{D}$
Views	Vi	Numerical value
Virtual reward	R	Value ranging from 0 to 1
Total number of comments	Co	Total number of comments

We propose a Trustability Metric TM as shown in Eq. 1, concerning individual social media accounts, thus follows:

$$TM = \left(F \times \overbrace{\frac{Tc - Df + L}{D}}^{CCR} \times \overbrace{\frac{1}{Co \times Vi \times R}}^{engagement} \right) \times (V + 1) \quad (1)$$

Our formula for computing TM takes into account the user engagement towards the account's produced content over the period on which it is active, yielding a measure of trust that could be used to decide whether to follow it for intelligence gathering. CCR takes all produced content Tc and discounts when the user first posted anything plus the last time they logged in over the day of registration. This is an attempt to determine engagement and avoid passive or camper users, i.e., those that just consume content without ever generating it.

One characteristic that does exist but we have not considered is the type of account (business or user) as renown organisations when publishing intelligence pieces could add more trustworthiness to the analysis. This will be the subject of future research. Table 3 tests the metric outlining synthetic accounts populated with quantitative random data.

Table 3. Evaluation of TM for randomly generated values in social media accounts.

Synthetic Account†	D	V	Df	L	F	Tc	CCR	Vi	R	Co	TM	TM'‡
`@abc123` Twitter	88	1	51	1	23,450	405	4.034	233,892	0.1	4,334	0.0004	2.729
`@hugh3` YouTube	5	0	5	0	100	2	−0.600	56	0.05	12	−1.7857	−0.252
`@kikin3tw` Instagram	102	1	10	2	1,302	25	0.167	8,391	0.1	1,221	0.0001	3.373
`@baba00b` Twitter	1,011	1	1,000	10	123,555	1,010	0.020	90,000	0.05	1,234	0.0002	3.055
`@ju_b1bopr` YouTube	123	0	23	20	111	5	0.016	590	0.1	10	0.0030	2.514

†These accounts might exist by pure chance.
‡Formula: $TM' = -log10(|TM|)$, higher is best

It is noticeable that TM prioritises quality and interaction over quantity. It privileges the amount of content over engagement and user interaction through comments, views, and so called virtual rewards, i.e., a number between 0 and 1 that indicates how many users actively clicked on any button representing agreement or disagreement (like/dislike, heart/*un-heart*, etc.).

Limitations: The metric is not authoritative, functioning as a suggestion to map and use a quantitative measure for trust, and there is a need for further research on the topic. Security and intelligence analysis must consider other approaches when choosing their sources to work. The idea here is to use publicly available measures to compute this index that are most likely available through API calls or straightforward crawling outputs (if permitted) within each platform.

The trustability metric is crucial to determine the quality of the sources under intelligence gathering that security analysts should consider and prioritise over other information venues. The mechanism we describe herein subscribes to key accounts and follow them in their respective platforms, having access to their stream and feeds for tracking worthy intelligence pieces altogether.

One alternative that could be used by analysts is to devise a bespoke index by adjusting TM' to a factor that address the community's support to a given account. Originally, the proposed trustability metric uses only quantitative data available from accounts and user interaction; using this factor might add to the index how trustworthy the community sees the accounts, which might foster better analysis throughout.

4 Case Study on Twitter: the CyberTweets Tool

In this paper we are interested in designing and implementing a tool that collects and organises OSINT-based data from social media. We have developed a tool called CyberTweets for extracting Twitter based data and convey it to end-users. It is a web-based tool which connects to Twitter API v2 to get cyber security related tweets and analyses them further to display the data to the user in a user-friendly way. CyberTweets website offers not only a nice interface but also many features which could be useful for cyber analysts or IT professionals.

4.1 Operational Details and Architecture

CyberTweets utilises natural language processing (NLP) techniques to detect useful information for threat intelligence. In terms of its architecture, it was built using React (18.2.0) for the front-end, NodeJS (16.14.2) and Express for the server side and MongoDB for the database. Figure 2 illustrates CyberTweets' basic architecture and interaction with other elements from the system.

We have used other auxiliary libraries and APIs to build up the application namely `CORS` (for cross-origin HTTP requests), `Dotenv` (to manage environment variables), `Mongoose` (connections to MongoDB), `Express-async-handler` (to simplify error handling), `Bcryptjs` (for basic encryption features), `Jsonwebtoken` (session management), `Axios` (library for making HTTP requests), `Node Cron` (for scheduling), `Node NLP` (analysing data for NLP), `MUI` (interfacing library), and Styled components (dynamic rendering of webpages). The tool was hosted at Amazon Web Services (AWS) for simplifying Continuous Integration and Continuous Deployment (CI/CD), among other benefits for the basic user account included in the offer. The application uses the Twitter API v2 and data matching pre-set requirements, such as domain, entity fields, hashtags, account ID, and the tweet ID. We feed this information to the MongoDB database as soon as the request processes finishes.

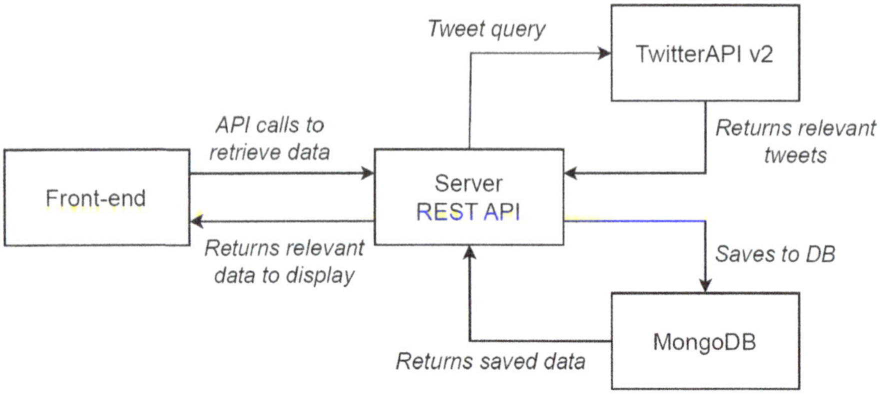

Fig. 2. Overview of CyberTweets' operational details and architecture.

4.2 Feature Set and Basic Screens

The tool allows users to filter tweets by date range, hashtags, search text, and named entities identified using the Node-NLP library. Additionally, users can save and download the text data from tweets. The project aim is to research and develop a useful tool which allows OSINT data gathering from Twitter and offers ways to analyse it further for threat identification, potentially helping many cyber security experts in their daily activities. Figure 3 highlights the opening screen for CyberTweets application, assuming the user has logged in and has had already chosen interesting topics and accounts to follow.

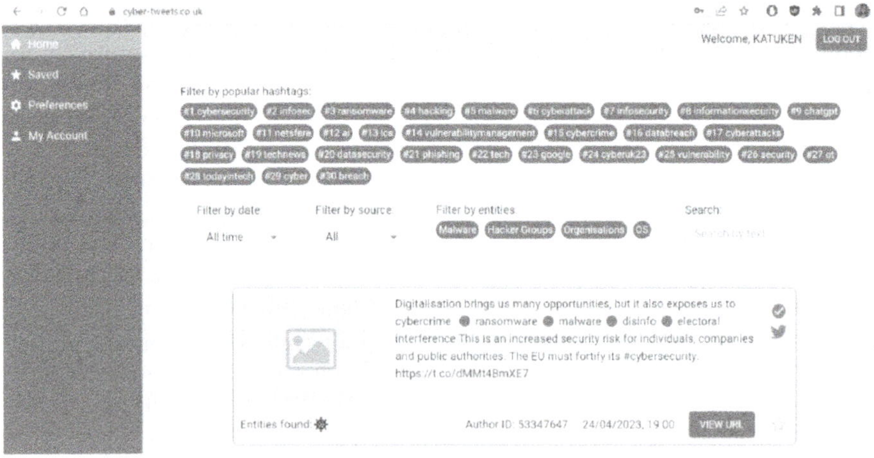

Fig. 3. Welcome screen for the CyberTweets application and basic feature set.

The tool shows current filters (logged users), list of applied filters and additional options (by date, by source, by entities, e.g., 'malware', 'hacker groups', or 'organisations'), plus a "Search" feature to look out pieces by providing text snippets according to user aims. Figure 4 shows how to set user preferences.

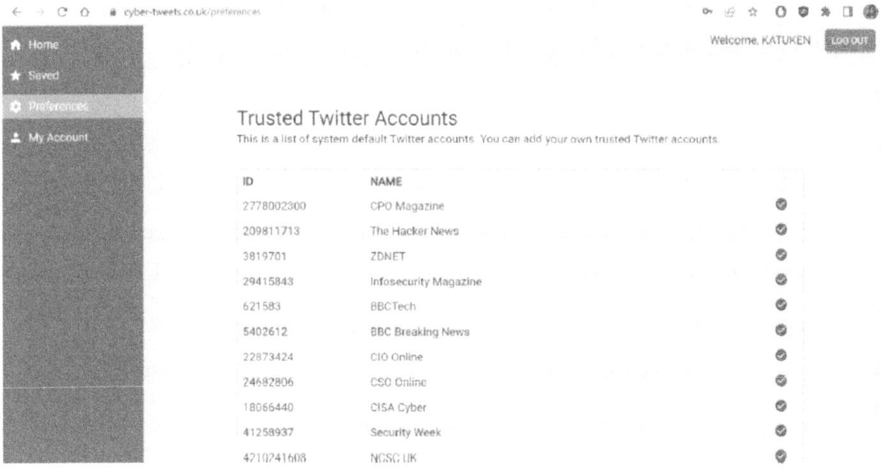

Fig. 4. Preferences for users, showing accounts that it is currently following.

In this current version, the application is manually following trusted accounts instead of using the trustability metric. In the near future, we envision to integrate and test using the metric to determine and suggest users other interesting accounts they should integrate into their analysis.

4.3 Analysis and End-User Evaluation

CyberTweets website has been evaluated by a few test users which have IT expertise to measure its potential use. We have conducted a basic usability testing over a reduced set of three users, using a qualitative approach to reason on less usable parts of the system and where improvements could be tackled for better understanding how to approach intelligence tasks. We have arranged interviews with users, where they were exposed to the tool, performed tasks, and answered a questionnaire following the process, so we understand their reasoning and overall perception whilst using the tool. We highlight a list of nine tasks we asked users to conduct, and the time they took to comply (following pattern `Task#n Description [average time, in seconds]`):

Task#1: Find tweets older than three days [17.3]
Task#2: Save a tweet [7.0]
Task#3: Find a tweet which has a hashtag you are interested in [15.3]

Task#4: Find a tweet which has an entity of potential interest to security [7.6]
Task#5: Change the list of trusted accounts (default accounts are added, add a new account with an ID number as `123456` and the name as `Test`) [36.3]
Task#6: Access your saved tweets [1.6]
Task#7: Change your name (note that your current name is set to `TestUser`, please change it to `UserTesting`) [8.3]
Task#8: Change your password (dummy password is `Testing123`, please change it to `Testing567`) [15.0]
Task#9: Find some specific information in the tweet text [10.3]

The most difficult task they performed was Task#5, when changing the list of trusted accounts. This has suggested us the need to improve ways when presenting users with simpler mechanisms for better understanding the concept of trusted accounts and how they could easily access it or present it in a seamless fashion. We present questions used in the interview with users:

1. What is your overall perception of the tool?
2. In your opinion, does it have the potential to attract other users?
3. Do you know any tool that is related to this one? If yes, what it is called?
4. Are icons easy to understand? For example, the tick, star etc.?
5. Was the website easy to use and navigate?
6. Were there any website features that you particularly liked or disliked?
7. Did you find the filters (date, hashtags, entities, search) helpful in narrowing down the tweets you wanted to see?
8. Did you find the information provided by the CyberTweets website useful?
9. Was there any other functionality you would have liked to see?
10. Do you have any recommendations to improve the tool?

We received feedback that was generally positive where users have provided valuable insights for improving the tool in future versions. Some users found the tasks very easy to do but some of them struggled, either not understanding it or it just was a user's preference to perform it in a different way. When asked to find a tweet by a popular hashtag one user used a search field and the other checked the tweet text manually. Another interesting observation was that when asked to add a new trusted twitter account none of the users clicked on `Preferences` tab first, most clicked on `My Account`. This indicates that perhaps the naming of Preferences should be changed.

5 Case Study on Reddit: Webcrawler to STIX Bundle

We proceed working with Reddit, a popular social news aggregator and discussion board. We have created an account for crawling data from specific directories (called 'subreddits' in the platform) namely cyber security related discussion fora. Having an account and authenticating in the platform will extend the limitations when retrieving data. The crawler is a Python script integrated with The Python Reddit API Wrapper (PRAW)[2].

[2] Link: https://github.com/praw-dev/praw.

After deciding which data for CTI, we will convert the set of strings into STIX [3,10] format and generate a STIX model that could be consumed by the cyberaCTIve tool [5,6]. This tool is publicly available[3] and allow users to directly insert CTI streams acting as a front-end to the STIX format. It presents users with available parameters (mandatory and optional) and offers interesting features such as attack timeline analysis and sharing STIX models (it dumps the model representation for storage and sharing into other tools).

Given the reduced set of attributed that can be retrieved by PRAW dictated by the platform's limits, we will need to modify the way we computed the trustability metric to accommodate the relevance of submissions into cyber threat analysis. For instance, the PRAW's object `Redditor` will only provide the user's name and `comment_karma` (this attribute is somewhat related to reputation) and the date they first logged in (under `created_utc` attribute) whilst for the object `Submission` we had available its `title`, `score`, `upvote_ratio` (i.e., the percentage of upvotes from all votes on the submission), `num_comments`, and `date_created` (unless detailed, these attributes are self-explanatory).

Figure 5 outlines our general process for gathering intelligence out of social media outlets, particularly Reddit.

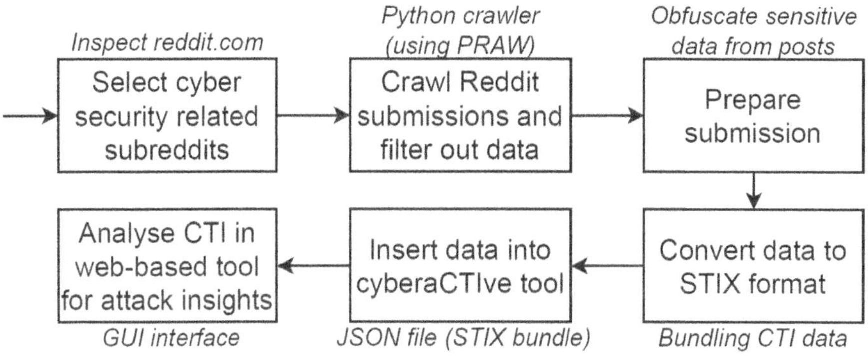

Fig. 5. Converting posts from Reddit to actionable CTI.

Reddit imposes limits to submission retrieval for non-authenticated and authenticated users/crawlers. As of Sep/2023 the documentation states that *"Any single reddit listing will display at most 1000 items."* and that *"Apps that make less than 100 queries per minute per OAuth ID can still use the free tier"*, i.e., one must resort to filter out submissions by `hot()`, `new()`, or `top()` (employing limits to the functions such as `subreddit.hot(limit=50)`) as data crawlers must comply with this to get any meaningful results.

Reddit offers a host of subreddits related to cyber security. One notices an active community involving non-technical, developers, designers, software quality and pentesters where cyber security is the focal point. Next, we present a

[3] Link: https://cyberactive.techster.uk.

list of subreddits that we could potentially employ to extract meaningful CTI. We note that this is not comprehensive, i.e., there will be many other subreddits within the platform that discuss the topic of cyber security. All links will work adding to the browser the prefix https://www.reddit.com/ followed by the subreddit's link as mentioned below. We also state the number of members within brackets ([N]) – as of September 2023 – and that can be used to prioritise certain subreddits for CTI as well. Unless stated otherwise, these subreddits are public.

- `r/BadApps` [2.7k]: all information about malware (focus on smart phone apps and Google's Play Store).
- `r/blackhat` [83.5k]: vulnerabilities and exploitation.
- `r/blueteamsec` [38.1k]: focuses on technical intelligence for blue teams.
- `r/computerforensics` [59.7k]: dedicated to recovery and investigation of cyber related materials.
- `r/ComputerSecurity` [31.6k]: provides curated list of links to IT security.
- `r/cyber` (private): covers the geopolitical and corporate CTI.
- `r/cybersecurity` [564k]: general discussion about cyber security, careers, developing threats.
- `r/ethicalhacking` [27.7k]: interest in computer hacking (ethically).
- `r/ExploitDev` [11.2k]: discusses software vulnerabilities and exploits.
- `r/fulldisclosure` [2.2k]: relates information about breaches, exploits, data leaks and vulnerabilities.
- `r/hackersec` (private): offers technical guides to interact and share information about cyber security.
- `r/hacking` [2.6 m]: dedicated to computer hackers and hacking in general.
- `r/Information_Security` [22.3k]: publishes information about security news and analysis.
- `r/Malware` [70.9k]: discussions on malware reports and related information.
- `r/pwned` (private): news about recent exploits and breaches, leaked data.
- `r/redteamsec` [25.1k]: converges red and blue teams to discuss malware, tradecraft and reverse engineering.
- `r/reverseengineering` [135k]: discusses topics related to reverse engineering software, breaking it apart and understanding it.
- `r/threatintel` [3.7k]: discusses threats and sharing information across stakeholders to thwart the advance of attacks.
- `r/websecurity` [6.2k]: covers links and discussions about development and security of websites, aggregating owners, developers and pentesters.

Out of this list of subreddits, we point out that `r/hacking` has about 2.6 million members so one must factor in the sheer amount of noise that such large community creates over time. On the other hand, it may act as a valuable source for useful CTI for understanding attacks. The main cyber security subreddit (`r/cybersecurity`) with 564 thousand users stands out as a valid alternative that might yield an interesting amount of data pieces for CTI.

5.1 Retrieving Data from Selected Subreddits into cyberaCTIve

For this work we have decided to retrieve only hot and new first 50 submissions and compute the trustability metric to determine which posts merited to be further analysed. Out of those, we extracted the submission's title and looked for interesting (with respect to CTI) descriptions worth creating STIX objects capable of feeding the cyberaCTIve on-line tool.

If we do not limit the list of subreddits to inspect, the script will produce an output that has a lot of noise to process. We have chosen to look into the following ones: `"r/cybersecurity"`, `"r/ethicalhacking"`, `"r/malware"`, `"r/threatintel"` and `"r/blueteamsec"`. In light of this fact we have chosen cyber security related subreddits to search for strings having the following:

```
regexes = [ "attack.*", "attacker.*", "cybersecurity.*", "CVE.*",
            "NVD.*", "security.*", "malware.*", "threat actor.*",
            "threat.*", "MS-Windows.*", "Android.*", "MacOS.*",
            "iOS.*", "GNU-Linux.*", "Linux.*", "vulnerability*" ]
```

where `regexes` is a Python data structure to withhold all our strings for pattern matching using regular expressions. This is a clear limitation of our approach as one must fine-tune it from time to time to capture other ways redditors are creating CTI related content.

For this task here, we are interested in running a periodic Python script that will traverse new posts, extract relevant CTI data, and convert to standardised formats (namely STIX) for later analysis. We are tracking each individual posts' identifiers to avoid creating repeated entries in JSON files.

Each post shall map into distinct STIX objects as follows. As STIX Domain Objects (SDO) we could add data into `infrastructure`, `malware`, `malware analysis`, `note`, `observed-data`, `opinion`, `report`, `threat-actor`, `tool`, and `vulnerability` and STIX Relationship Objects (SRO) such as the `relationship` type. For STIX Cyber-observable Objects (SCO), we could potentially use `file`, `ipv4-addr/ipv6-addr`, `network-traffic`, `software`, `url`, and `user-account`, to name a few. The mapping will depend on our ability to understand the post and assign meaning to it, in the hope of extracting useful and actionable CTI.

We present Algorithm 1 (named `Reddit2CTI_Converter`) that crawls Reddit for CTI-related content as explained next.

From the list of subreddits and the regular expressions to perform the pattern matching, the script will traverse the list of posts per subreddit and select likely CTI to populate cyberaCTIve tool. The function `crawl_reddit` does the data extraction within Reddit whereas the `assign_type` will determine which STIX object to assign to the post. Function `compute_trustability` will take the new entry and the discussion, extract the current Redditor and determine the trustability metric as explained in Sect. 3.1. We have created a function called `acceptable(tm)` that evaluates the trustability metric and determines whether the piece of data merits further analysis, i.e., insertion into the CTI tool. Finally, the function `convert` will transform the post into a JSON file

Algorithm 1 Reddit2CTI_Converter

```
subreddits ← list of selected (relevant) to cyber security Reddit subreddits
regexes ← list of strings related to CTI tracking
for all subreddit : subreddits do                      ▷ traverse the list of selected subreddits
    discussions ← get_discussions(subreddit, regexes)              ▷ match discussions
    for all discussion : discussions do                        ▷ process all discussions
        entry_new ← crawl_reddit(subreddit, regexes)               ▷ match discussions
        tm ← compute_trustability(entry_new, discussion)
        if acceptable(tm) & unique(entry_new) then                ▷ If this is a new item
            type ← assign_type(entry_new)        ▷ set STIX objects: SDO, SRO, SCO
            entry_json ← convert(entry_new, type)      ▷ returns JSON file for entry
            insert(entry_json)                      ▷ Insert JSON file into cyberaCTIve
        end if
    end for
end for
```

and function `insert` that could feed it into the cyberaCTIve tool[4]. The function will also create a new STIX model, assign temporary names and STIX objects parameters depending on each entry.

We have implemented the algorithm explained in previous section as a Python script integrated with PRAW. Next, we highlight some Python code excerpts to showcase our approach:

```
import praw # if not present, run 'pip install praw'

def main():
    reddit = praw.Reddit(
        client_id=client_id,            # given by Reddit
        client_secret=client_secret,    # given by Reddit
        password=my_pass,               # chosen by user
        username=my_user,               # chosen by user
        user_agent=my_useragent,        # create a mock user agent
        check_for_async=False           # prevent warning
    )
    my_subreddits = [
        "cybersecurity",
        "ethicalhacking",
        "malware",
        "threatintel",
        "blueteamsec"
    ]
    regexes = [
        "attack.*", "attacker.*", "cybersecurity.*",
        "security.*", "malware.*", "threat.*",
        "threat actor.*", "CVE.*", "NVD.*", "vulnerability*",
        "MS-Windows.*", "Android.*", "MacOS.*",
        "iOS.*", "GNU-Linux.*", "Linux.*"
```

[4] Note that this feature is not yet implemented in the Python crawler described herein.

```
    ]
    combined = "(" + ")|(".join(regexes) + ")"
    for mysubreddit in my_subreddits:
        subreddit = reddit.subreddit(mysubreddit)
        i=0
        print("Subreddit: " + mysubreddit)
        #pick one method for retrieving posts out of this options:
        #submissions = subreddit.stream.submissions()
        #submissions = subreddit.new()
        #submissions = reddit.subreddit("all").search(mysubreddit,
            sort="hot", syntax=None, limit=LIMIT)
                # 'sort': "relevance", "hot", "top", "new", or "comments".
        submissions = subreddit.hot(limit=LIMIT)
        for submission in submissions:
          if (hasattr(submission.author, 'name') and   # checks valid user
            user_exists(reddit, submission.author) and # checks valid user
            submission.stickied == False and           # checks only 'unpinned'
                                                       #  ('unstickied') items
            re.search(combined, submission.title)):
            i=i+1
            process_submission(i, submission)
    file1.close()

def user_exists(reddit, name):
    try:
        if hasattr(reddit.redditor(name), 'id'):
            reddit.redditor(name).id
    except NotFound:
        return False
    return True

def process_submission(i, submission):
    file1.write("\n\nProcessing submission [" + submission.permalink + "]")
    if hasattr(submission.author, 'created_utc'):
        date = arrow.get(submission.author.created_utc).to('local').humanize()
    file1.write("---\nRedditor: " + submission.author.name +
          " (karma: " + (str(submission.author.comment_karma)
               if hasattr(submission.author, 'comment_karma') else "") +  ")")
    file1.write("\Title: " + str(i) + ": " + submission.title +
          ", score:" + str(submission.score) +
          ", upvote_ratio: " + str(submission.upvote_ratio) +
          ", num comments: " + str(submission.num_comments)
          "")

if __name__ == "__main__":
    main()
```

The idea is to crawl Reddit for specific data concerning cyber security and process it in our end to filter out unwanted results and prioritise elements we deem important.

Next, we show one instance of our *proof-of-concept script* (subject to further validation in the near future) return to showcase how the conversion to STIX could work (note that each redditor's name was obfuscated) from the subreddit `r/Malware`.

```
Permalink: /r/Malware/comments/15136a4/malware_delivery_
           via_microsoft_teams_law_firms/
Redditor: dkal33ks2 (karma: 8)
Title: Malware delivery via Microsoft Teams, law firms under
       cyberattack, CVSS 4.0 is out
Statistics: Score= 6, upvote_ratio= 0.75, num comments= 3
```

In terms of converting these data intelligence, it consists on creating a STIX model with a pre-selected name and create a bundle in JSON format. For the first item, one might come up with the following ***excerpt*** of STIX model:

```
{ "type": "bundle",
  "id": "bundle--ba83f63f-72ff-4f49-9fca-616f2d29e13c",
  "objects": [
  {
    "type": "infrastructure",
    "id": "infrastructure--ed75baaf-54eb-472c-b68a-4cdd0731fa13",
    "name": "Company PC on third floor"
  }, {
    "type": "malware",
    "name": "reddit-delivery-via-ms-teams",
    "malware_types": [ "backdoor" ],
    "implementation_languages": [ "c++" ]
  }, {
    "type": "relationship",
    "id": "relationship--0aaab1f3-e296-4860-8980-238d3d2abf10",
    "source_ref": "infrastructure--ed75baaf-54eb-472c-b68a-4cdd0731fa13",
    "target_ref": "malware--30494a3a-899f-451e-ad10-264eb7873c53"
  }, { ... } ] }  # as the STIX model will have more entries
```

The difficult part is not the conversion to STIX itself, but to have interesting intelligence pieces as input for the implementation. Developers working on a subsequent tool should focus on the Reddit crawler, i.e., determining what is and what it is not considered intelligence, and then calling a conversion function.

5.2 Discussion

Extracting CTI out of Reddit is not trivial given the multiple ways the community is creating messages and discussions across varied topics. We stress that a lot of internal details from this tool were omitted here, specially when converting posts into the STIX format and general modelling.

PRAW is a satisfactory tool with simple API to access Reddit, however, creating working Python scripts requires a lot of tweaking and checks to make it work. The way of sorting posts should employ programming after the crawling process altogether, i.e., the API is limited, perhaps to prevent abusing the platform through scripting. Sometimes data does not exist (e.g., has been removed by the platform, however, it still returns the post by the API), the user has been removed, or the post has specific attributes (stick or flagged) by moderators, among other issues.

6 Conclusion

Present work has two main contributions, firstly, it has shown how to employ social networks data sources as complementary intelligence gathering (secondary sources), and secondly, case studies in Twitter and Reddit, showcasing interesting examples of how to build a tiered system for handling intelligence. We have highlighted the main issues and concerns when implementing such systems, discussing a design framework that meets social networks elements and quantitative data that can be used to compute a trustability metric.

There has been interesting discussions, challenges, and open research ideas on how to best approach OSINT to explore its use in daily cyber security mitigation efforts for both end-users and organisations [16]. As future work for CyberTweets we will integrate user feedback and expand the feature set with other suggestions, coupling the system with automated account subscription emerging in social networks, adding more filtering options, and collating data from multiple platforms altogether.

For Reddit-based CTI retrieval there is the need to fine-tune the search strings to match more meaningful data items out of the platform as well as increasing the number of subreddits to inspect. One notices that expressing the most relevant way to extract intelligence from these social networks is not trivial and merits further research.

Ultimately, CTI is about achieving a balance among employing high-quality sources, timeliness, and quickly separating signals from noise for quick analysis and response. As a final note, we are conscious of current efforts on employing and combining ideas in Artificial Intelligence/Machine Learning (AI/ML) in OSINT-based research, exploring natural language processing and integrating with other information systems in organisations.

References

1. Abu, M.S., Selamat, S.R., Ariffin, A., Yusof, R.: Cyber threat intelligence-issue and challenges. Indonesian J. Electr. Eng. Comput. Sci. **10**(1), 371–379 (2018)
2. Aïmeur, E., Amri, S., Brassard, G.: Fake news, disinformation and misinformation in social media: a review. Soc. Netw. Anal. Min. **13**(1), 30 (2023)
3. Barnum, S.: Standardizing cyber threat intelligence information with the structured threat information eXpression (STIX). Mitre Corporation **11**, 1–22 (2012)
4. Czekster, R.M.: Leveraging cyber threat intelligence in smart devices. In: Information Security and Privacy in Smart Devices: Tools, Methods, and Applications, pp. 71–95. IGI Global (2023)
5. Czekster, R.M., Metere, R., Morisset, C.: cyberaCTIve: a STIX-based Tool for Cyber Threat Intelligence in Complex Models (2022). https://doi.org/10.48550/ARXIV.2204.03676

6. Czekster, R.M., Metere, R., Morisset, C.: Incorporating cyber threat intelligence into complex cyber-physical systems: a STIX model for active buildings. Appl. Sci. **12**(10), 5005 (2022)
7. Daud, N.N., Ab Hamid, S.H., Saadoon, M., Sahran, F., Anuar, N.B.: Applications of link prediction in social networks: a review. J. Netw. Comput. Appl. **166**, 102716 (2020)
8. Gräve, J.F.: What KPIs are key? Evaluating performance metrics for social media influencers. Soc. Media+ Soc. **5**(3), 2056305119865475 (2019)
9. Hoppa, M.A., Debb, S.M., Hsieh, G., KCa, B.: TwitterOSINT: automated open source intelligence collection, analysis & visualization tool. Ann. Rev. Cyberther. Telemed. **121** (2019)
10. Jordan, B., Piazza, R., Darley, T.: STIX Version 2.1. OASIS Standard (2021). https://docs.oasis-open.org/cti/stix/v2.1/os/stix-v2.1-os.html. Accessed 01 Sep 2023
11. Kong, X., Shi, Y., Yu, S., Liu, J., Xia, F.: Academic social networks: modeling, analysis, mining and applications. J. Netw. Comput. Appl. **132**, 86–103 (2019)
12. Kuss, D.J., Griffiths, M.D.: Social networking sites and addiction: ten lessons learned. Int. J. Environ. Res. Public Health **14**(3), 311 (2017)
13. Le Sceller, Q., Karbab, E.B., Debbabi, M., Iqbal, F.: SONAR: automatic detection of cyber security events over the twitter stream. In: Proceedings of the 12th International Conference on Availability, Reliability and Security, pp. 1–11 (2017)
14. Mavroeidis, V., Bromander, S.: Cyber threat intelligence model: an evaluation of taxonomies, sharing standards, and ontologies within cyber threat intelligence. In: 2017 European Intelligence and Security Informatics Conference (EISIC), pp. 91–98. IEEE (2017)
15. Niakanlahiji, A., Safarnejad, L., Harper, R., Chu, B.T.: IoCMiner: automatic extraction of indicators of compromise from Twitter. In: 2019 IEEE International Conference on Big Data (Big Data), pp. 4747–4754. IEEE (2019)
16. Pastor-Galindo, J., Nespoli, P., Mármol, F.G., Pérez, G.M.: The not yet exploited goldmine of OSINT: opportunities, open challenges and future trends. IEEE Access **8**, 10282–10304 (2020)
17. Peters, K., Chen, Y., Kaplan, A.M., Ognibeni, B., Pauwels, K.: Social media metrics-a framework and guidelines for managing social media. J. Interact. Mark. **27**(4), 281–298 (2013)
18. Riebe, T., et al.: CySecAlert: an alert generation system for cyber security events using open source intelligence data. In: International Conference on Information and Communications Security, pp. 429–446. Springer (2021). https://doi.org/10.1007/978-3-030-86890-1_24
19. Sapienza, A., Ernala, S.K., Bessi, A., Lerman, K., Ferrara, E.: Discover: mining online chatter for emerging cyber threats. In: Companion Proceedings of the The Web Conference 2018, pp. 983–990 (2018)
20. Schlette, D., Böhm, F., Caselli, M., Pernul, G.: Measuring and visualizing cyber threat intelligence quality. Int. J. Inf. Secur. **20**, 21–38 (2021)
21. Soomro, T.R., Hussain, M.: Social media-related cybercrimes and techniques for their prevention. Appl. Comput. Syst. **24**(1), 9–17 (2019)
22. Stottlemyre, S.A.: HUMINT, OSINT, or something new? Defining crowdsourced intelligence. Int. J. Intell. Counter Intell. **28**(3), 578–589 (2015)
23. Strom, B.E., Applebaum, A., Miller, D.P., Nickels, K.C., Pennington, A.G., Thomas, C.B.: MITRE ATT&CK: design and philosophy. Technical report (2018)
24. Strom, B.E., et al.: Finding cyber threats with ATT&CK-based analytics. The MITRE Corporation, Bedford, MA, Technical Report No. MTR170202 (2017)

25. Tabassum, S., Pereira, F.S., Fernandes, S., Gama, J.: Social network analysis: an overview. Wiley Interdiscip. Rev. Data Min. Knowl. Discov. **8**(5), e1256 (2018)
26. Tounsi, W.: What is cyber threat intelligence and how is it evolving? Cyber-Vigilance and Digital Trust: Cyber Security in the Era of Cloud Computing and IoT, pp. 1–49 (2019)
27. Wasserman, S., Faust, K.: Social network analysis: Methods and applications. Cambridge University Press (1994)
28. Williams, H.J., Blum, I.: Defining second generation open source intelligence (OSINT) for the defense enterprise. Rand Corporation Santa Monica (2018)
29. Xiong, W., Legrand, E., Åberg, O., Lagerström, R.: Cyber security threat modeling based on the MITRE Enterprise ATT&CK Matrix. Softw. Syst. Model. **21**(1), 157–177 (2022)
30. Yadav, A., Kumar, A., Singh, V.: Open-source intelligence: a comprehensive review of the current state, applications and future perspectives in cyber security. Artif. Intell. Rev., 1–32 (2023). https://doi.org/10.1007/s10462-023-10454-y
31. Yeboah-Ofori, A., Brimicombe, A.: Cyber intelligence and OSINT: developing mitigation techniques against cybercrime threats on social media. Int. J. Cyber-Sec. Digit. Forensics (IJCSDF) **7**(1), 87–98 (2018)

System Biology

Attractor and Slicing Analysis of a T Cell Differentiation Model Based on Reaction Systems

Linda Brodo[1], Roberto Bruni[2], Moreno Falaschi[3], Roberta Gori[2], and Paolo Milazzo[2(✉)]

[1] Dipartimento di Scienze Economiche e Aziendali, University of Sassari, Via Muroni 25, 07100 Sassari, Italy
brodo@uniss.it

[2] Department of Computer Science, University of Pisa, Largo B. Pontecorvo 3, 56127 Pisa, Italy
{roberto.bruni,roberta.gori,paolo.milazzo}@unipi.it

[3] Department of Information Engineering and Mathematics, University of Siena, Via Roma 56, 53100 Siena, Italy
moreno.falaschi@unisi.it

Abstract. Reaction Systems (RSs) were introduced in the field of natural computing as a qualitative model inspired by biological systems. In a RS, each reaction comprises a set of reactants that generate products unless inhibited by reaction inhibitors. We propose a method for analyzing the *attractors* of a RS model (the states to which the system converges) and for identifying the entities responsible for their attainment. Our approach builds on (i) the construction of a Labeled Transition System (LTS) based on a formal SOS semantics of RSs, and (ii) the application of a slicing method to the trajectories within the LTS. Our model analysis provides new insights with respect to previous studies. We illustrate our methodology on a case study that demonstrates its capability to identify stimulus combinations that lead to specific phenotypes, but also to elucidate the involvement of proteins within T cells in each scenario. These findings allow for a better understanding of the phenomenon and for the identification of potential drug targets for diseases.

Keywords: Systems Biology · LTS · Slicing · Attractors

Supported by project "MEDICA" (2022RNTYWZ) funded by MUR-PRIN_2022, by PNRR ECS00000017 - "THE - Tuscany Health Ecosystem" - Spokes 3 and 6 - CUP I53C22000780001 funded by the EC under the NextGeneration EU programme, by the Italian MUR PRIN 2022 PNRR project *Resource Awareness in Programming: Algebra, Rewriting, and Analysis* (P2022HXNSC), and by the INdAM–GNCS project CUP_E53C22001930001.

G. Broccia and A. Cerone (Eds.): DataMod 2023, LNCS 14618, pp. 69–89, 2025.
https://doi.org/10.1007/978-3-031-87217-4_4

1 Introduction

Reaction Systems (RSs) [17,18] are a successful computational framework inspired by biochemical systems. They offer a broad and flexible platform for constructing qualitative models, abstracting away the specific count of modeled entities (e.g., molecules). A RS comprises a finite set of reactions, where each reaction is a triple (R, I, P), with R, I, and P being finite, non-empty sets of entities defined over a fixed finite set S called the *background set*. A computation in a RS begins with an initial state (a finite set of entities) and, at each step, repeatedly generates new entities by applying all enabled reactions to the current state. Each reaction (R, I, P) contributes to the new state only if all entities in R (the reactants) and no element in I (the inhibitors) are present in the current state. If these two conditions are met, the set P (the products) is included in the next state. The union of the products of all reactions determines the new state.

RSs are an interactive model of computation that can be fed with an ordered sequence of states (sets of entities) called *context sequence*. Then, the i-th state in a computation will be determined by the result of the application of the reactions to the previous state, together with the set of entities in the i-th set of the context sequence.

In this paper, we present a methodology for analyzing the attractors of a RS model, which represent the set of states towards which the system converges, and for identifying biological entities responsible for their attainment. Exploiting the operational semantics defined in [11], our method starts by computing a Labeled Transition System (LTS) describing all the possible behaviours of the RS model. Subsequently, we employ an automated methodology, known as slicing (see [12]), to simplify the trajectories described by the LTS.

To demonstrate the effectiveness of our methodology, we apply it to a case study, focusing on the analysis of a model representing T cell differentiation in the immune system. This model encompasses reactions enabling T cells to manifest various phenotypes in response to environmental stimuli. Our analysis unveils novel insights compared to previous studies, revealing the combinations of stimuli associated with each phenotype and identifying the specific proteins within T cells implicated in each scenario.

Several tools find fruitful application in our study. The first is BioReSolve [5], a freely available tool that we have previously developed: it implements RSs in SWI-Prolog, along with a slicing analysis method. In order to develop the analysis of attractors, we have designed and implemented a new Python script leveraging the `networkx` package. Our script interacts with BioReSolve through the Python-to-Prolog binding facilitated by the `swiplserver` Python package.

Roughly, our methodology consists of the following steps: firstly, we utilise BioReSolve to run our RS model, obtained through automatic translation from the Boolean network to the corresponding RS. Subsequently, we add the contexts which are necessary to start a computation in BioReSolve by considering a non-deterministic context which provides all combinations of entities/stimuli as different initial alternatives. The computation proceeds along each path by repeating the same initial context of that path until reaching a loop in the computation graph. BioReSolve returns a representation of the LTS as a graph in dot format, which can be loaded by our Python script. Our Python script conducts an analysis of the attractors, considering different *targets* corresponding to the different combinations of phenotypes that a T cell can exhibit. The slicing tool, which performs a form of causality analysis, is used to simplify the computation traces, retaining only the information pertinent to producing a *target* of our analysis. This enables us to uncover significant facts, such as identifying the genes necessary for the expression of a target transcription factor.

Our methodology is general, and hence it could be applied to many other case studies, such as the ones in the public data base *Cell Collective* [28], which contains our current case study. Moreover, our methodology introduces an original analysis of attractors combined with a slicing algorithm that provides a deeper understanding of the evolution of the system and the entities involved. This can have a significant impact in drug design, since understanding which genes are necessary or, more generally, contribute to the expression of some other genes or transcription factors involved in a disease can be helpful for the identification of potential drugs or vaccine targets.

Related Work. This paper contributes to the research in computational modelling and analysis of gene regulatory networks [4,22]. In particular, the attractors and slicing analyses, combined together, constitute a new methodology for the investigation of causality properties in such networks. Causality properties can be studied by running simulations [24,29], to investigate the role of initial configurations of active genes and identify attractors. Moreover, formal causality approaches have been investigated for biological applications in [7,16], and in particular for RSs in [1,2]. Compared to these approaches, ours provides information about the role of both the environmental stimuli (or the "input" nodes of the networks) and the intermediate genes involved in the achievement of a given target, computed in an integrated way and with scalable performances.

Structure of the Paper. in Sect. 2, we present the basic framework of RSs and the slicing algorithm. Then, Sect. 3 presents the implementation of our methodology. In Sect. 4 we define the RS model of T cell differentiation whose analysis is described in Sect. 5. We draw some concluding remarks and sketch future work in Sect. 6.

2 Reaction Systems and Slicing Analysis

In this section we recall background notions about the Reaction Systems, as well as the definition of a SOS semantics and of a slicing analysis method.

2.1 Reaction Systems

The theory of Reaction Systems (RSs) [9] was born in the field of natural computing to model the qualitative behavior of biochemical reactions in living cells.

We recall here the main concepts and we use the term *entities* to denote generic molecular substances (e.g., atoms, ions, molecules) that may be present in the states of a biochemical system.

Let S be a finite set of entities, a reaction in S is a triple $r = (R, I, P)$, where $R, I, P \subseteq S$ are non empty sets and $R \cap I = \emptyset$. The sets R, I, P are the *reactants*, *inhibitors*, and *products*, respectively. All reactants have to be present in the current state for the reaction to take place. The presence of any of the inhibitors blocks the reaction. Products are the outcome of the reaction, to be released in the next state. Given a state $W \subseteq S$, the result of a reaction $r = (R, I, P)$ on W, denoted by $res_r(W)$, is defined as follows, where $en_r(W)$ is called the *enabling predicate*:

$$res_r(W) \triangleq \begin{cases} P & \text{if } en_r(W) \\ \emptyset & \text{otherwise} \end{cases} \qquad en_r(W) \triangleq R \subseteq W \ \wedge \ \mathrm{I} \cap W = \emptyset$$

A Reaction System is a pair $\mathcal{A} = (S, A)$ where S is the set of entities, and A is a finite set of reactions over S. Given $W \subseteq S$, the result of the reactions A on W, denoted $res_A(W)$, is $res_A(W) \triangleq \bigcup_{r \in A} res_r(W)$.

Since living cells can react to environmental stimuli, the behavior of a RS $\mathcal{A} = (S, A)$ is formalized as an *interactive process*. An n-step *interactive process* in $\mathcal{A}$, with $n \geq 0$, is a pair $\pi = (\gamma, \delta)$ s.t. $\gamma = \{C_i\}_{i \in [0,n]}$ is the *context sequence* and $\delta = \{D_i\}_{i \in [0,n]}$ is the *result sequence*, where $C_i, D_i \subseteq S$ for $i \in [0, n]$, $D_0 = \emptyset$, and $D_{i+1} = res_A(D_i \cup C_i)$ for $i \in [0, n-1]$. The context sequence γ represents the environment, while the result sequence δ is determined by γ and A. We call $\tau = W_0, \ldots, W_n$ the *state sequence*, with $W_i \triangleq C_i \cup D_i$ for $i \in [0, n]$.

Example 1. We consider a toy RS defined as $\mathcal{A} \triangleq (S, A)$ where $S \triangleq \{\mathsf{a}, \mathsf{b}, \mathsf{c}\}$, and the set $A \triangleq \{r_1\}$ only contains the reaction $r_1 \triangleq (\{\mathsf{a}, \mathsf{b}\}, \{\mathsf{c}\}, \{\mathsf{b}\})$ (written as $(\mathsf{ab}, \mathsf{c}, \mathsf{b})$ for short). Then, we consider a 4-steps interactive process $\pi \triangleq (\gamma, \delta)$, where $\gamma \triangleq \{C_0, C_1, C_2, C_3\}$, with $C_0 \triangleq \{\mathsf{a}, \mathsf{b}\}$, $C_1 \triangleq \{\mathsf{a}\}$, $C_2 \triangleq \{\mathsf{c}\}$, and $C_3 \triangleq \{\mathsf{c}\}$; and $\delta \triangleq \{D_0, D_1, D_2, D_3\}$, with $D_0 \triangleq \emptyset$, $D_1 \triangleq \{\mathsf{b}\}$, $D_2 \triangleq \{\mathsf{b}\}$, and $D_3 \triangleq \emptyset$. Then, the resulting state sequence is $\tau = W_0, W_1, W_2, W_3 = \{\mathsf{a}, \mathsf{b}\}, \{\mathsf{a}, \mathsf{b}\}, \{\mathsf{b}, \mathsf{c}\}, \{\mathsf{c}\}$. In fact, it is easy to check that, e.g., $W_0 = C_0$, $D_1 = res_A(W_0) = res_A(\{\mathsf{a}, \mathsf{b}\}) = \{\mathsf{b}\}$ because $en_{r_1}(W_0)$, and $W_1 = C_1 \cup D_1 = \{\mathsf{a}\} \cup \{\mathsf{b}\} = \{\mathsf{a}, \mathsf{b}\}$.

2.2 SOS Rules for Reaction Systems

Our methodology exploits the algebraic syntax and the formal semantics for RSs introduced in [11]. As in process algebras such as CCS [27], SOS inference rules define the behavior of each operator. This induces a LTS semantics for RSs, where states are terms of the algebra, transitions correspond to steps of the RS, and their labels retain information on the entities needed to perform each step.

Definition 1. (RS processes). *Let S be a finite set of entities. A* RS process P *is any term defined by the following grammar:*

$$\mathsf{P} := [\mathsf{M}] \qquad \mathsf{M} := (R, I, P) \mid D \mid \mathsf{K} \mid \mathsf{M}|\mathsf{M} \qquad \mathsf{K} ::= \mathbf{0} \mid X \mid C.\mathsf{K} \mid \mathsf{K} + \mathsf{K} \mid \mathsf{rec}\ X.\ \mathsf{K}$$

where $R, I, P, C, D \subseteq S$, $R, I, P \neq \emptyset$, *and* X *belongs to the set of process variables.*

A RS process P embeds a *mixture* process M obtained as the parallel composition of some reactions (R, I, P), some set of current entities D (possibly the empty set), and some *context* K. We write $\prod_{j \in J} \mathsf{M}_j$ for the parallel composition of all M_j with $j \in J$. A context process K is a possibly non-deterministic and recursive system: the nil context $\mathbf{0}$ stops the computation; the prefixed context $C.\mathsf{K}$ makes the entities C available to the reactions, and then leaves K be the context offered at the next step; the non-deterministic choice $\mathsf{K}_1 + \mathsf{K}_2$ allows the context to behave as either K_1 or K_2; X is a process variable, and $\mathsf{rec}\ X.\ \mathsf{K}$ is the usual recursive operator of process algebras.

We say that P and P' are structurally equivalent, written $\mathsf{P} \equiv \mathsf{P}'$, when they denote the same term up to the laws of commutative monoids (unit, associativity and commutativity) for parallel composition $\cdot|\cdot$, with $\emptyset$ as the unit, and the laws of idempotent and commutative monoids for choice $\cdot + \cdot$, with $\mathbf{0}$ as the unit. We also assume $D_1|D_2 \equiv D_1 \cup D_2$ for any $D_1, D_2 \subseteq S$.

Definition 2. (RSs as RS processes). *Let* $\mathcal{A} = (S, A)$ *be a RS, and* $\pi = (\gamma, \delta)$ *an* n*-step interactive process in* $\mathcal{A}$*, with* $\gamma = \{C_i\}_{i \in [0,n]}$ *and* $\delta = \{D_i\}_{i \in [0,n]}$*. For any step* $i \in [0, n]$*, the corresponding RS process* $[\![\mathcal{A}, \pi]\!]_i$ *is defined as follows:*

$$[\![\mathcal{A}, \pi]\!]_i \triangleq \left[\prod_{r \in A} r \mid D_i \mid \mathsf{K}_{\gamma^i} \right]$$

where $\mathsf{K}_{\gamma^i} \triangleq C_i.C_{i+1}.\cdots.C_n.\mathbf{0}$ *is the serialization of the entities offered by* γ^i *(the shifting of* γ *at the i-th step). We write* $[\![\mathcal{A}, \pi]\!]$ *as a shorthand for* $[\![\mathcal{A}, \pi]\!]_0$*.*

Example 2. The encoding of the RS $\mathcal{A} = (S, A)$, in Example 1, is as follows:

$$\mathsf{P} \triangleq [\![\mathcal{A}, \pi]\!] = [\![(\{\mathsf{a},\mathsf{b},\mathsf{c}\}, \{(\mathsf{ab},\mathsf{c},\mathsf{b})\}), \pi]\!] = [(\mathsf{ab},\mathsf{c},\mathsf{b}) \mid \emptyset \mid \mathsf{K}_\gamma] \equiv [(\mathsf{ab},\mathsf{c},\mathsf{b}) \mid \mathsf{K}_\gamma]$$

where $\mathsf{K}_\gamma = \{\mathsf{a},\mathsf{b}\}.\{\mathsf{a}\}.\{\mathsf{c}\}.\{\mathsf{c}\}.\mathbf{0}$ (written as $\mathsf{ab.a.c.c}.\mathbf{0}$ for short), and $D_0 = \emptyset$ can be discarded thanks to structural congruence.

A transition label ℓ is a tuple $\langle (D, C) \rhd R, I, P \rangle$ with $D, C, R, I, P \subseteq S$. The sets D, C record the entities currently in the system; R records entities whose presence is assumed (acting as reactants or as inhibitors); I records entities whose absence is assumed (acting as inhibitors or as missing reactants); P records the products of enabled reactions.

The operational semantics of RS processes is defined by the SOS rules in Fig. 1. Process $\mathbf{0}$ does nothing. Rule (*Ent*) makes available the entities in the (possibly empty) set D, then reduces to $\emptyset$. In rule (*Cxt*), a prefixed context process $C.\mathsf{K}$ makes available the entities in C and then reduces to K. (*Rec*) is the classical rule for recursion. Rules (*Suml*) and (*Sumr*) select a move of either the left or the right component, resp., discarding the other one. Rule (*Pro*) executes the reaction (R, I, P) (its reactants, inhibitors, and products are recorded in the label), and remains available at the next step together with P. Rule (*Inh*) applies if the reaction (R, I, P) can not be executed; the label records the causes

$$\frac{}{D \xrightarrow{\langle (D,\emptyset) \rhd \emptyset,\emptyset,\emptyset \rangle} \emptyset}\ (Ent) \qquad \frac{}{C.\mathsf{K} \xrightarrow{\langle (\emptyset,C) \rhd \emptyset,\emptyset,\emptyset \rangle} \mathsf{K}}\ (Cxt)$$

$$\frac{\mathsf{K}_1 \xrightarrow{\ell} \mathsf{K}_1'}{\mathsf{K}_1 + \mathsf{K}_2 \xrightarrow{\ell} \mathsf{K}_1'}\ (Suml) \qquad \frac{\mathsf{K}_2 \xrightarrow{\ell} \mathsf{K}_2'}{\mathsf{K}_1 + \mathsf{K}_2 \xrightarrow{\ell} \mathsf{K}_2'}\ (Sumr) \qquad \frac{\mathsf{K}[{}^{\mathsf{rec}\ X.\mathsf{K}}/_X] \xrightarrow{\ell} \mathsf{K}'}{\mathsf{rec}\ X.\ \mathsf{K} \xrightarrow{\ell} \mathsf{K}'}\ (Rec)$$

$$\frac{}{(R,I,P) \xrightarrow{\langle (\emptyset,\emptyset) \rhd R,I,P \rangle} (R,I,P) \mid P}\ (Pro) \qquad \frac{J \subseteq I \quad Q \subseteq R \quad J \cup Q \neq \emptyset}{(R,I,P) \xrightarrow{\langle (\emptyset,\emptyset) \rhd J,Q,\emptyset \rangle} (R,I,P)}\ (Inh)$$

$$\frac{\mathsf{M}_1 \xrightarrow{\ell_1} \mathsf{M}_1' \quad \mathsf{M}_2 \xrightarrow{\ell_2} \mathsf{M}_2' \quad \ell_1 \frown \ell_2}{\mathsf{M}_1 \mid \mathsf{M}_2 \xrightarrow{\ell_1 \cup \ell_2} \mathsf{M}_1' \mid \mathsf{M}_2'}\ (Par) \qquad \frac{\mathsf{M} \xrightarrow{\langle (D,C) \rhd R,I,P \rangle} \mathsf{M}' \quad R \subseteq D \cup C}{[\mathsf{M}] \xrightarrow{\langle (D,C) \rhd R,I,P \rangle} [\mathsf{M}']}\ (Sys)$$

Fig. 1. SOS semantics of the RS processes.

that disable the reaction: some inhibitors ($J \subseteq I$) are present or some reactants ($Q \subseteq R$) are missing, with $J \cup Q \neq \emptyset$. The rule (*Par*) puts two processes in parallel by joining all the set components of the labels. The check $\ell_1 \frown \ell_2$ guarantees that reactants and inhibitors are consistent (we let $W_i \triangleq D_i \cup C_i$):

$$\langle (D_1, C_1) \rhd R_1, I_1, P_1 \rangle \frown \langle (D_2, C_2) \rhd R_2, I_2, P_2 \rangle \triangleq (W_1 \cup W_2 \cup R_1 \cup R_2) \cap (I_1 \cup I_2) = \emptyset$$

In the conclusion of rule (*Par*) $\ell_1 \cup \ell_2$ stands for the component-wise union of labels (see definition below, where the notation $X_{1,2} \triangleq X_1 \cup X_2$ is used):

$$\langle (D_1, C_1) \rhd R_1, I_1, P_1 \rangle \cup \langle (D_2, C_2) \rhd R_2, I_2, P_2 \rangle \triangleq \langle (D_{1,2}, C_{1,2}) \rhd R_{1,2}, I_{1,2}, P_{1,2} \rangle$$

Rule (*Sys*) requires that all the processes of the system have been considered, and checks that all the needed reactants are available in the system ($R \subseteq D \cup C$).

Example 3. The RS process $\mathsf{P}_0 \triangleq [(\mathsf{ab}, \mathsf{c}, \mathsf{b}) \mid \mathsf{ab.a.c.c.0}]$ from Example 2, and its next state P_1 have a unique outgoing transition:

$$[(\mathsf{ab}, \mathsf{c}, \mathsf{b}) \mid \mathsf{ab.a.c.c.0}] \xrightarrow{\langle (\emptyset,\mathsf{ab}) \rhd \mathsf{ab},\mathsf{c},\mathsf{b} \rangle} [(\mathsf{ab}, \mathsf{c}, \mathsf{b}) \mid \mathsf{b} \mid \mathsf{a.c.c.0}] \xrightarrow{\langle \mathsf{b},\mathsf{a} \rhd \mathsf{ab},\mathsf{c},\mathsf{b} \rangle} [(\mathsf{ab}, \mathsf{c}, \mathsf{b}) \mid \mathsf{b} \mid \mathsf{c.c.0}]$$

From $\mathsf{P}_2 = [(\mathsf{ab}, \mathsf{c}, \mathsf{b}) \mid \mathsf{b} \mid \mathsf{c.c.0}]$, three transitions lead to the same state $\mathsf{P}_3 \triangleq [(\mathsf{ab}, \mathsf{c}, \mathsf{b}) \mid \mathsf{c.0}]$, each with a different cause why reaction $(\mathsf{ab}, \mathsf{c}, \mathsf{b})$ is not enabled:

1. $\mathsf{P}_2 \xrightarrow{\langle (\mathsf{b},\mathsf{c}) \rhd \mathsf{c},\emptyset,\emptyset \rangle} \mathsf{P}_3$ the presence of c inhibits the reaction;
2. $\mathsf{P}_2 \xrightarrow{\langle (\mathsf{b},\mathsf{c}) \rhd \emptyset,\mathsf{a},\emptyset \rangle} \mathsf{P}_3$ the absence of a inhibits the reaction;
3. $\mathsf{P}_2 \xrightarrow{\langle (\mathsf{b},\mathsf{c}) \rhd \mathsf{c},\mathsf{a},\emptyset \rangle} \mathsf{P}_3$ this label summarizes the two previous ones.

From now on, we assume transitions $\mathsf{P} \xrightarrow{\langle (D,C) \rhd R,I,P \rangle} \mathsf{P}'$ to maximize the sets J and Q in applying rule (*Inh*) (see [11]). In [11], Theorem 19, we have shown that the set-theoretic dynamics of a RS matches the SOS semantics of its RS process.

2.3 Attractors

In biological systems, attractors depict an equilibrium dynamics where a finite set of states repeats infinitely in an ordered manner. Thus, in RSs an attractor is defined as a cyclic set of states, whose behaviour is repeated identically forever or until an external condition changes and differently stimulates the system. The number of states composing an attractor defines its size.

2.4 SOS Rules for a Slicing Computation

A slicing computation, presented in the next subsection, needs a slightly different state configuration that includes the whole past state sequence $W_i = C_i \cup D_i$. To do that, we add as a prefix to the state configuration $[\mathsf{M}]$ the list of the previous result and context sets, written $(\mathsf{D},\mathsf{C})[\mathsf{M}]$, where (D,C) stands for the list $(D_0, C_0), \ldots, (D_n, C_n)$. Definition 1 is thus updated to carry on such a history.

Definition 3. (RS processes with history). *Let* $\mathcal{A} = (S, A)$ *be a RS, and* $\pi = (\gamma, \delta)$ *an* n*-step interactive process in* $\mathcal{A}$*, with* $\gamma = \{C_i\}_{i\in[0,n]}$ *and* $\delta = \{D_i\}_{i\in[0,n]}$*. For any step* $i \in [0, n]$*, the new process configuration* $[\![\mathcal{A}, \pi]\!]_i$ *is defined as:*

$$[\![\mathcal{A}, \pi]\!]_i \triangleq (\mathsf{D},\mathsf{C})[\mathsf{M}]$$

where $(\mathsf{D},\mathsf{C}) \equiv (D_0, C_0), \ldots, (D_{i-1}, C_{i-1})$*, and,* $[\mathsf{M}] = \left[\prod_{r\in A} r \mid D_i \mid \mathsf{K}_{\gamma^i}\right]$.

The next step consists in enriching the operational semantics to deal with the history. We only have to modify the (Sys) inference rule in Fig. 1 as follows:

$$\frac{\mathsf{M} \xrightarrow{\langle (D,C)\rhd R,I,P\rangle} \mathsf{M}' \quad R \subseteq D \cup C}{(\mathsf{D},\mathsf{C})[\mathsf{M}] \xrightarrow{\langle (D,C)\rhd R,I,P\rangle} (\mathsf{D},\mathsf{C}) :: (D, C)[\mathsf{M}']} \ (HistSys)$$

where, given the history $(\mathsf{D},\mathsf{C}) = (D_0, C_0), \ldots, (D_{i-1}, C_{i-1})$, we let the notation $(\mathsf{D},\mathsf{C}) :: (D, C)$ stand for the history $(D_0, C_0), \ldots, (D_{i-1}, C_{i-1}), (D, C)$.

2.5 Slicing RS Computations

In the context of programming, dynamic slicing is a technique that helps a user to debug a program by simplifying a partial execution trace, by pruning parts which are irrelevant and highlighting parts of the program which have been wrongly ignored during execution. Our slicing technique for RSs is defined in [12]. We resume it here. The technique consists of three steps.

Enriched Semantics (Step S1). The slicing process requires some extra information from the execution of the processes. More precisely, (1) at each operational step we need to highlight the reactions that have been applied; and (2) we need to determine the part of the context which adds to the previous state the entities which are necessary to produce the marked entities in the following state. For solving (1) and (2), in Sect. 2.4 we have introduced an enriched

Input: - a trace $(D_0, C_0) \xrightarrow{N_1} \cdots \xrightarrow{N_m} (D_m, C_m)$
- a marking $D_{sliced} \subseteq D_m$

Output: a sliced trace $(D'_0, C'_0) \xrightarrow{N'_1} \cdots \xrightarrow{N'_m} (D_{sliced}, C_m)$

begin
  let $D'_m = D_{sliced}$
  for $i = m$ *to* 1 **do**
    let $D'_{i-1} = \emptyset \wedge C'_{i-1} = \emptyset \wedge N'_i = \emptyset$
    for $j \in N_i$ *where* $r_j = (R_j, I_j, P_j)$, *such that* $(D'_i \cap P_j \neq \emptyset)$ **do**
      let $N'_i = N'_i \cup \{j\}$
      if $\neg en_{r_j}(D_{i-1})$, **then**
      $C'_{i-1} = C'_{i-1} \cup (R_j \setminus D_{i-1}) \wedge D'_{i-1} = D'_{i-1} \cup \{R_j \cap D_{i-1}\}$
      else $D'_{i-1} = D'_{i-1} \cup R_j$
    end
  end
end

Algorithm 1: Trace Slicer

semantics that records computation sequences. We need to keep track of the state sequence of the computation for the slicing process, by keeping separated the produced entities D_i in a computation step from the context C_i.

Marking the State (Step S2). Let the final configuration in a partial computation be (D_m, C_m). The user (or a logical formula expressed by a monitor [12]) selects a subset $D_{sliced} \subseteq D_m$ that may explain the behavior of the program.

Trace Slice (Step S3). Starting from the pair (D_{sliced}, C_m) denoting the user's (or monitor) marking, we get a slicing step deleting from the execution trace all information not related to D_{sliced}.

Marking Algorithm. Let us now explain how the slicing Algorithm 1 works. We assume that the reactions are numbered consecutively by positive integer numbers, and denote the j-th reaction in the RS by the notation r_j. Please notice also that each history $(D_0, C_0)::\cdots::(D_m, C_m)$ computed in m steps by Definition 3, defines a *trace* $(D_0, C_0) \xrightarrow{N_1} \cdots \xrightarrow{N_m} (D_m, C_m)$ on which we perform the slicing computation, where N_i is the set of reactions applied in the i-th computation step. Here, each reaction is represented by its numeric position in the list of reactions, i.e., $N_i = \{j \mid en_{r_j}(D_{i-1} \cup C_{i-1})\}$ for any $i \in [1, m]$. Abusing the notation, we write $r_j \in N$ whenever $j \in N$.

Our algorithm returns a sliced trace which contains only the (usually small) subset of the entities which are necessary for deriving the marked entities. Let us consider the more complex case of context dependent computations. First of all, the user (or a logic formula expressed by a monitor [12]) has to indicate the subset D_{sliced} of the entities in the last state of the computation D_m that she wants to mark. Then, the backward slicing process can start. Now, let us consider the iteration i of the slicer. Marking the relevant information in previous state (D_{i-1}, C_{i-1}) requires analyzing the rules which have been applied at step $i-1$. So, if $r_j \in N_{i-1}$ and $r_j = (R_j, I_j, P_j)$, we need to check if r_j produces at least one entity which is marked in the next state. If this is the case, j is added to the set of marked rules. Then, it is necessary to check if the context C_{i-1} was essential for applying rule r_j, or if all necessary entities were already included in D_{i-1}. Thus, it is necessary to compute the entities in C_{i-1} which are missing in D_{i-1} in order for rule r_j to be enabled, and those entities are marked in (added to) context C'_{i-1}. The elements in R_j are added to the marked entities in D'_{i-1}.

3 Implementation of the Analyzer

Our experimentation exploits BioReSolve [5], a tool implementing the SOS semantics of RSs and the slicing analysis methods described in the previous section. It has been developed in SWI-Prolog [31] by some of the authors of this paper, according to the specifications given in [10] and [12].

To apply our method in the analysis of gene regulatory networks, we interface with BioReSolve through a Python script. This script makes it possible (i) to exploit Python packages such as `networkx` to process the LTS generated by BioReSolve for identifying attractors, and (ii) to automate the execution of the slicing analysis method for multiple gene targets and LTS states. This interaction is made possible by the usage of the `swiplserver` Python package, allowing to run SWI-Prolog code via Python function invocations.

More precisely, the Python script performs the following steps:

1. it loads an LTS generated by BioReSolve in dot format and uses it to create a `networkx DiGraph` object;
2. it initializes the list of targets of the analysis as a list of objects of a class `Target` with two fields, `present` and `absent`, denoting the genes that have to be expressed and non expressed, respectively, in the states of attractors that have to be considered as target;
3. it defines a few functions that will be used during the attractor analysis:
   - function `check_node(node)` checks whether the LTS state `node` belongs to an attractor of the LTS (i.e., it is in a cycle);
   - function `compute_attractor(node)` returns the list of genes that are present in states of the attractor reachable from state `node`[1];
   - function `target_computations(target)` selects the LTS traces that lead to attractors in target `target`, and for each of them it provides a description of the corresponding context sequences;
4. it executes the main loop that, for every target to be investigated, invokes the `target_computation` function and then for every state of every attractor of such a target, asks BioReSolve to compute the sliced computation leading to that state. Entities mentioned in a sliced computation are then collected in a set representing the entities that actually played a role for the presence of the target genes in the attractor. Finally, the set of entities obtained for each target are used to compute two results: the union of all of them (representing those entities that *may* play a role to achieve the target) and the intersection of all of them (representing those entities that *must* play a role).

[1] We will show that the LTS for the analysis described in this paper are such that every state, apart from the initial one, leads to exactly one attractor.

The Python script we developed, along with the BioReSolve specification of the RS model to be analysed in this paper, are freely available at [19].

4 RS Model of T Cell Differentiation

In this section we define the RS model of T cell differentiation on which we demonstrate our attractor and slicing analyses. The model is based on the Boolean network model proposed in [29].

4.1 The Boolean Network Model

T cell differentiation is a widely studied biological phenomenon for which several Boolean network models have been proposed [29,30,32]. We considered the model investigated in [29] and available on CellCollective [20]. The analysis performed in [29] is based on the simulation method provided by such a platform.

We choose this model since it describes a realistic regulation system that is involved in many diseases [21,23,26] and it has been investigated under both the viewpoints of causality (effect of environmental conditions) and of reachability (reachable phenotypes). The Boolean network model is graphically represented as shown in Fig. 2 and is fully specified by the Boolean update formulas shown in Fig. 3. It includes 9 *input* nodes (orange), that correspond to stimuli that the T cell can receive by the external environment. Then, it contains 23 nodes representing relevant T cell genes, and 6 nodes representing secreted cytokines.

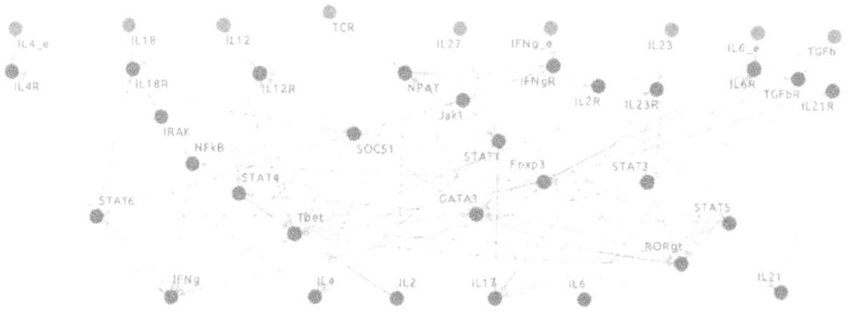

Fig. 2. Graphical representation of the Boolean network model of T Cell differentiation from [29]. The model is available in electronic format at [28].

T cells can differentiate by expressing four different phenotypes, denoted Th1, Th2, Th17 and iTreg. Such phenotypes correspond to the expression of four different trancription factors included in the model: Tbet (for Th1), GATA3 (for Th2), RORgt (for Th17) and Foxp3 (for iTreg). There exists experimental evidence that a T cell can express more than one phenotype (hence, more than

```
   Jak1 = IFNgR and not SOCS1
   IL21 = STAT3 and NFAT
  IL18R = IL18 and IL12 and not STAT6
  SOCS1 = STAT1 or Tbet
    IL6 = RORgt
  STAT5 = IL2R
   IL17 = (RORgt and not STAT1)
          or (STAT3 and IL17 and IL23R and not STAT1 and not STAT5)
  STAT4 = IL12R and IL12 and not GATA3
  IFNgR = (IFNg_e and NFAT) or (IFNg and NFAT)
  STAT6 = IL4R and not IFNg and not SOCS1
  GATA3 = (STAT6 and NFAT and not TGFb and not RORgt and not Foxp3
          and not Tbet) or (GATA3 and not Tbet)
          or (STAT5 and not TGFb and not RORgt and not Foxp3 and not Tbet)
    IL4 = GATA3 and NFAT and not STAT1
   NFkB = IRAK and not Foxp3
    IL2 = NFAT and NFkB and not Tbet
  IL23R = (IL23 and STAT3 and not Tbet) or STAT3
   Tbet = (STAT4 and not RORgt and not Foxp3)
          or (STAT1 and not RORgt and not Foxp3)
          or (Tbet and not IL12 and not IFNg and not RORgt and not Foxp3)
  TGFbR = TGFb and NFAT
  RORgt = TGFbR and ((STAT3 and IL21R) or (STAT3 and IL6R)) and not Tbet
          and not GATA3 and not Foxp3
   IL6R = IL6 or IL6_e
  IL21R = IL21
  Foxp3 = (TGFbR and not (IL6R and STAT3) and not IL21R and not GATA3)
          or (STAT5 and not (IL6R and STAT3) and not IL21R and not GATA3)
   IRAK = IL18R
  IL12R = (IL12 and NFAT) or (STAT4 and not GATA3) or Tbet or (TCR and not GATA3)
   IL2R = IL2 and NFAT
  STAT3 = IL21R or IL23R or IL6R
   IFNg = NFkB or (STAT4 and NFkB and NFAT and not STAT3 and not STAT6)
          or (Tbet and not STAT3)
   NFAT = TCR and not Foxp3
  STAT1 = (IL27 and NFAT) or Jak1
   IL4R = (IL4 and not SOCS1) or IL4_e
```

Fig. 3. Update rules of the Boolean network model of T Cell differentiation from [29]. Available in electronic format at [28].

one of the associated transcription factors) [25]. Moreover, through the computational analysis performed in [29], the authors hypothesize that T cells may express also other combinations of phenotypes, that might include three or even four of them. Finally, the case in which none of the four relevant transcription factors is expressed (i.e. no phenotype) is denoted as Th0.

4.2 The RS Model

Translating a Boolean network model into an equivalent RS can be done by turning every Boolean formula of the network into disjunctive normal form. Then, every term of the disjunction (which is a conjunction of atoms, possibly negated) is translated into a reaction in which (i) reactants are the positive atoms, (ii) inhibitors are the negated atoms and (iii) the (only) product is the Boolean variable that is updated through the considered formula. For example, the Boolean formula for IL12R, namely:

```
IL12R = (IL12 and NFAT) or (STAT4 and not GATA3) or Tbet or (TCR and not GATA3)
```

is translated into the following four reactions:

$$(\{\text{IL12}, \text{NFAT}\}, \emptyset, \{\text{IL12R}\}) \quad (\{\text{STAT4}\}, \{\text{GATA3}\}, \{\text{IL2R}\})$$
$$(\{\text{Tbet}\}, \emptyset, \{\text{IL12R}\}) \quad (\{\text{TCR}\}, \{\text{GATA3}\}, \{\text{IL12R}\})$$

that, in BioReSolve syntax, are coded as follows:

```
react([il12,nfat],[void],[il12r]),  react([stat4],[gata3],[il2r]),
react([tbet],[void],[il12r]),       react([tcr],[gata3],[il12r])
```

Even more complex forms of Boolean networks (such as Threshold Boolean Networks [8]) can be translated into RSs, as we demonstrated in [3].

The RS model of T cell differentiation obtained from the translation of the Boolean model is given in Fig. 4.

```
react([il4r],[socs1,ifng],[stat6]),          react([tgfb,nfat],[void],[tgfbr]),
react([tbet],[void],[il12r]),                react([stat4],[gata3],[il2r]),
react([tcr],[gata3],[il12r]),                react([il12,nfat],[void],[il12r]),
react([il2r],[void],[stat5]),                react([gata3],[tbet],[gata3]),
react([stat5],[tgfb,rorgt,foxp3,tbet],[gata3]),
react([stat6,nfat],[tgfb,rorgt,foxp3,tbet],[gata3]),
react([stat3],[void],[il23r]),               react([il23,stat3],[tbet],[il23r]),
react([tbet],[stat3],[ifng]),                react([nfkb],[void],[ifng]),
react([stat4,nfkb,nfat],[stat6,stat3],[ifng]),
react([tgfbr,stat3,il6r],[tbet,gata3,foxp3],[rorgt]),
react([tgfbr,stat3,il21r],[tbet,gata3,foxp3],[rorgt]),
react([il21],[void],[il21r]),                react([il18,il12],[stat6],[il18r]),
react([il6e],[void],[il6r]),                 react([il6],[void],[il6r]),
react([il18r],[void],[irak]),                react([il12r,il12],[gata3],[stat4]),
react([tbet],[void],[socs1]),                react([stat1],[void],[socs1]),
react([gata3,nfat],[stat1],[il4]),           react([stat3,nfat],[void],[il21]),
react([rorgt],[void],[il6]),                 react([stat5],[il21r,il6r,gata3],[foxp3]),
react([stat5],[il21r,stat3,gata3],[foxp3]),  react([tgfbr],[il21r,il6r,gata3],[foxp3]),
react([tgfbr],[il21r,stat3,gata3],[foxp3]),  react([tbet],[ifng,il12,rorgt,foxp3],[tbet]),
react([stat4],[rorgt,foxp3],[tbet]),         react([stat1],[rorgt,foxp3],[tbet]),
react([il27,nfat],[void],[stat1]),           react([jak1],[void],[stat1]),
react([il21r],[void],[stat3]),               react([il23r],[void],[stat3]),
react([il6r],[void],[stat3]),                react([ifngr],[socs1],[jak1]),
react([il2,nfat],[void],[il2r]),             react([il4e],[void],[il4r]),
react([il4],[socs1],[il4r]),                 react([irak],[foxp3],[nfkb]),
react([tcr],[foxp3],[nfat]),                 react([stat3,il17,il23r],[stat1,stat5],[il17]),
react([rorgt],[stat1],[il17]),               react([nfat,nfkb],[tbet],[il2]),
react([ifng,nfat],[void],[ifngr]),           react([ifnge,nfat],[void],[ifngr])
```

Fig. 4. Reactions of the RS model in BioReSolve syntax.

5 Attractors and Slicing Analyses

In this section we describe the analyses we performed on the RS model of T Cell differentiation. We describe both the methodology we applied and the results we obtained. We start from the generation of the LTS obtained by the execution of BioReSolve. Then, we perform an analysis aimed at identifying attractors and characterizing environmental configurations (i.e., RS contexts) leading to them. Finally, we perform the slicing analysis in order to identify relevant and crucial internal regulators for the expression of the different phenotypes.

5.1 Generation of the LTS

The LTS of the RS model is generated by invoking the `main_do(digraph)` directive of BioReSolve after providing model and context specifications in the expected syntax. In order to test all of the possible configurations of the environment, the RS context in the BioReSolve specification is defined as a process that, at the first step, chooses in a non-deterministic way the set of environmental stimuli that have to be present. Then, the chosen stimuli will persist in the context. According to the syntax of RS processes given in Definition 1, this is expressed by the following parallel composition of context processes:

$$\mathsf{rec}\ \mathsf{x11.TGFb.x11} + \mathsf{rec}\ \mathsf{x0}.\emptyset.\mathsf{x0} \mid \ldots \mid \mathsf{rec}\ \mathsf{x91.TCR.x91} + \mathsf{rec}\ \mathsf{x0}.\emptyset.\mathsf{x0}$$

which, in the BioReSolve model specification, is expressed as follows:

```
myenvironment('[ x1 = ({tgfb}.x11 + {}.x0), x2 = ({il23}.x21 + {}.x0),
                 x3 = ({il12}.x31 + {}.x0), x4 = ({il18}.x41 + {}.x0),
                 x5 = ({il4e}.x51 + {}.x0), x6 = ({il27}.x61 + {}.x0),
                 x7 = ({il6e}.x71 + {}.x0), x8 = ({ifnge}.x81 + {}.x0),
                 x9 = ({tcr}.x91 + {}.x0),
                 x11 = {tgfb}.x11, x21 = {il23}.x21, x31 = {il12}.x31,
                 x41 = {il18}.x41, x51 = {il4e}.x51, x61 = {il27}.x61,
                 x71 = {il6e}.x71, x81 = {ifnge}.x81, x91 = {tcr}.x91,
                 x0 = {}.x0 ]').
mycontext("[x1,x2,x3,x4,x5,x6,x7,x8,x9]").
```

```
react([il4r],[socs1,ifng],[stat6]),          react([tgfb,nfat],[void],[tgfbr]),
react([tbet],[void],[il12r]),                react([stat4],[gata3],[il2r]),
react([tcr],[gata3],[il12r]),                react([il12,nfat],[void],[il12r]),
react([il2r],[void],[stat5]),                react([gata3],[tbet],[gata3]),
react([stat5],[tgfb,rorgt,foxp3,tbet],[gata3]),
react([stat6,nfat],[tgfb,rorgt,foxp3,tbet],[gata3]),
react([stat3],[void],[il23r]),               react([il23,stat3],[tbet],[il23r]),
react([tbet],[stat3],[ifng]),                react([nfkb],[void],[ifng]),
react([stat4,nfkb,nfat],[stat6,stat3],[ifng]),
react([tgfbr,stat3,il6r],[tbet,gata3,foxp3],[rorgt]),
react([tgfbr,stat3,il21r],[tbet,gata3,foxp3],[rorgt]),
react([il21],[void],[il21r]),                react([il18,il12],[stat6],[il18r]),
react([il6e],[void],[il6r]),                 react([il6],[void],[il6r]),
react([il18r],[void],[irak]),                react([il12r,il12],[gata3],[stat4]),
react([tbet],[void],[socs1]),                react([stat1],[void],[socs1]),
react([gata3,nfat],[stat1],[il4]),           react([stat3,nfat],[void],[il21]),
react([rorgt],[void],[il6]),                 react([stat5],[il21r,il6r,gata3],[foxp3]),
react([stat5],[il21r,stat3,gata3],[foxp3]), react([tgfbr],[il21r,il6r,gata3],[foxp3]),
react([tgfbr],[il21r,stat3,gata3],[foxp3]), react([tbet],[ifng,il12,rorgt,foxp3],[tbet]),
react([stat4],[rorgt,foxp3],[tbet]),         react([stat1],[rorgt,foxp3],[tbet]),
react([il27,nfat],[void],[stat1]),           react([jak1],[void],[stat1]),
react([il21r],[void],[stat3]),               react([il23r],[void],[stat3]),
react([il6r],[void],[stat3]),                react([ifngr],[socs1],[jak1]),
react([il2,nfat],[void],[il2r]),             react([il4e],[void],[il4r]),
react([il4],[socs1],[il4r]),                 react([irak],[foxp3],[nfkb]),
react([tcr],[foxp3],[nfat]),                 react([stat3,il17,il23r],[stat1,stat5],[il17]),
react([rorgt],[stat1],[il17]),               react([nfat,nfkb],[tbet],[il2]),
react([ifng,nfat],[void],[ifngr]),           react([ifnge,nfat],[void],[ifngr])
```

Fig. 5. Overall representation of the LTS as a graph without labels. Enlargments of this image are available in Figs. 6 and 7.

Since we have 9 input entities representing the possible stimuli, this definition of the context process leads to an LTS with an initial branching into 2^9 different states, each being the start of a deterministic computation (i.e. a linear trace).

To give an idea of the structure of the LTS, in Fig. 5 we show its representation as a graph (without labels). Moreover, in Fig. 6 and Fig. 7 we zoom on some portions of the graph. In particular, Fig. 6 shows the initial state of the LTS and a few alternative traces all ending with a self-loop in the final state that corresponds to an attractor of size 1 (a steady state). On the other hand, Fig. 7 shows some examples of traces ending with attractors of different sizes.

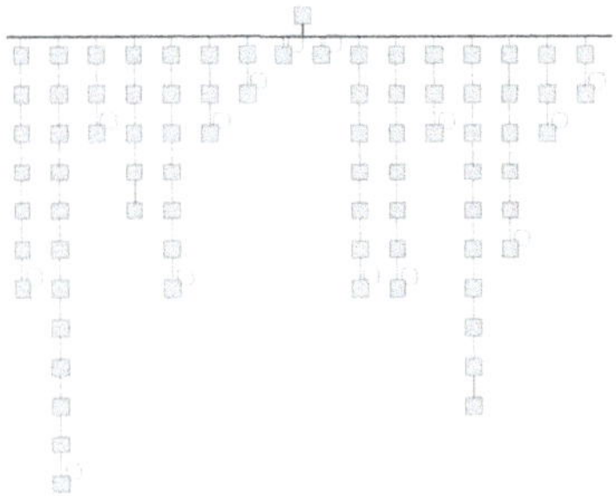

Fig. 6. Central part of the LTS depicted in Fig. 5. The node on top is the initial state, from which several independent branches start.

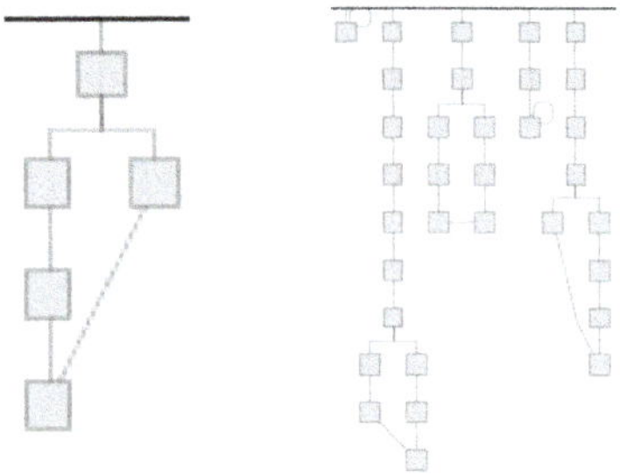

Fig. 7. Two fragments of the LTS with a trace leading to an attractor of size four (left), and a few traces leading to attractors of different sizes (right).

5.2 Attractors Analysis

BioReSolve returns the LTS as a graph in dot format, which is then loaded by our Python script. Then, attractors related with a target of interest are identified by looking for cycles in the LTS. Due to the LTS structure, this is particularly simple, and it is done in the `target_computations` function defined in our Python script by invoking repeatedly the `find_cycle` function provided by `networkx` package.

The analysis is performed by considering different *targets* corresponding to the different combinations of phenotypes that a T cell can express. As we described in Sect. 4.1, T cells can exhibit four phenotypes, Th1, Th2, Th17 and iTreg, represented by the expression of the four transcription factors Tbet, GATA3, RORgt and Foxp3, respectively. Since we are interested also in combinations of phenotypes, we consider all of the 2^4 combinations of such transcription factors: each of them will be a target of our analysis (hence, 16 targets overall).

For each target, we identify the attractors that include states in which the target transcription factors are expressed (not all necessarily in the same state), and in which the other transcription factors are not expressed. For example, for the target containing the combination of transcription factors {Tbet,GATA3}, we select the attractors (i.e., the cycles) that include at least one state in which Tbet is present, at least one state (possibly the same) in which GATA3 is present, and no state in which either RORgt or Foxp3 are present.

The filtering procedure just described gives as a result the subset of the attractors that correspond to the achievement of the considered target. Each of these attractors is reachable by making a different choice of environmental stimuli in the first step. The collection of all of those choices allows us to determine, for each target, which combinations of stimuli lead to it.

In Table 1 we report the number of different contexts (choices of environmental stimuli) that lead to each target. The table shows only targets that can be reached, and they result to be those in which only one transcription factor is expressed, and those in which Tbet is expressed together with another transcription factor. For each target, the contexts leading to it are summarized in the table by a Boolean formula, while in Fig. 8 they are depicted graphically.

Table 1. Summary of contexts leading to each reachable target.

Target	Contexts	Formula
Tbet	76	(not X11) and (X91) and (((not X31) and (X61)) or ((not X31) and (not X61) and (X71) and (X81)) or ((not X31) and (not X51) and (not X61) and (not X71) and (X81)) or ((X31) and (X71)))
GATA3	8	(not X11) and (not X31) and (X51) and (not X61) and (not X81) and (X91)
Foxp3	72	(not X71) and (not X91) and (((X11) and (not X61) and (not X81)) or (X31))
RORgt	16	(X11) and (not X31) and (not X61) and (X71) and (X91)
Tbet,GATA3	4	(not X11) and (not X31) and (X51) and (not X61) and (not X71) and (X81) and (X91)
Tbet,Foxp3	24	(X11) and (not X31) and (not X71) and (X91) and ((X61) or (X81))
Tbet,RORgt	48	(X11) and (X71) and (X91) And ((X31) or (X61))
TOTAL	**248**	

Analysis results show that 248 contexts (out of 512) lead to the expression of at least one of the four transcription factors under study. Tbet, corresponding to phenotype Th1, is expressed in the majority of the cases (152 out of 248), half of the times in combination with another transcription factor (in 76 cases out of 152). Also Foxp3 is often expressed (in 96 cases out of 248), while RORgt and GATA3 are less frequent (64 and 12 cases, respectively).

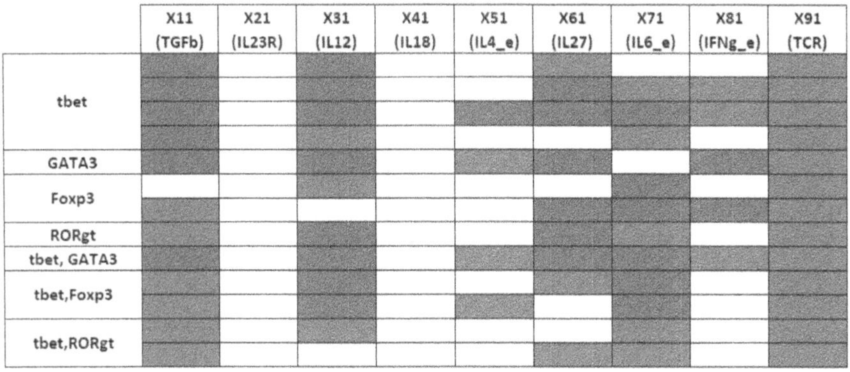

Fig. 8. Graphical representation of the Boolean formula given in Table 1 and characterizing contexts leading to each reachable target. Green cells denote that the corresponding environmental stimulus has to be present, red cells denote absences, and white cells denote that the stimulus is irrelevant. (Color figure online)

Figure 8 allows us to make the following main observations about the role of the environment in the T cell differentiation process:

- TCR has to be present in order to express any of the phenotypes
- IL23R and IL18R do not contribute to determine any of the phenotypes
- The presence of TGFb mostly discriminates between the expression of either Foxp3/RORgt or tbet/GATA3.

Moreover, the detailed characterization of the contexts leading to the expression of each phenotype could allow several more specific observations to be done.

The results of the analysis we conducted partially agree with those of a similar analysis done in [29]. However, there are also some significant differences between the results of the two studies. First of all, in [29] the authors show that it is also possible to reach configurations in which three or four (i.e., all) phenotypes are expressed. Morevoer, they show that a configuration in which only RORgt is expressed cannot be reached. The Boolean network we started from is exactly the same as the one considered in [29]. The main difference between the two analysis approaches lies in the semantics of the environment: in our case the environment is modelled by a context process that remains the same after the initial non-deterministic choice, while in [29] the analysis is performed by applying a simulation method that allows activity levels and noise to be taken into account for the input species. Hence, the method applied in [29] can lead to a larger range of hypotheses about the modelled system behaviours (such as the possibility for T cell to express more than two phenotypes), while ours is more conservative and consistent with the standard simulation approaches.

5.3 Slicing Analysis

For each target, slicing analysis is conducted by invoking the `main_do(slice,S)` directive of BioReSolve for each state of each attractor of the target. This is obtained by implementing suitable nested loops in the Python script that, at each iteration, execute BioReSolve through the Python-to-Prolog binding provided by the `swiplserver` package.

Slicing analysis in BioReSolve requires, in addition to the RS reactions, to provide the specification of a monitor (i.e., a logic formula) to collect the proper information during the model execution (see [12] for details). Monitored entities are only the transcription factors that the target requires to be present.

Moreover, the context specification now does not contain the non deterministic choice of the general RS model: it is immediately initialized with a specific configuration of environmental stimuli. Here we show an example of specification of both the context and the monitor for the slicing analysis of one of the states of the target { Tbet, RORgt } reachable when the context does not provide IL12, IL4_e and INFg_e (denoted as `x31` `x51` and `x81`, respectively):

```
mycontext("[x11,x21,x0,x41,x0,x61,x71,x0,x91]").
mymonitor("[ m0 ]").
mymondef("[ m0 = ([{il12r,il21,il21r,il23r,il6r,nfat,rorgt,
                    socs1,stat1,stat3,tbet,tgfbr} inW].no({tbet,rorgt})
                + [-({il12r,il21,il21r,il23r,il6r,nfat,rorgt,
                     socs1,stat1,stat3,tbet,tgfbr} inW)].m0) ]").
```

Results of slicing analysis are summarized in Fig. 9, where it is possible to see, for each target, which internal genes are *strictly necessary* and which are somehow *relevant* for the expression of the transcription factor of the target. We remark that this is a form of causality analysis: for example, one gene that results to be necessary may cause the execution of a chain of reactions leading after some steps to the expression of one of the target transcription factors.

Once necessary and relevant genes for one target are identified, we can look for them in the results of the analysis conducted for the other targets. This leads to a notion of *specificity* that is very important. For example, a gene that is necessary for the expression of a phenotype and that is not relevant for the expression of the other phenotypes (i.e., it is highly specific) is a perfect candidate as a target for a drug aimed at inhibiting the expression of its phenotype.

The table in Fig. 9 allows us to assess necessity, relevance and specificity of each internal gene for each phenotype. In particular, for the four phenotypes characterized by a single transcription factor we can observe that:

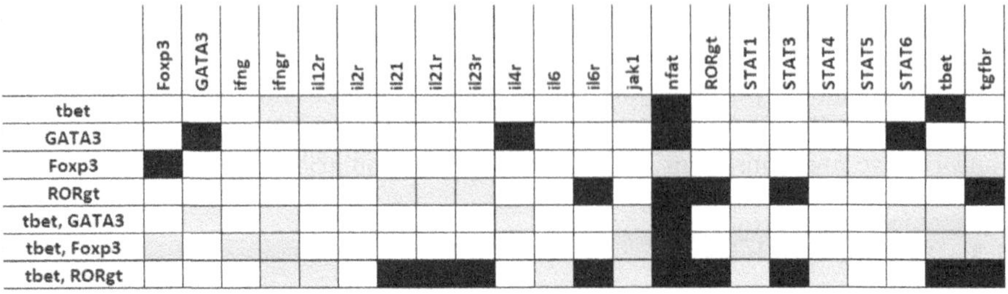

Fig. 9. Results of slicing analysis. Black cells identify genes (in columns) that are strictly necessary for the achievement of each target (in rows). Gray cells identify relevant genes. White cells identify genes that are not relevant.

- for target Tbet, the analysis suggests that IFNgR and Jak1 are two relevant genes with high specificity, although they are not strictly necessary for the achievement of the target (i.e., their inhibition or knock-out does not guarantee that the target will not be reached);
- for target GATA3, the analysis suggests that IL4R and STAT6 are strictly necessary and highly specific;
- for target Foxp3, the analysis suggests that IL2R and STAT5 are relevant and highly specific, although not strictly necessary; and
- for target RORgt, the analysis suggests that IL6R and STAT3 are strictly necessary and highly specific, but also IL21, IL21R and IL23 result to be particularly important and specific (as also pointed out in [25]).

6 Conclusions and Future Work

In this paper we have presented a methodology for analyzing the attractors of a RS model and for identifying the biological entities that are responsible for their achievement. Our methodology considers an operational semantics of RSs which allows us to construct Labeled Transition Systems (LTSs) to describe the behaviours of the model. Then, we apply a slicing algorithm to identify the minimal entities which describe a behaviour that we analyse.

Our methodology can be applied to Boolean network models of gene regulation, by translating them into RSs. We remark that such a translation emphasizes the different causes for the activation of each gene (representing them as different reactions). Moreover, it enables the application of analysis tools already developed for RSs.

We have applied our analysis to a model of T cell differentiation in the immune system. The analysis of the model allowed us to determine which combinations of stimuli lead to each phenotype, and also which proteins inside T cells are involved in each case. This analysis contributes to the understanding of the behaviour of the model, to correct it in case some mistakes are identified and to use it for identifying drug targets. We discussed the relation with other approaches in the literature.

Our methodology is general and can be applied to the (large number of) case studies in the public database on the CellCollective platform [20], as well as to other Boolean network models.

As a future work we plan to extend our methodology in several ways, for instance by deriving information on the number of paths in which important molecules for a given target are used, by considering subsets of molecules and by counting the paths in which a (set of) molecule(s) is present. Our method might also be combined with other analyses (e.g. [6,11,13,14]) which are based on quantitative extensions of RSs, in order to define models which can express directly properties which require to count the number of entities in the system, or to express the time and speed of a reaction. The slicing might also be improved by considering the role of inhibitors as it was done in [15], where we defined a predictor analysis of causality in RSs based on static analyses.

References

1. Barbuti, R., Gori, R., Levi, F., Milazzo, P.: Investigating dynamic causalities in reaction systems. Theor. Comput. Sci. **623**, 114–145 (2016). https://doi.org/10.1016/j.tcs.2015.11.041
2. Barbuti, R., Gori, R., Levi, F., Milazzo, P.: Generalized contexts for reaction systems: definition and study of dynamic causalities. Acta Informatica **55**, 227–267 (2018)
3. Barbuti, R., Gori, R., Milazzo, P.: Encoding Boolean networks into reaction systems for investigating causal dependencies in gene regulation. Theoret. Comput. Sci. **881**, 3–24 (2021). https://doi.org/10.1016/j.tcs.2020.07.031
4. Barbuti, R., Gori, R., Milazzo, P., Nasti, L.: A survey of gene regulatory networks modelling methods: from differential equations, to Boolean and qualitative bioinspired models. J. Membrane Comput. **2**, 207–226 (2020). https://doi.org/10.1007/s41965-020-00046-y
5. BioReSolve web page, a prolog interpreter for Reaction Systems analysis. http://pages.di.unipi.it/bruni/LTSRS/. Accessed 18 Mar 2024
6. Bodei, C., Brodo, L., Gori, R., Levi, F., Bernini, A., Hermith, D.: A static analysis for brane calculi providing global occurrence counting information. Theor. Comput. Sci. **696**, 11–51 (2017). https://doi.org/10.1016/J.TCS.2017.07.008
7. Bodei, C., Gori, R., Levi, F.: Causal static analysis for brane calculi. Theoret. Comput. Sci. **587**, 73–103 (2015)
8. Bornholdt, S.: Boolean network models of cellular regulation: prospects and limitations. J. Royal Soc. Interface **5**(suppl_1), S85–S94 (2008). https://doi.org/10.1098/rsif.2008.0132.focus
9. Brijder, R., Ehrenfeucht, A., Main, M., Rozenberg, G.: A tour of reaction systems. Int. J. Found. Comput. Sci. **22**(07), 1499–1517 (2011). https://doi.org/10.1142/S0129054111008842
10. Brodo, L., Bruni, R., Falaschi, M.: A process algebraic approach to reaction systems. Theoret. Comput. Sci. **881**, 62–82 (2021). https://doi.org/10.1016/j.tcs.2020.09.001

11. Brodo, L., Bruni, R., Falaschi, M.: A logical and graphical framework for reaction systems. Theoret. Comput. Sci. **875**, 1–27 (2021). https://doi.org/10.1016/j.tcs.2021.03.024
12. Brodo, L., Bruni, R., Falaschi, M.: Dynamic slicing of reaction systems based on assertions and monitors. In: Hanus, M., Inclezan, D. (eds.) Proc. of Practical Aspects of Declarative Languages - 25th Int. Symp., PADL 2023. LNCS, vol. 13880, pp. 107–124. Springer (2023). https://doi.org/10.1007/978-3-031-24841-2_8
13. Brodo, L., Bruni, R., Falaschi, M., Gori, R., Levi, F., Milazzo, P.: Exploiting modularity of SOS semantics to define quantitative extensions of reaction systems. In: Aranha, C., Martín-Vide, C., Vega-Rodríguez, M.A. (eds.) Proc. of TPNC 2021. LNCS, vol. 13082, pp. 15–32. Springer (2021). https://doi.org/10.1007/978-3-030-90425-8_2
14. Brodo, L., Bruni, R., Falaschi, M., Gori, R., Levi, F., Milazzo, P.: Quantitative extensions of reaction systems based on SOS semantics. Neural Comput. Appl. **35**(9), 6335–6359 (2023)
15. Brodo, L., et al.: Causal analysis of positive reaction systems (2024). submitted for publication
16. Clark, A., Galpin, V., Gilmore, S., Guerriero, M.L., Hillston, J.: Formal methods for checking the consistency of biological models. In: Advances in Systems Biology, pp. 461–475. Springer (2012).https://doi.org/10.1007/978-1-4419-7210-1_27
17. Ehrenfeucht, A., Rozenberg, G.: Reaction systems. Fundamenta Informaticae **76**, 1–18 (2006). https://content.iospress.com/articles/fundamenta-informaticae/fi75-1-4-15
18. Ehrenfeucht, A., Rozenberg, G.: Reaction systems: a formal framework for processes based on biochemical interactions. Electron. Commun. EASST **26**, 1–10 (2010). https://doi.org/10.1007/978-3-642-02424-5_3
19. Github repository with the python script developed for this paper. https://github.com/Unipisa/TCell-AttractorsSlicingAnalyses. Accessed 18 Mar 2024
20. Helikar, T., et al.: The cell collective: toward an open and collaborative approach to systems biology. BMC Syst. Biol. **6**(1), 1–14 (2012). https://doi.org/10.1186/1752-0509-6-96
21. Hirahara, K., Nakayama, T.: CD4+ T-cell subsets in inflammatory diseases: beyond the T h 1/T h 2 paradigm. Int. Immunol. **28**(4), 163–171 (2016). https://doi.org/10.1093/intimm/dxw006
22. Karlebach, G., Shamir, R.: Modelling and analysis of gene regulatory networks. Nat. Rev. Mol. Cell Biol. **9**(10), 770–780 (2008). https://doi.org/10.1038/nrm2503
23. Lafaille, J.J.: The role of helper T cell subsets in autoimmune diseases. Cytokine Growth Factor Rev. **9**(2), 139–151 (1998). https://doi.org/10.1016/s1359-6101(98)00009-4
24. Li, F., Long, T., Lu, Y., Ouyang, Q., Tang, C.: The yeast cell-cycle network is robustly designed. Proc. Natl. Acad. Sci. **101**(14), 4781–4786 (2004). https://doi.org/10.1073/pnas.0305937101
25. Luckheeram, R.V., Zhou, R., Verma, A.D., Xia, B.: CD4+ T cells: differentiation and functions. Clin. Dev. Immunol. **2012** (2012). https://doi.org/10.1155/2012/925135
26. Meng, X., et al.: Regulatory T cells in cardiovascular diseases. Nat. Rev. Cardiol. **13**(3), 167–179 (2016). https://doi.org/10.1038/nrcardio.2015.169
27. Milner, R.: A calculus of communicating systems, LNCS, vol. 92. Springer (1980). https://doi.org/10.1007/3-540-10235-3

28. Puniya, B.L.: CD4+ T cell differentiation model webpage on the CellCollective platform. https://research.cellcollective.org/?dashboard=true#module/6678:1/cd4-t-cell-differentiation/1. Accessed 18 Mar 2024
29. Puniya, B.L., Todd, R.G., Mohammed, A., Brown, D.M., Barberis, M., Helikar, T.: A mechanistic computational model reveals that plasticity of CD4+ T cell differentiation is a function of cytokine composition and dosage. Front. Physiol. **9**, 878 (2018). https://doi.org/10.3389/fphys.2018.00878
30. Saez-Rodriguez, J., et al.: A logical model provides insights into T cell receptor signaling. PLoS Comput. Biol. **3**(8), e163 (2007). https://doi.org/10.1371/journal.pcbi.0030163
31. SWI-Prolog home page. https://www.swi-prolog.org/. Accessed 18 Mar 2024
32. Thakar, J., Albert, R.: Boolean models of within-host immune interactions. Curr. Opin. Microbiol. **13**(3), 377–381 (2010). https://doi.org/10.1016/j.mib.2010.04.003

Preliminary Results on Shapley Value Notions and Propagation Methods for Boolean Networks

Giang Pham and Paolo Milazzo(✉)

Department of Computer Science, University of Pisa, Largo B. Pontecorvo 3, 56127 Pisa, Italy
tranhuong.giangpham@phd.unipi.it, paolo.milazzo@unipi.it

Abstract. The Shapley value is a concept in coalition game theory, with applications extending across various fields, including computational biology. In this domain, the Shapley value is primarily used to assess the importance of nodes within biological networks. In this study, we tackle the problem of evaluating the significance of nodes in gene regulatory networks modeled as Boolean networks. We introduce two game settings for Boolean networks, along with three different notions of the Shapley value. Furthermore, we present preliminary results on a propagation method that enables the Shapley value to be extended from one set of nodes to others within the network.

Keywords: Boolean networks · Shapley value · Game theory · Network propagation · Gene regulatory networks

1 Introduction

In game theory, particularly within coalition games, the Shapley value addresses the challenge of fairly distributing the total payoff obtained by a coalition among its individual members [1]. The Shapley value's appealing properties have led to its widespread application in various fields, including computational biology. A common use in this domain is to evaluate the significance of nodes within a biological network. In 2004, Keinan *et al.* [2] introduced its application for quantifying the contribution of network elements to the network's overall outcome. Here, the complete set of nodes represents the "carrier" of the game or, equivalently, the set of players, which also forms the grand coalition wherein all players participate. By selectively removing nodes from this set in all possible combinations, other coalitions are created, evaluated (based on their potential payoffs), and subsequently used to compute each node's Shapley value. A similar approach for calculating the importance of nodes in a biological network is the Multi-perturbation Shapley Analysis (MSA) [2], which assesses the functional performance of a biological system following deletions, mutations, or lesions of its elements.

G. Broccia and A. Cerone (Eds.): DataMod 2023, LNCS 14618, pp. 90–112, 2025.
https://doi.org/10.1007/978-3-031-87217-4_5

In 2007, Moretti *et al.* introduced a new class of game called *microarray game* [3]. This study applied Shapley value to construct a relevance index for genes by using microarray data. The obtained relevance index shows how much a particular gene contributes to a disease. Another quantity to measure the centrality of a co-expression network has also been developed, based on the Shapley value by Moretti [4]. A co-expression network is an undirected graph in which the undirected edges relates genes that are often express together. By computing the Shapley value as the power value from the *association game* (a game of N "ordinary" genes as players with a payoff function giving the number of "key" genes $\subseteq K$ interacting with a set of "ordinary" genes) and *graph restricted game* (the game of N "ordinary" genes with the payoff function giving the sum of all connected components' payoff value from the association game) and taking the difference between the two power values, we can obtain the centrality measurement for the co-expression networks.

In this paper, we address the challenge of determining the importance of nodes within a gene regulatory network represented as a Boolean network. In this framework, nodes represent genes, each of which can be either active or inactive. The network's directed edges, which come in two types, indicate either a positive or negative influence of one gene on another. A positive influence implies that when the source gene is active, it promotes the activation of the target gene. Conversely, a negative influence means that when the source gene is active, it favors the inactivation of the target gene. This representation of gene interactions can be ambiguous; for instance, if two genes both positively influence the same target gene, it may be unclear whether the activation of only one gene is sufficient to activate the target. To address this, Boolean networks are typically specified using Boolean update functions (represented as Boolean logic formulas) that allow simulations of the evolution of gene states over time. With these functions, the graph representation of the network serves as an abstraction of the underlying formulas, useful for visualization and for applying abstract analysis techniques.

Determining the importance of nodes within a gene regulatory network modeled as a Boolean network is a significant research problem, as it can aid in identifying key regulators of cellular biological processes. Identifying these regulators may, in turn, enhance our understanding of the biological causes of diseases and help identify promising target genes for therapeutic interventions.

We focus specifically on Boolean networks in which a subset of nodes, termed *input nodes*, act as input collectors. These nodes are not associated with an update formula; rather, they can be set to an initial active or inactive state, which remains stable. The importance of network nodes will therefore be assessed by considering all possible initial combinations of active/inactive states for the input nodes.

The remainder of this paper is structured as follows: we begin by reviewing foundational concepts of Boolean networks and the Shapley value. Next, we introduce three candidate Shapley value variants for this context: the *input* Shapley value, the *layered* Shapley value, and the *knockout* Shapley value. We explore the relationships between these three variants and discuss potential applications for each. We then focus on the knockout Shapley value and present preliminary findings on how this value can be propagated from the network's input nodes to internal nodes without requiring recomputation. While these initial results are demonstrated on a simplified class of Boolean networks, they indicate that propagation can significantly reduce the complexity of analyzing the entire network. Finally, we discuss potential further developments of this approach and outline future research directions.

2 Boolean Networks

In this section, we begin by presenting a general definition of Boolean networks, establishing the foundational concepts relevant to this study. Following this, we narrow our focus to two specific subclasses of Boolean networks: layered and tree-shaped networks. We examine the structural characteristics and properties of each subclass, which will play a key role in the subsequent analysis.

2.1 General Definition

The Boolean network formalism was first introduced by S. A. Kauffman in 1969 as a model for gene regulatory networks [5]. It remains one of the simplest models for studying the dynamics of biological systems [6]. A Boolean network consists of a set of n Boolean variables $(x_1, x_2, ..., x_n)$, along with a set of Boolean functions $f_{m+1}, f_{m+2}, ..., f_n$ (where $m \geq 0$) that update these variables. Not all variables require an update function; the m variables that lack one can take any value in $\{0, 1\}$ and are treated as inputs to the Boolean network. We refer to the set of input nodes for a given Boolean network as M.

For all other variables, the value of x_i at time $t+1$ is calculated based on the values of k other variables $x_{j1}, x_{j2}, ..., x_{jk}$ at time step t by the Boolean function $f_i : \{0,1\}^k \rightarrow \{0,1\}$, namely::

$$x_i(t+1) = f_i(x_{j1}(t), x_{j2}(t), ..., x_{jk}(t)) \tag{1}$$

The Boolean function f_i is composed of Boolean variables and operations. In this paper, we omit the time step indices t and $t+1$ from all formulas. We denote the OR operator by $+$, the AND operator by $\cdot$, and the NOT operator by $\neg$. Additionally, the constants 0 and 1 may be used as Boolean literals within the formulas. Any Boolean function can be expressed in *disjunctive normal form (DNF)* as a summation (a sequence of $+$) of terms, where each term is a multiplication (a sequence of $\cdot$) of possibly negated variables (i.e., variables with or without a $\neg$ prefix). For simplicity, we use capital letters $A, B, C, \ldots$ to denote variables instead of the traditional notation $x_1, x_2, x_3, \ldots$.

We provide the following example to illustrate a Boolean network:

$$\begin{aligned} C &= A + B \\ D &= \neg C \\ E &= C \cdot (\neg D) \end{aligned} \tag{2}$$

with $M = \{A, B\}$ input nodes.

A Boolean network can also be represented as a graph, where each variable corresponds to a node. This graph representation provides an abstract view of the system. Boolean networks are typically depicted as directed graphs with two types of edges: promotion (shown as an arrow with a ↑-head) and inhibition (shown as an arrow with a ⊤-head). Node A is said to promote node B when A appears in one of the terms in the DNF of B's update function f_B in a positive form, and it inhibits B when it appears in a negative form. In this graphical representation, variables without update functions (inputs) are depicted as nodes without incoming edges and are considered input nodes. However, the reverse does not hold, as some nodes may lack incoming edges but have a constant update function that fixes their value to either 0 or 1 (meaning they are not input nodes). Thus, input nodes would typically be marked in the graph, but as we do not consider examples with constant update functions in this paper, we omit such markings, assuming instead that nodes without incoming edges correspond to the network's input nodes.

As an example, we revisit the Boolean network presented in Eq. (2) and display its graphical representation in Fig. 1. This representation alone does not capture the exact Boolean operators between nodes; for instance, in Fig. 1, it is unclear whether $C = A + B$ or $C = A \cdot B$. Therefore, while the graphical representation cannot replace the detailed specification of update functions, it is useful for visualization and for applying abstract analytical methods.

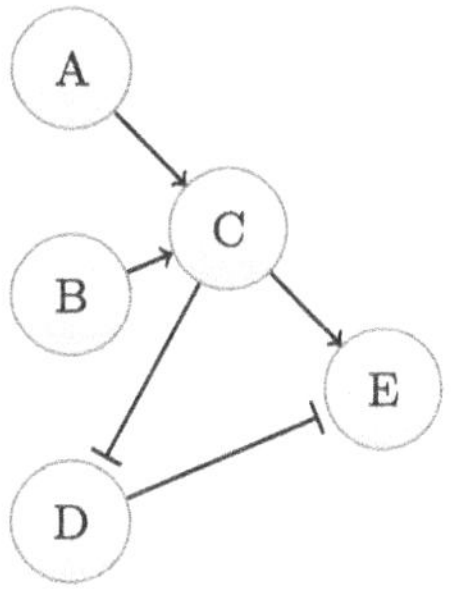

Fig. 1. The graph representation of the Boolean network in Eq. (2).

A Boolean network can reveal valuable insights into the biological system it represents. The graph representation highlights the interactions among its components, while the network's dynamical properties can capture the system's behavioral patterns. The dynamics of a Boolean network is studied by simulating the network. At each time step t, the current values of all variables collectively define the network's state. A state transitions to another by applying the Boolean functions to update the variables. In this process, two alternative update schemes are commonly considered in the literature. The first scheme, known as *asynchronous*, updates only one Boolean variable (a randomly selected node) at each time step, using its associated update function. The second scheme, called *synchronous*, applies all update functions simultaneously to update all Boolean variables (all nodes) at once. In this study, we focus on the synchronous update scheme, which is often favored for its deterministic nature [7].

Simulating a Boolean network generates a *state graph*. Figure 2 displays the state graph for the Boolean network shown in Fig. 1 under the synchronous update scheme. There are two input nodes, A and B, which can each take any value in $\{0, 1\}$, giving us 2^2 initial states (shown in bold) with various values for these nodes, while all other node variables are initialized to zero. Node values are listed in alphabetical order; for example, 10101 represents the state in which $A = 1$, $B = 0$, $C = 1$, $D = 0$, and $E = 1$.

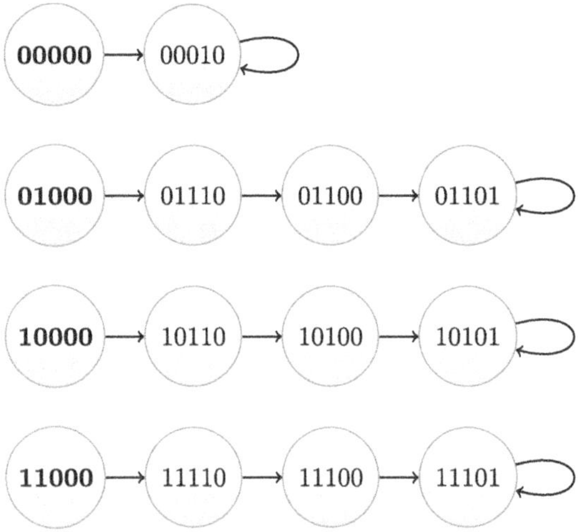

Fig. 2. The state graph of the Boolean network in Fig. 1 (Eq. (2)) under the synchronous update scheme.

The way we defined input nodes (as nodes without an update function) causes the state graph to be partitioned into disconnected subgraphs, each corresponding to a different initial state. Loops in the state graph of a Boolean network are called *attractors*. For example, in Fig. 2, there are four attractors, each containing a single state (00010, 01101, 10101, and 11101), each originating from a different starting state.

The attractors obtained from simulations across all $2^{|M|}$ input configurations can be collectively represented in a truth table, where each row shows the values of all variables in the corresponding attractors for each input combination. In general, an attractor may form a loop involving multiple states. Thus, if a node appears in at least one state within the attractor, it is considered present in the attractor and is assigned a value of 1 in the truth table.

The truth table for the network defined in Eq. (2), depicted graphically in Fig. 1 and with its state graph shown in Fig. 2, is as in Table 1.

Table 1. Truth table for the network defined in Eq. 2, depicted in Fig. 1.

A	B	C	D	E
0	0	0	1	0
0	1	1	0	1
1	0	1	0	1
1	1	1	0	0

The table has $2^{|M|} = 2^2 = 4$ rows and one column for every node. Since all attractors in the state graph in Fig. 2 involve only one state, the truth table contains exactly the representation of such states.

Attractors are interesting because they capture the steady state behaviour of the system. Many analysis techniques for Boolean network focus on identification and analysis of attractors.

2.2 Layered and Tree-Shaped Boolean Networks

We introduce a class of Boolean networks with straightforward structures, termed layered Boolean networks. In these networks, nodes are organized into distinct, non-overlapping groups known as layers. Layers are sequentially numbered, starting from 0, and nodes in each layer i depend exclusively on the nodes in layer $i-1$. Consequently, nodes in layer 0 function as the input nodes of the network.

The motivation for focusing on layered Boolean networks lies in their structural simplicity. Under a synchronous update scheme, nodes in layer i reach their final values at the ith step of the simulation, retaining these values up to the attractor state. Therefore, to compute the steady-state value of a node in layer i, it suffices to examine only the nodes from the input layer (layer 0) up to layer i, disregarding nodes in subsequent layers. In such cases, we consider the node of interest as the output node of the network and assume it resides in the final layer. Generally, a network may contain multiple output nodes, but for the scope of this paper, we focus on layered Boolean networks with a single output node located in the last layer.

To represent the partitioning of nodes into layers, we will use the following notation. Nodes in layer 0, the input nodes, are denoted as $I_1, I_2, \ldots$; nodes in layer 1 as $A, A_1, A_2, \ldots$; nodes in layer 2 as $B, B_1, B_2, \ldots$; and so forth. For example, consider the following (layered) Boolean network:

$$\begin{aligned} A_1 &= I_1 + I_2 \\ A_2 &= I_2 \cdot (\neg I_3) \\ B &= A_1 + A_2 \end{aligned} \tag{3}$$

The network has three input nodes, $M = \{I_1, I_2, I_3\}$, which constitute layer 0. Additionally, it includes two nodes in layer 1, labeled A_1 and A_2. Finally, it contains a single layer 2 node, B, which serves as the output node of the network.

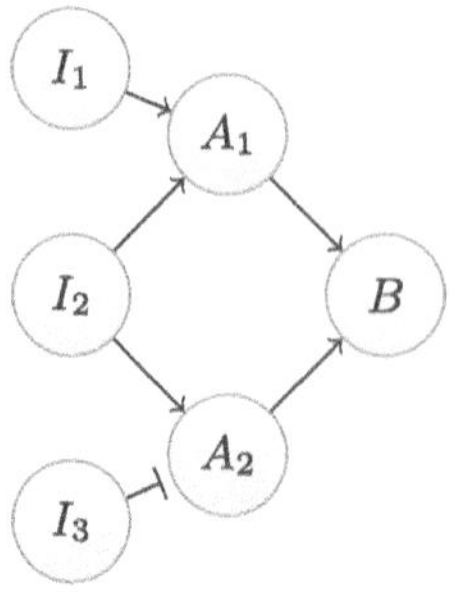

Fig. 3. The graphical representation of the Boolean network in Eq. (3).

Figure 3 provides a graphical representation of this network, with layers visually emphasized by the vertical alignment of the nodes.

A further constrained subclass of layered Boolean networks is the class of *tree-shaped Boolean networks*, where no two nodes at any layer i depend on the same node in the preceding layer, $i - 1$. Thus, the graphical representation of a network in this class forms a tree rooted at the output node. The Boolean network presented in Eq. (3) and depicted in Fig. 3 is not tree-shaped, as both A_1 and A_2 depend on I_2. An example of a tree-shaped Boolean network, along with its graphical representation, is provided in Eq. 4 and Fig. 4.

$$\begin{aligned} A_1 &= I_1 \cdot (\neg I_2) \\ A_2 &= I_3 \\ B &= A_1 + A_2 \end{aligned} \tag{4}$$

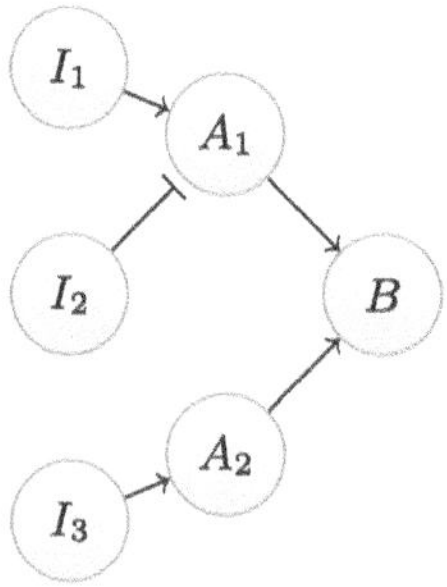

Fig. 4. The graphical representation of the Boolean network in Eq. (4).

This network has three input nodes: I_1, I_2, and I_3, resulting in $2^3 = 8$ possible input configurations. The truth table summarizing the attractors from the network simulation is presented in Table 2.

Layered and tree-shaped Boolean networks can also be interpreted as representations of the abstract syntax tree of a standard Boolean function. For

Table 2. Truth table for the Boolean network defined in Eq. (4), and depicted in Fig. 4.

I_1	I_2	I_3	A_1	A_2	B
0	0	0	0	0	0
0	0	1	0	1	1
0	1	0	0	0	0
1	0	0	1	0	1
0	1	1	0	1	1
1	0	1	1	1	1
1	1	0	0	0	0
1	1	1	0	1	1

example, the layered Boolean network in Eq. (3) and Fig. 3 can represent the Boolean function $(I_1+I_2)+(I_2\cdot(\neg I_3))$. Tree-shaped Boolean networks, in particular, correspond to *read-once* Boolean functions [8]. This correspondence could be useful for leveraging certain properties of these Boolean function classes (such as their conversion to a compact DNF) to simplify the analysis methods proposed in this paper. However, because our long-term goal is to generalize these methods to broader classes of Boolean networks, we choose not to rely on these simplifications here, as they may not scale to the general case.

3 Shapley Value Notions for Boolean Networks

Given a (layered) Boolean network, there are multiple approaches to model a coalition game and calculate the corresponding Shapley value, each offering a distinct interpretation. In this section, we first present some general background concepts on Shapley value calculation. Following this, we introduce new concepts of coalition game and Shapley value specifically for Boolean networks.

3.1 Background on the Shapley Value

The concept of game theory has deep historical roots, but modern game theory is generally considered to have been formally introduced in 1944 by John von Neumann and Oskar Morgenstern in their book Theory of Games and Economic Behavior [9]. They formalized the idea of assigning a numerical value to each alternative that individuals (referred to as players) encounter in games. One class of games, known as coalition games or cooperative games, involves players cooperating to form coalitions rather than acting independently. Such games are typically modeled by a set of players N (the carrier) and a payoff function v.

Given a finite set of players N and a function v from $2^N \to \mathbb{R}$ (where $v(\emptyset) = 0$), called the *payoff function*, which assigns a real value to each subset S of players within N. The set N, containing all players in the game, is referred to as the *grand coalition*. The game is considered super-additive if:

$$v(S) \geq v(S \cap T) + v(S \setminus T) \text{ with } S, T \subseteq N \tag{5}$$

The central challenge in this game is determining how to divide the payoff among the players. Lloyd Shapley [1] proposed that a solution ϕ should satisfy three axioms: symmetry, carrier, and additivity, described as follows:

- Symmetry: If two players, i and j, contribute equally to every coalition they join, they should receive the same payoff.
- Carrier: The total payoff shared among all players in the carrier N must equal the payoff earned by this carrier, i.e., $\sum_{i \in N} \phi_i(v) = v(N)$. This axiom implies an additional rule for a *null player* or *dummy player* i, such that $\phi_i(v) = 0$ if i contributes nothing to all the coalitions it joins.
- Additivity: For any two games v and w, the Shapley value of the combined game $(v + w)$ should equal the sum of the individual values, $\phi(v + w) = \phi(v) + \phi(w)$, where $(v + w)(S) = v(S) + w(S)$ for any coalition S. This axiom is crucial for defining the uniqueness of $\phi(v)$, as it ensures the value of each game is coherently related to others [10].

In 1953, Lloyd Shapley introduced a unique value that satisfies the three aforementioned axioms [1]. For each player i in a game with N players and a payoff function v (not necessarily super-additive), the *Shapley value* $\phi_i(v)$ of player i is calculated as follows:

$$\phi_i(v) = \sum_{S \subseteq N, i \in S} \frac{(|S| - 1)!(|N| - |S|)!}{|N|!} [v(S) - v(S \setminus \{i\})] \tag{6}$$

that can be slightly simplified into the following equivalent form:

$$\phi_i(v) = \sum_{S \subseteq N \setminus \{i\}} \frac{|S|!(|N| - |S| - 1)!}{|N|!} [v(S \cup \{i\}) - v(S)] . \tag{7}$$

Intuitively, $\phi_i(v)$ represents the average of player i's marginal contributions to each coalition S, defined as the difference in payoff, $[v(S) - v(S \setminus i)]$ in Eq. (6) or $[v(S \cup i) - v(S)]$ in Eq. (7). This average is weighted by the term $\frac{(|S|-1)!(|N|-|S|)!}{|N|!}$ in Eq. (6) or $\frac{|S|!(|N|-|S|-1)!}{|N|!}$ in Eq. (7), which is inversely proportional to the number of ways coalition S can be formed. In Eq. (6), player i's marginal contribution is assessed by removing player i from the coalition S that initially includes i. Meanwhile, Eq. (7) calculates this by adding player i to coalition S, formed as a subset of $N \setminus \{i\}$ where i is intentionally left out to be added later. Despite these different approaches, both formulas yield the same Shapley value for player i. An alternative, equivalent formulation of $\phi_i(v)$ is:

$$\phi_i(v) = \frac{1}{|N|} \sum_{S \subseteq N \setminus \{i\}} \frac{1}{\binom{|N|-1}{|S|}} [v(S \cup \{i\}) - v(S)] . \tag{8}$$

This formula offers a more abstract view. Similar to Eq. (7), the term $[v(S \cup i) - v(S)]$ represents the marginal contribution of player i to coalition S. This term is summed across all possible coalitions S, weighted by the probability of forming S from $N \setminus \{i\}$, given by $\frac{1}{\binom{|N|-1}{|S|}}$. Here, it becomes clearer that the weight assigned to player i's marginal contribution to coalition S is inversely proportional to the number of ways coalition S of size $|S|$ can be formed from the set $N \setminus \{i\}$. Player i is initially excluded to allow for measuring its contribution when added (in $v(S \cup i)$). Throughout the remainder of the paper, we will refer to one of these three formulas in whichever form best serves our purpose.

To illustrate the Shapley value concept, we refer to an example from [10]. Consider a trading game with three players-1, 2, and 3-where player 1 is a seller offering goods at a price of \$10. Players 2 and 3 are buyers, offering to pay \$20 and \$30, respectively. Transactions require the seller's involvement. This game can be modeled as a coalition game (N, v), where $N = \{1, 2, 3\}$ is the player set, and v is the payoff function, defined as $v(\emptyset) = v(\{2\}) = v(\{\ 3\}) = v(\{2, 3\}) = 0$, $v(\{1\}) = 10$, $v(\{1, 2\}) = 20$, $v(\{1, 3\}) = v(\{1, 2, 3\}) = 30$. The Shapley value for each of the three players is calculated based on Eq. (8) as:

$$\phi_1(v) = \frac{1}{3}[\frac{1}{\binom{2}{0}}(v(\{1\}) - v(\emptyset)) + \frac{1}{\binom{2}{1}}(v(\{1,2\}) - v(\{2\}))$$
$$+\frac{1}{\binom{2}{1}}(v(\{1,3\}) - v(\{3\})) + \frac{1}{\binom{2}{2}}(v(\{1,2,3\}) - v(\{2,3\}))] = 21\frac{2}{3}$$

$$\phi_2(v) = \frac{1}{3}[\frac{1}{\binom{2}{0}}(v(\{2\}) - v(\emptyset)) + \frac{1}{\binom{2}{1}}(v(\{1,2\}) - v(\{1\}))$$
$$+\frac{1}{\binom{2}{1}}(v(\{2,3\}) - v(\{3\})) + \frac{1}{\binom{2}{2}}(v(\{1,2,3\}) - v(\{1,3\}))] = \frac{5}{3}$$

$$\phi_3(v) = \frac{1}{3}[\frac{1}{\binom{2}{0}}(v(\{3\}) - v(\emptyset)) + \frac{1}{\binom{2}{1}}(v(\{1,3\}) - v(\{1\}))$$
$$+\frac{1}{\binom{2}{1}}(v(\{2,3\}) - v(\{2\})) + \frac{1}{\binom{2}{2}}(v(\{1,2,3\}) - v(\{1,2\}))] = \frac{20}{3}$$

3.2 Summary of Shapley Value Notions for Boolean Networks Presented in This Paper

We propose three variants of the Shapley value for Boolean networks, referred to as the *input Shapley value*, *layered Shapley value*, and *knockout Shapley value*. The first two variants are computed based on a coalition game model we term the *Boolean network game*, while the third variant is derived from a different game setting, which we call the *knockout game*. In the following subsections, we introduce these two game models and present the corresponding Shapley value definitions for each.

While we will define different notions of the Shapley value for both general and layered Boolean networks, we illustrate them using a simple, tree-shaped network defined in Eq. (4) and shown in Fig. 4. Additionally, we refer to the truth table for this network, provided in Table 2.

3.3 The Boolean Network Game

Game definition. Given a layered Boolean network[1] with input nodes $M = I_1, \ldots, I_m$ and an output node O (i.e., the only node in the final layer), the *Boolean network game* is a coalition game where players correspond to the input nodes. A coalition $S \subseteq M$ represents an input configuration in which each input node I_i is set to 1 if and only if $I_i \in S$. The coalition wins the game if this input configuration results in $O = 1$ in the attractor (i.e., in the corresponding row of the truth table); otherwise, the coalition loses. Consequently, the coalition's payoff $v(S)$ is the value of O in the attractor: either 1 (win) or 0 (lose). In this game setting, we introduce two notions of the Shapley value: the first, called the *input Shapley value*, and the second, the *layered Shapley value*.

Input Shapley value. In the context of a Boolean network game, by directly applying the classical notion of Shapley value for coalition games, as given in Eq. (7), to the network's input nodes (i.e., the players), we can determine the Shapley value of each input node. This value indicates the significance of each input node in activating the output node within the attractor. For instance, in the toy network described in Eq. (4), Fig. 4, and Table 2, where B is the output node, the Shapley values for inputs I_1, I_2, and I_3 are:

$$\begin{aligned}
\phi_{I_1}(v) &= \frac{1}{3} \sum_{S \subseteq \mathcal{P}(\{I_2, I_3\})} \frac{v(S \cup \{I_1\}) - v(S)}{\binom{2}{|S|}} = \\
&= \frac{1}{3}[\frac{(v(\{I_1\}) - v(\emptyset))}{\binom{2}{0}} + \frac{(v(\{I_1, I_2\}) - v(\{I_2\}))}{\binom{2}{1}} + \\
&\quad + \frac{(v(\{I_1, I_3\}) - v(\{I_3\}))}{\binom{2}{1}} + \frac{(v(\{I_1, I_2, I_3\}) - v(\{I_2, I_3\}))}{\binom{2}{2}}] \\
&= \frac{1}{3}(\frac{1-0}{1} + \frac{0-0}{2} + \frac{1-1}{2} + \frac{1-1}{1}) = 0.333
\end{aligned} \tag{9}$$

[1] The Boolean network game can also be defined for general Boolean networks.

For I_2:

$$\begin{aligned}\phi_{I_2}(v) &= \frac{1}{3}\sum_{S\subseteq\mathcal{P}(\{I_1,I_3\})}\frac{v(S\cup\{I_2\})-v(S)}{\binom{2}{|S|}} = \\ &= \frac{1}{3}[\frac{(v(\{I_2\})-v(\emptyset))}{\binom{2}{0}}+\frac{(v(\{I_2,I_1\})-v(\{I_1\}))}{\binom{2}{1}}+ \\ &+\frac{(v(\{I_2,I_3\})-v(\{I_3\}))}{\binom{2}{1}}+\frac{(v(\{I_1,I_2,I_3\})-v(\{I_1,I_3\}))}{\binom{2}{2}}] \\ &= \frac{1}{3}(\frac{0-0}{1}+\frac{0-1}{2}+\frac{1-1}{2}+\frac{1-1}{1}) = -0.167\end{aligned} \tag{10}$$

Similarly for I_3:

$$\phi_{I_3}(v) = \frac{1}{3}\sum_{S\subseteq\mathcal{P}(\{I_1,I_2\})}\frac{v(S\cup\{I_3\})-v(S)}{\binom{2}{|S|}} = 0.833. \tag{11}$$

The negative value of I_2 indicates that its presence in the network inhibits the activation of the output node B, as confirmed by the Boolean formulas in Eq. 4. However, it is somewhat counterintuitive that the absolute values of I_1 and I_2 differ (0.333 and 0.167) even though $A_1 = I_1 \cdot (\neg I_2)$. This difference arises because, as in the standard Shapley value definition (see Eq. 7), node I_1 acts as a determining player (causing a win) in the coalition I_1 (with only 1 player), while I_2 is a determining player (causing a loss) in the coalition I_1, I_2 (with 2 players). Since the absolute value of the payoff depends on the size of the coalition considered, I_1 and I_2 end up with payoffs of different absolute magnitudes.

As we have seen, the input Shapley value can be calculated for the input nodes of a Boolean network to assess their importance in activating the output. It would be highly useful to apply a similar evaluation to the intermediate nodes; however, these nodes are not players in the game. To assign a value to intermediate nodes, one could modify the game definition to treat all nodes as players. However, non-input nodes cannot assume arbitrary values (i.e., they cannot 'play' independently) because their values are constrained by nodes from lower levels. In the Boolean network's truth table-used as the data source for computing Shapley values-intermediate nodes do not appear with all possible value combinations, unlike input nodes. For instance, in Table 2, the intermediate node A_1 takes a value of 1 in only two out of eight cases. This uneven distribution complicates the calculation of the node's marginal contribution, $[v(S \cup i) -$ v(S)], in Eq. (7). Consequently, although this Shapley value approach is highly effective for evaluating input nodes, we must consider alternative methods to evaluate intermediate nodes.

Layered Shapley Value. In the context of layered Boolean networks, we can define a Shapley value for intermediate nodes within a Boolean network game by sequentially removing layers, starting from layer 0, and at each step, treating the remaining (sub)network as the active network for the game. In the i-th step of this iterative layer-removal procedure, all nodes from layers 0 to $i-1$ are removed along with their connecting edges. The nodes in layer i then become the new input nodes, allowing the Shapley value to be computed similarly to the input Shapley value.

For example, in the toy network described in Eq. (4), Fig. 4 and Table 2, the layered Shapley value for layer 0 (input) nodes I_1, I_2 and I_3 would coincide with the input Shapley value for them. The layered Shapley value for layer 1 nodes A_1 and A_2, instead, would be computed by removing I_1, I_2 and I_3 and by considering A_1 and A_2 as input nodes. This corresponds to transforming the Boolean network into the following one:

$$B = A_1 + A_2$$

We note that, as illustrated in the toy example, the layered Shapley value can be regarded as a generalization of the input Shapley value. These values are identical for the input nodes, but only the layered Shapley value extends to intermediate nodes.

This notion of Shapley value provides insight into each node's contribution within its layer toward activating the output node, independently of the specific input node configuration. All preceding layers are removed, so the structural information from the input layer (layer 0) up to the current layer-which determines how input configurations affect intermediate nodes at that layer-is disregarded.

For instance, in the toy example, we find that $\phi_{A_1} = \phi_{A_2} = 0.5$. This result reflects that, if we disregard the dependency of A_1 and A_2 on the inputs, both nodes become equally important in determining B.

In this setting, intermediate nodes are assumed to be capable of taking any value, which may not always be realistic. However, analyzing an intermediate node's role independently of input configurations can be valuable in various applications. For example, in a Boolean network modeling a gene regulatory network, this information could reveal an intermediate gene's potential influence on activating the target gene represented by the output node. In a disease-related gene regulatory network where the target gene is misregulated, identifying an influential intermediate gene could suggest a potential target for a new drug.

3.4 The Knockout Game

We propose a new game for Boolean networks, termed the *knockout game*, which conceptually resembles the MSA method introduced in [2]. In this approach, the marginal contribution of each node X is assessed by comparing the payoff from each input configuration where X functions according to its update function f_X with the payoff from the same configurations when X's update function is replaced by the constant function $f'_X = 0$. This substitution is analogous to 'knocking out'[2] node X. The behavior of a Boolean network with a node knocked out can then be represented by a modified truth table.

[2] Gene knock-out is a standard concept and experimental method in gene regulatory networks.

For instance, in the toy network described in Eq. (4), illustrated in Fig. 4 and represented in Table 2, if we assume node A_2 is knocked out, the network with A_2 removed transforms as follows:

$$\begin{aligned} A_1 &= I_1 \cdot (\neg I_2) \\ A_2 &= 0 \\ B &= A_1 + A_2 \end{aligned} \tag{12}$$

allowing us to compute the attractors and build the truth table as shown in Table 3.

Table 3. Truth table corresponding to the Boolean network defined in Eq. (12).

I_1	I_2	I_3	A_1	A_2	B
0	0	0	0	0	0
0	0	1	0	0	0
0	1	0	0	0	0
1	0	0	1	0	1
0	1	1	0	0	0
1	0	1	1	0	1
1	1	0	0	0	0
1	1	1	0	0	0

Comparing this truth table with Table 2, we observe that knocking out A_2 results in three instances where B is no longer activated. These correspond to the input configurations $I_1 = 0, I_2 = 0, I_3 = 1$; $I_1 = 0, I_2 = 0, I_3 = 1$; and $I_1 = 1, I_2 = 1, I_3 = 1$.

Game Definition. Given a layered Boolean network[3] with input nodes $M = I_1, \ldots, I_m$ and output node O (i.e., the only node in the last layer), the *knock-out game* is defined as the Boolean network game. The only difference is that, in addition to the payoff function $v(S)$ that determines the reward obtained by coalition S, each node X in the Boolean network has an associated knockout payoff function $v_{\bar{X}}(S)$, defined analogously to $v(S)$ but computed on the attractors (i.e., the truth table) of the Boolean network in which f_X, the update function for X, is replaced by the constant function $f'_X = 0$. In this setting, we can define a notion of *knockout Shapley value.*

Knockout Shapley Value. The knockout Shapley value is computed similarly to the input Shapley value, with the key distinction that the marginal contribution of each node X is determined by the difference between the standard payoff function v and the knockout payoff function $v_{\bar{X}}$.

[3] The knockout game can also be defined for general Boolean networks.

Although the players in the knockout game correspond to the input nodes M (similar to the Boolean network game), the knockout Shapley value can be computed for both input and internal nodes. Formally, the knockout Shapley value for every node X in the Boolean network is calculated as follows:

$$\phi_X^{ko}(v) = \sum_{S \subseteq M} \frac{|S|!(|M| - |S|)!}{|M|!}[v(S) - v_{\bar{X}}(S)] \tag{13}$$

which can be equivalently formulated as:

$$\phi_X^{ko}(v) = \sum_{S \subseteq M} \frac{1}{\binom{|M|}{|S|}}[v(S) - v_{\bar{X}}(S)]\,. \tag{14}$$

Equation (13) differs from the standard Shapley value definition (Eq. (6), which is also used for the input Shapley value) in two main aspects. The first difference is simply that $v(S \setminus i)$ is replaced by $v_{\bar{X}}$, a distinction we have already discussed. The second difference is that $|S-1|!$ is replaced by $|S|!$. This change is intuitively motivated by the fact that we are not considering coalitions S in which the node under study is present (and will be removed), which would imply a number of ways to choose the other nodes proportional to $|S-1|!$. Instead, we consider all possible coalitions S, with the node under study (which could also be an intermediate node) remaining in S and being used to compute $v_{\bar{X}}$. Consequently, the number of ways to form S is proportional to $|S|!$.

This *knockout Shapley value* reveals the importance of each input and intermediate node in the overall network by assessing the impact of its presence on the output. The Shapley values calculated in this manner for the toy network described in Eq. (4), as illustrated in Fig. 4 and summarized in Table 2, are:

$$\begin{aligned}
\phi_{I_1}^{ko}(v) &= \sum_{S \subseteq M} \frac{|S|!(|M| - |S|)!}{|M|!}[v(S) - v_{\bar{I}_1}(S)] = 0.333.\\
\phi_{I_2}^{ko}(v) &= \sum_{S \subseteq M} \frac{|S|!(|M| - |S|)!}{|M|!}[v(S) - v_{\bar{I}_2}(S)] = -0.333.\\
\phi_{I_3}^{ko}(v) &= \sum_{S \subseteq M} \frac{|S|!(|M| - |S|)!}{|M|!}[v(S) - v_{\bar{I}_3}(S)] = 1.667.\\
\phi_{A_1}^{ko}(v) &= \sum_{S \subseteq M} \frac{|S|!(|M| - |S|)!}{|M|!}[v(S) - v_{\bar{A}_1}(S)] = 0.333\\
\phi_{A_2}^{ko}(v) &= \sum_{S \subseteq M} \frac{|S|!(|M| - |S|)!}{|M|!}[v(S) - v_{\bar{A}_2}(S)] = 1.667
\end{aligned} \tag{15}$$

The knockout Shapley values for I_3 and A_2 are the highest (1.667), indicating that their (forced) absence strongly inhibits the activation of the output node B across multiple input configurations. In contrast, I_1 and A_1 have smaller positive values, meaning that knocking out either of them makes it less likely for B to switch from active to inactive. As for the negative value of I_2, this reflects that knocking out I_2 actually increases the likelihood of B becoming activated.

The knockout Shapley values calculated for the toy example closely align with the intuitive roles of each node, as suggested by the graphical representation of the Boolean network in Fig. 4. Notably, unlike the input Shapley values, nodes I_1 and I_2 receive values with opposite signs but the same absolute magnitude. This symmetry in absolute value arises from the fact that $\binom{3}{1} = \binom{3}{2}$ (see the definition of $\phi_X^{ko}(v)$ in Eq. (14)), though this relationship does not hold in general.

The interpretation of the knockout Shapley value is straightforward. A node's (absolute) value increases in proportion to how much forcing it to be 0 raises the likelihood of inactivating the output node. This approach parallels the way biological circuits are often examined in wet labs: genes of interest are knocked out by artificially mutating them or applying inhibitors, and the resulting effects are observed. Thus, while the other Shapley value definitions we have introduced hold theoretical and practical interest, we proceed with our study using the knockout Shapley value.

4 Preliminary Results About Shapley Value Propagation

In this section, we present observations and preliminary results on a propagation method for the knockout Shapley value. The idea is to compute this value for the input nodes only, then propagate it to intermediate nodes without needing to recompute it for each. This approach could greatly reduce the computational cost of analyzing the entire set of nodes within the Boolean network under study.

We focus on the knockout Shapley value as it applies to both input and internal nodes and shows particular promise for applications in gene regulatory networks, where knockouts are a standard concept.

In this preliminary study, we consider a very restricted class of Boolean networks, specifically *tree-shaped Boolean networks without negation*, meaning we assume the negation operator $\neg$ is not used in the Boolean update functions. This choice simplifies the presentation of our initial results; however, we believe that incorporating negation is also feasible and plan to address this in future work.

Network propagation methods, such as the PageRank algorithm [11], are commonly used to study information flow in networks. For the restricted class of Boolean networks considered here, we define Shapley value propagation by proposing a recursive definition for $\phi_X^{ko}(v)$ without introducing any approximation. For larger classes of Boolean networks (e.g., non-tree-shaped), defining a recursive approach may be challenging, so we plan to explore a PageRank-based approximation in future work.

To establish propagation rules, we begin with some motivating observations made on examples of Boolean networks.

4.1 Motivating Observations

This subsection provides general observations on the knockout Shapley value of nodes under various conditions, highlighting specific cases that reveal important patterns and insights. Through these examples, we aim to illustrate how the knockout Shapley value reflects each node's influence within the network and how these values change depending on the structural properties and interactions of the nodes. These observations lay the groundwork for understanding how knockout effects propagate and inform subsequent analysis.

Observation #1 Identical Variables: It is clear that when a node simply adopts the value of another node, it should inherit that node's knockout Shapley value (i.e., if the update function for node B is $B = A$, then $\phi_B^{ko} = \phi_A^{ko}$). For example, in the network shown in Fig. 5, each intermediate node A_i inherits the same value as the input node I_i from which it directly derives. This is demonstrated by calculating the knockout Shapley values using Eq. (13). The result for $\phi_{I_i}^{ko}(v)$ is 0.25, and for $\phi_{A_i}^{ko}(v)$ it is also 0.25, for all $i \in \{1, 2, 3, 4\}$. Similarly, in the slightly more complex network in Fig. 6, the knockout Shapley value of A_2 matches that of the input node I_5, which is 0.2.

$$
\begin{aligned}
A_1 &= I_1 \\
A_2 &= I_2 \\
A_3 &= I_3 \\
A_4 &= I_4 \\
B &= A_1 + A_2 + A_3 + A_4
\end{aligned}
$$

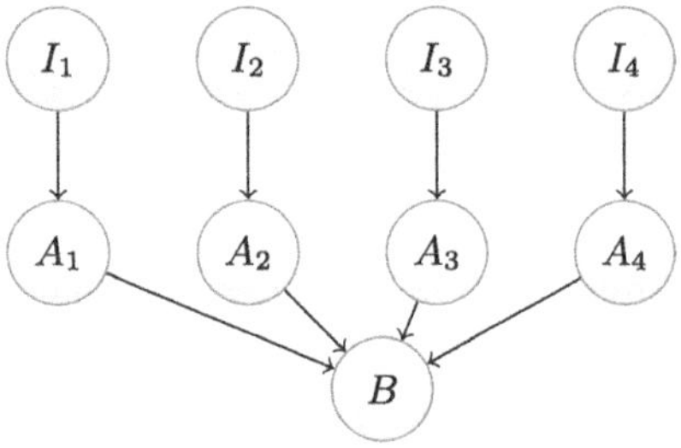

Fig. 5. Update functions and graphical representation of a Boolean network.

$$
\begin{aligned}
A_1 &= I_1 + I_2 + I_3 + I_4 \\
A_2 &= I_5 \\
B &= A_1 + A_2
\end{aligned}
$$

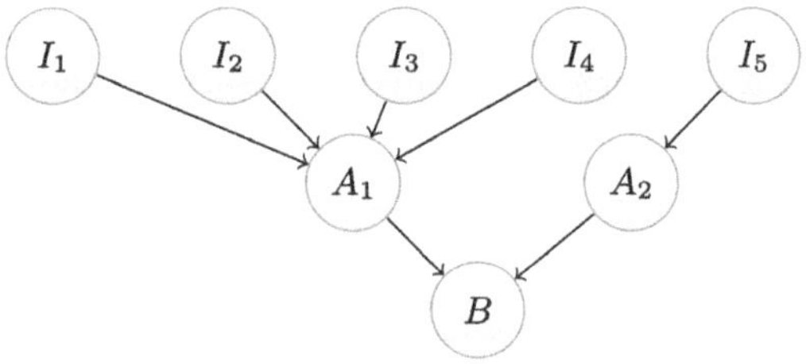

Fig. 6. Update functions and graphical representation of a Boolean network.

Observation #2 "AND" Relation: If a node B is active only when all nodes A_i ($i \in \{1, \ldots, k\}$) are active (i.e., if $B = A_1 \cdot \ldots \cdot A_k$), then knocking out node

B has the same effect as knocking out any node A_i. Furthermore, each node A_i contributes equally to the activation of B, meaning they all share the same Shapley value. This can be formalized as follows: if $B = A_1 \cdot \ldots \cdot A_k$, then $\phi_B^{ko}(v) = \phi_{A_1}^{ko}(v) = \ldots = \phi_{A_k}^{ko}(v)$. For example, in Fig. 7, the knockout Shapley value for each I_i with $i \in \{1, 2, 3, 4\}$ equals the knockout Shapley value of A_1, which is 0.067.

$$A_1 = I_1 \cdot I_2 \cdot I_3 \cdot I_4$$
$$A_2 = I_5 + I_6$$
$$B = A_1 + A_2$$

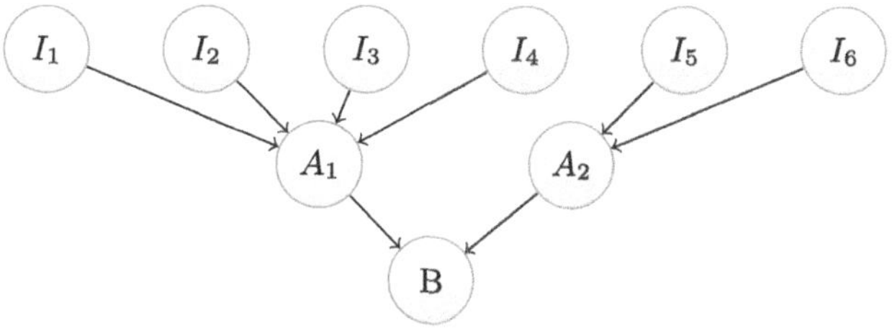

Fig. 7. Update functions and graphical representation of a Boolean network.

Observation #3 "OR" Relation: Consider the simple network shown in Fig. 8. The knockout Shapley values for the input nodes are: $\phi_{I_1}^{ko}(v) = \phi_{I_2}^{ko}(v) = 0.5$. Meanwhile, the knockout Shapley value of the intermediate node A is $\phi_A^{ko}(v) = 2.0$. Since $A = I_1 + I_2$, node A transmits the activation information for I_1, I_2, as well as for the combined case $I_1 \cdot I_2$, where both are active simultaneously. Therefore, the Shapley value of A, $\phi_A^{ko}(v)$, should be greater than the sum of $\phi_{I_1}^{ko}(v)$ and $\phi_{I_2}^{ko}(v)$ and should also account for $\phi_{A'}^{ko}(v')$, where $A' = I_1 \cdot I_2$ represents a node in a Boolean network with I_1 and I_2 connected by AND rather than OR, and v' is the payoff function for this configuration. Given that $\phi_{A'}^{ko}(v') = 1$, it follows that $\phi_A^{ko}(v) = \phi_{I_1}^{ko}(v) + \phi_{I_2}^{ko}(v) + \phi_{A'}^{ko}(v') = 2$.

Now, let's consider the more complex example in Fig. 9. Here, since $A_1 = I_1 + I_2 + I_3 + I_4$, the Shapley value of A_1 should account for all cases where each individual I_i, with $i \in \{1, 2, 3, 4\}$, is the only active node, as well as all pairwise cases where I_i and I_j (for $i, j \in \{1, 2, 3, 4\}$ and $i \neq j$) are active, and similarly for triples and the full quartet (I_1, I_2, I_3, I_4). Beyond the sum of $\phi_{I_i}^{ko}(v)$, the Shapley value for A_1 should also include terms for these groups of I_i considered in an AND configuration. Thus, we have $\phi_{A_1}^{ko}(v) = \sum_{i \in 1,2,3,4} \phi_{I_i}^{ko}(v) + \sum_{i,j \in 1,2,3,4, i \neq j} \phi_{A'_{ij}}^{ko}(v'_{ij}) + \sum_{i,j,k \in 1,2,3,4, i \neq j, i \neq k, j \neq k} \phi_{A'_{ijk}}^{ko}(v'_{ijk}) + \phi_{A'}^{ko}(v')$, where $A'_{ij} = I_i \cdot I_j$, $A'_{ijk} = I_i \cdot I_j \cdot I_k$, and $A' = I_1 \cdot I_2 \cdot I_3 \cdot I_4$ in Boolean networks derived by modifying the original configuration, with v'_{ij}, v'_{ijk}, and v' as their corresponding payoff functions.

While all of this requires formal definition and introduces considerable complexity, we will not pursue this formalization here, as Observation #4 will allow us to simplify the scenario.

$$A = I_1 + I_2$$
$$B = A$$

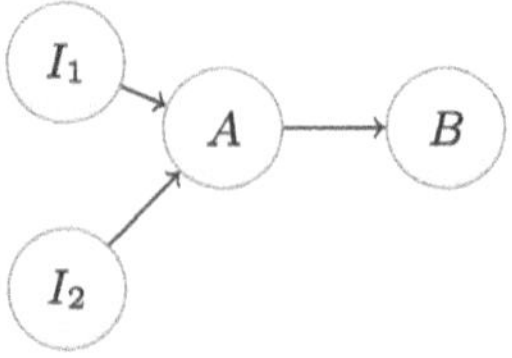

Fig. 8. Update functions and graphical representation of a Boolean network.

$$A_1 = I_1 + I_2 + I_3 + I_4$$
$$A_2 = I_5 + I_6$$
$$B = A_1 + A_2$$

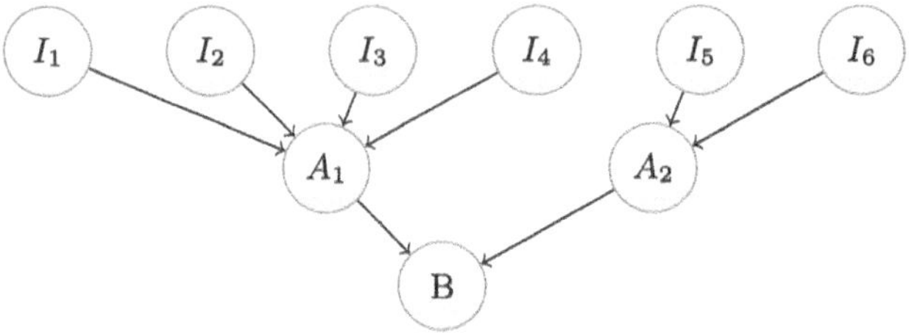

Fig. 9. Update functions and graphical representation of a Boolean network.

Observation #4 Equivalent Binary Tree: Any tree-shaped Boolean network can be transformed into an equivalent binary tree-shaped Boolean network, where each node depends on at most two other nodes. Figure 10 illustrates this with a simple example. In general, the equivalent binary form is achieved by converting each Boolean update formula into disjunctive normal form, then constructing the Boolean network directly from the abstract syntax tree of the resulting formula, with $+$ and $\cdot$ as binary operators.

Fig. 10. Graphical representation of the Boolean network $A_1 = I_1 + I_2 + I_3$, and of the equivalent binary version given by $I'_{12} = I_1 + I_2$, $I'_3 = I_3$ and $A'_1 = I'_{12} + I'_3$.

4.2 Preliminary Propagation Method

In this section, we provide a preliminary definition of a propagation method for the knockout Shapley value in Boolean networks. For simplicity, we focus on *binary tree-shaped Boolean networks without negation.* Negation is excluded to simplify the presentation, and the restriction to tree-shaped networks is aimed at achieving a foundational result that can be expanded upon in future work. The binary constraint, meanwhile, allows for more straightforward definitions without loss of generality (as discussed in Sect. 4.1, Observation #4).

The idea behind propagation is that we can compute the knockout Shapley value solely for the input nodes of the network, then derive values for the other nodes from these initial computations. For general Boolean networks, this approach may be challenging or even infeasible[4] and might require approximations. However, for tree-shaped Boolean networks, exact propagation can be achieved using the following recursive definition of the knockout Shapley value, building on the observations discussed in Sect. 4.1:

$$\phi_B^{ko}(v) = \begin{cases} \phi_A^{ko}(v) & \text{if } B = A \\ \phi_{A_1}^{ko}(v) \;\; (= \phi_{A_2}^{ko}(v)) & \text{if } B = A_1 \cdot A_2 \\ \phi_{A_1}^{ko}(v) + \phi_{A_2}^{ko}(v) + \phi_{B'}^{ko}(v') & \text{if } B = A_1 + A_2 \end{cases} \tag{16}$$

where $B' = A_1 \cdot A_2$ and v' is the payoff function for the network with B replaced by B'. Calculating $\phi_{B'}^{ko}(v')$ would require constructing a different Boolean network and redoing the analysis on this new network. To avoid this, we define an equivalent reformulation of the equation in which $\phi_{B'}^{ko}(v')$ is replaced by a computation that remains within the original Boolean network, leveraging the fact that we are interested only in cases where both A_1 and A_2 are active-cases that are also captured by the truth table of the original network.

$$\phi_B^{ko}(v) = \begin{cases} \phi_A^{ko}(v) & \text{if } B = A \\ \phi_{A_1}^{ko}(v) \;\; (= \phi_{A_2}^{ko}(v)) & \text{if } B = A_1 \cdot A_2 \\ \phi_{A_1}^{ko}(v) + \phi_{A_2}^{ko}(v) & \\ \quad + \displaystyle\sum_{R \in \mathcal{P}(N), \{A_1, A_2\} \subseteq R, S = R \cap M} \frac{[v(S) - v_{\bar{A}_1 \bar{A}_2}(S)]}{\binom{|M|}{|S|}} & \text{if } B = A_1 + A_2 \end{cases} \tag{17}$$

In this second formulation, $\phi_{B'}^{ko}(v')$ is replaced by a summation over $R \in \mathcal{P}(N)$. Here, N denotes the complete set of all nodes in the Boolean network, and $\mathcal{P}(N)$ represents the set of all rows in the network's truth table. In each row R, all nodes in that specific configuration are included, and $S = R \cap M$ refers specifically to the subset of input nodes within R. Here, $v_{\bar{A}_1 \bar{A}_2}$ denotes the payoff function for the network with both A_1 and A_2 knocked out. This formula explicitly conveys that we aim to compute the contribution when both A_1 and A_2 are set to 0. This computation can be performed using the already-established truth table of the Boolean network with payoff function v.

In the example shown in Fig. 11, the knockout Shapley values for the input nodes, calculated using Eq. (13), are as follows: $\phi_{I_1}^{ko}(v) = \phi_{I_2}^{ko}(v) = 0.1$ and $\phi_{I_3}^{ko}(v) = \phi_{I_4}^{ko}(v) = \phi_{I_5}^{ko}(v) = 0.4$. By applying the propagation formula from Eq. (17), the propagated values for A_1 and A_2 are straightforwardly determined

[4] We have not yet investigated this generalization.

to be $\phi^{ko}_{A_1}(v) = 0.1$ and $\phi^{ko}_{A_2}(v) = 0.4$. The propagated value for A_3 is then calculated as:

$$\phi^{ko}_{A_3}(v) = \phi^{ko}_{I_4}(v) + \phi^{ko}_{I_5}(v) + \sum_{R \in \mathcal{P}(N), \{I_4, I_5\} \subseteq R, S = M \cap R} \frac{v(S) - v_{\bar{I}_4 \bar{I}_5}(S)}{\binom{5}{|S|}} = \\ = 0.4 + 0.4 + \frac{1}{10} + \frac{1}{10} + \frac{1}{10} = 1.1 \tag{18}$$

Three terms $\frac{1}{10}$ come from the summation of the weighted gains A_3 obtains when $v(S) - v_{\bar{I}_4 \bar{I}_5}(S)$ is equal to one. This comes from three subsets: $\{I_4, I_5, A_3, B_2\}$ (giving $\frac{1}{\binom{5}{2}}$), $\{I_2, I_4, I_5, A_3, B_2\}$ (giving $\frac{1}{\binom{5}{3}}$), and $\{I_1, I_4, I_5, A_3, B_2\}$ (giving $\frac{1}{\binom{5}{3}}$). These sets which bring non zero gain can be found in the truth table of the Boolean network.

The value for B_2, according to the second case of Eq. (17), is equal to the value of A_3, so $\phi^{ko}_{B_2}(v) = 1.1$. Meanwhile, the value for the node B_1 can be calculated from the third case of Eq. (17) as:

$$\phi^{ko}_{B_1}(v) = \phi^{ko}_{A_1}(v) + \phi^{ko}_{A_2}(v) + \sum_{R \in \mathcal{P}(N), \{A_1, A_2\} \subseteq R, S = M \cap R} \frac{v(S) - v_{\bar{A}_1 \bar{A}_2}(S)}{\binom{5}{S}} = \\ = 0.1 + 0.4 + \frac{1}{10} = 0.6 \tag{19}$$

The term $\frac{1}{10} = \frac{1}{\binom{5}{3}}$ comes from the set $S = \{I_1, I_2, I_3, A_1, A_2, B_1\}$, which is the only one giving non zero gain.

The values for intermediate nodes A_1, A_2, A_3, B_1, B_2 given by Eq. (17) agree with the knockout Shapley value for these nodes given by Eq. (13).

$$\begin{aligned} A_1 &= I_1 \cdot I_2 \\ A_2 &= I_3 \\ A_3 &= I_4 + I_5 \\ B_1 &= A_1 + A_2 \\ B_2 &= A_3 \\ C &= B_1 + B_2 \end{aligned}$$

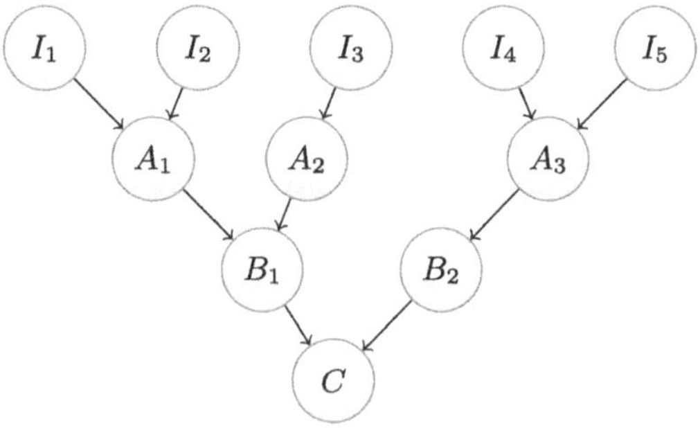

Fig. 11. Update functions and graphical representation of a Boolean network.

Discussion: The proposed propagation method enables us to bypass the need for simulating knockouts on intermediate nodes when calculating the knockout Shapley value. Propagation in cases involving identical update functions or the AND operator can be achieved in constant time. Although propagation with the OR operator is more complex, it still requires less computation than directly applying the knockout Shapley value definition.

5 Conclusion and Future Work

In this study, we introduced an approach to apply coalition game theory to Boolean networks through two game settings, which we referred to as the Boolean network game and the knockout game. Based on these games, we presented three notions of the Shapley value, along with their interpretations within biological systems. For the knockout Shapley value, we also proposed preliminary results for a propagation method that extends the Shapley value calculated for input nodes to intermediate nodes, thereby reducing computational effort.

These initial results apply only to Boolean networks with a binary tree structure. Addressing more general network structures and incorporating negation (inhibition) effects will be key areas for future work. Another promising direction would be to assign different weights, such as probabilities, to input configurations.

Acknowledgments. This work is supported by project "MEDICA" (2022RNTYWZ) funded by MUR-PRIN_2022, and by PNRR ECS00000017 - "THE - Tuscany Health Ecosystem" - Spoke 6 - CUP I53C22000780001 funded by the EC under the NextGeneration EU programme.

Disclosure of Interests. The authors declare that they have no conflicts of interest related to this work.

References

1. Shapley, L.S., et al.: A value for n-person games (1953)
2. Keinan, A., Sandbank, B., Hilgetag, C.C., Meilijson, I., Ruppin, E.: Fair attribution of functional contribution in artificial and biological networks. Neural Comput. **16**(9), 1887–1915 (2004)
3. Moretti, S., Patrone, F., Bonassi, S.: The class of microarray games and the relevance index for genes. TOP **15**, 256–280 (2007)
4. Moretti, S., Fragnelli, V., Patrone, F., Bonassi, S.: Using coalitional games on biological networks to measure centrality and power of genes. Bioinformatics **26**(21), 2721–2730 (2010)
5. Kauffman, S.A.: Metabolic stability and epigenesis in randomly constructed genetic nets. J. Theor. Biol. **22**(3), 437–467 (1969)
6. Schwab, J.D., Kühlwein, S.D., Ikonomi, N., Kühl, M., Kestler, H.A.: Concepts in boolean network modeling: what do they all mean? Comput. Struct. Biotechnol. J. **18**, 571–582 (2020)
7. Barbuti, R., Gori, R., Milazzo, P., Nasti, L.: A survey of gene regulatory networks modelling methods: from differential equations, to boolean and qualitative bioinspired models. J. Membrane Comput. **2**, 207–226 (2020)

8. Lozin, V., Razgon, I., Zamaraev, V., Zamaraeva, E., Zolotykh, N.: Linear read-once and related boolean functions. Discret. Appl. Math. **250**, 16–27 (2018)
9. Von Neumann, J., Morgenstern, O.: Theory of Games and Economic Behavior, 2nd rev (1947)
10. Roth, A.E.: The Shapley Value: Essays in Honor of Lloyd S. Cambridge University Press, Shapley (1988)
11. Cowen, L., Ideker, T., Raphael, B.J., Sharan, R.: Network propagation: a universal amplifier of genetic associations. Nat. Rev. Genet. **18**(9), 551–562 (2017)

Formal Methods in Healthcare

Towards a Flexible Approach for Understanding and Comparing Traces

Juliana K. F. Bowles[1,2(✉)]

[1] SCCH, Softwarepark 32a, 4232 Hagenberg, Austria
[2] School of Computer Science, University of St Andrews, St Andrews KY16 9SX, UK
jkfb@st-andrews.ac.uk

Abstract. We assume given a set of behavioural models of computation (event structures) that can be extracted from specifications, processes, code and/or data depending on the application, and have labels containing additional information of interest (e.g., an integer variable representing a measure in the context of the computation). In this paper we present our vision towards a formal flexible approach to search for optimal traces of execution with respect to different parameters of interest (e.g., time, efficacy, cost and/or concurrency), enriched with a mechanism to understand the difference between (sub-optimal) traces and their formalisation as explanations. The underlying idea of the approach is to be generalisable and hence suited to tackle practical problems in a variety of domains from aerospace, automotive and automation industries, as well as systems and applications developed for healthcare. Our examples here come from a healthcare based context.

Keywords: Event Structures · Traces · Optimisation · SMT solvers

1 Introduction

Complex software systems have become the heart of the world's economy, society and infrastructure. Consequently, software vulnerabilities and errors in these systems can have substantial global impact and need resilient approaches and solutions able to tackle them.

Formal verification techniques, including model checking, can be used to analyse properties over such systems but require the existence of system models (labelled transition systems, variants of automata, Markov-based models, and so on) which can be checked against properties of interest written in a suitable temporal logic (LTL, CTL, timed/stochastic extensions, etc.). Given a system model, model checking explores exhaustively all possible states in the model (either explicitly or implicitly) to find executions that violate certain constraints or conversely satisfy certain properties, and if the approach permits,

This work has been supported by the Austrian Funding Council (FWF) under Meitner M 3338-N.

G. Broccia and A. Cerone (Eds.): DataMod 2023, LNCS 14618, pp. 115–126, 2025.
https://doi.org/10.1007/978-3-031-87217-4_6

within certain timed bounds and probabilities. Despite the benefits of using logic and formal techniques for finding bugs in the hardware and software industries, it remains challenging in practice: techniques often do not scale, and system behavioural models may be incomplete or poorly understood.

By contrast, there are many complex problems in modern systems that can be encoded in first-order logic and benefit from the use of efficient SMT solvers: finding design errors in the logical functioning of modern digital electronic chips; solving scheduling and planning problems; validating cyber-physical systems; generating test inputs for safety-critical embedded software; detecting security vulnerabilities through an SMT-based technique called *Automatic Exploit Generation* [1]; amongst many others.

In this paper, we take the formalisation of (parts of) models of computation as sets of constraints given in first-order logic and enriched with parameters (e.g., an integer variable x representing a measure in the context of the computation), to search for executions that satisfy particular properties. More concretely, we use SMT solvers to search within models of computation for executions that optimise a given parameter (e.g., maximise x) whilst always satisfying a certain property (e.g., a boolean variable that must always be true). Our models of computation, (in our case, labelled event structures), are abstractions that can be extracted from specifications, processes, code and/or data depending on the application. The information contained in the labels of an event, for instance in relation to the value of x, is used when searching for the execution that optimises that parameter. The flexible and scalable nature of SMT solvers such as Z3 [23] make them a suitable choice in practice.

We envisage an approach which makes it possible to understand the obtained optimal computation (trace of execution aka solution) given by the solver, and (if applicable) whether there are several solutions that should be considered. In the latter case, a notion of *distance* is needed to help to characterise, differentiate and explain solutions, and consequently be used to justify a selected preferred one. This paper presents the background, context and a practical problem from the medical domain for our proposed approach. It discusses the challenges and open problems that have to be tackled to achieve this vision.

2 Background

A Boolean satisfiability problem, or SAT for short, is the problem of determining whether there is an assignment for all variables in a propositional formula such that the formula evaluates to true, that is, the formula is *satisfiable*. Many problems can be formulated in this way and are solved very efficiently by modern SAT solvers. Furthermore, modern SAT solvers have become core technology of many model checkers and are particularly suited to prove invariants as well as reachability properties through what is known as *bounded model checking* [4] and further enhanced through powerful approaches such as k-induction which, much like mathematical induction, use induction to increase the depth of the bound [14]. Efficient modern SAT solvers (and SMT solvers) are expected to continue to contribute to essential redevelopments of a new generation of model checkers which scale better and can handle infinite-state models.

Some problems require more expressive logics, such as first-order or higher-order logics, and include non-Boolean variables, functions and predicate symbols and quantifiers. To keep such problems decidable, it is usually necessary to constrain the interpretations of the functions and/or predicate symbols. This means that we assume some logical background *theory* (e.g., theory of equality, of integer numbers, of real numbers, and so on), and we are concerned with *satisfiability modulo theories* (SMT) [2,3], that is, determining the satisfiability of a formula φ with respect to an interpretation in a given theory T. To determine the satisfiability of formulae, SMT solvers make use of efficient reasoning techniques specific to the selected theory T. SMT solvers are particularly powerful because they can handle and combine many different kinds of theories, and can also be extended to include new theories to deal with new application domains. In addition, the standardisation efforts of SMT-LIB[1] have contributed to driving progress in SMT-based technology further.

Searching for traces of execution involves the use of a solver. Introducing non-Boolean variables, functions, predicate symbols and quantifiers, forces us to go beyond SAT solvers, and use SMT solvers for finding solutions which optimise parameters of interest. There is a wide range of possibilities for solvers that can be used to solve constraints involving non-Boolean variables, including, among others, Minion [16], FlatZinc and MiniZinc [25]. Modern SMT solvers such as Z3 allow the inclusion of heuristics also known as strategies [22]. In addition, when reasoning about the model of choice it can be useful to use a theorem prover Isabelle [27] to generate SMT-Lib code and link it to solvers such as Z3 and CVC5.For the underlying chosen model, we need to define notions of computation distance and explainability. Reasoning on those may be facilitated through the use of a theorem prover.

For a given abstraction from code, we may want to find executions that are computationally more efficient, have the highest degree of concurrency or consume less energy, using criteria such as performance, time, energy, efficacy, cost, and so on. We assume that statements in code may have annotated measures which can be used to search for execution runs that are optimal wrt those measures. The ability to evaluate and compare different optimal computations for different purposes can be used to gain further insights on the abstraction itself.

Let us consider the setting of improving treatment plans for patients with multiple chronic conditions where it is important to be certain that medications prescribed for different purposes do not lead to adverse reactions or undesired side effects: *is there a better combination of medications that avoids harmful adverse reactions and improves the quality of life of the patient?* Or even more fundamentally: *what is the difference between two solutions provided by a solver in terms of treatment efficacy or side effects?* It may be important to understand the difference between proposed treatments in cases where certain medications may not be available.

[1] http://smtlib.org.

3 Approach

3.1 Overview

The vision of our approach is sketched in Fig. 1. For a given input, here seen as one or more models of computation (e.g., event structures), converted into an SMT encoding (step ①) and passed to an SMT solver with arithmetic optimisation such as Z3 (step ②), we obtain (if solutions exist) one optimal solution (computation or trace of execution) with respect to the parameters of interest, and through a number of calls to the SMT solver (step ③), this may lead to one or more solutions: sol1, sol2, sol3, etc.

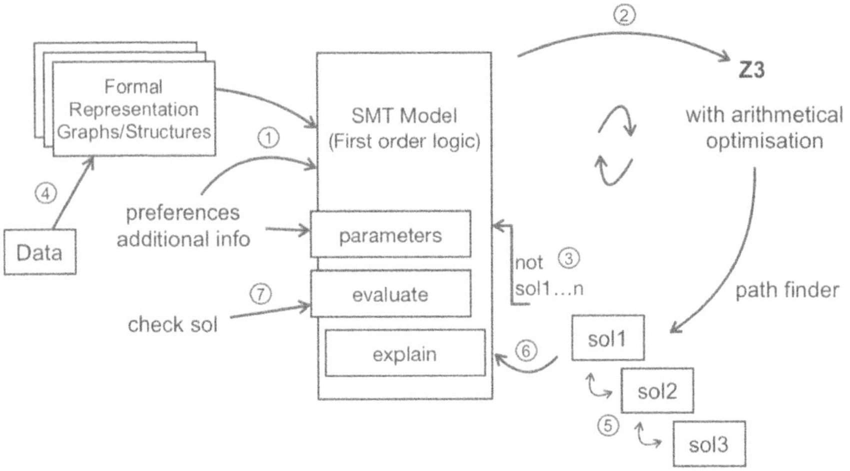

Fig. 1. Overview of the approach

Our earlier work (cf. [8–11]) offers partial contributions to steps ①, ② and ③, but needs to be extended to address preferences and additional information more accurately in step ①. In our earlier work, we have also used the theorem prover Isabelle [27] to generate SMT code automatically and provide additional aid in proving the correctness of properties as needed.

Challenges arise when there are no models available from which we can derive a formal representation or only partial information is available. Step ④ addresses this by enabling the inference of additional information from data, such as additional structures/paths, probabilities associated to different choices, etc. One option here is to follow a similar approach to CP-nets [5] where preferences are represented as a partial order with added priorities and optimisation criteria, but adapted to our richer event structures, and combine them with the remaining models when obtaining the SMT encoding (step ①). The advantage of our approach is that it will use the same abstract representation to capture different aspects and sources of information required for the search.

To create practical solutions of real value, we need to be able to explain generated solutions as well as their difference. Step ⑤ deals with the formalisation and understanding of differences between solutions, and how solutions are explained in step ⑥. Of added value is also to be able to evaluate how good a particular solution may be in the overall spectrum of possible solutions (step ⑦), making use of the notion of *solution distance* from step ⑤. Concerning step ⑥, we have explored the use of argumentation theory for explaining medication choices in [29,30]. Instead we may take a simpler approach and focus on the first-order logical statements associated to paths obtained and notions of computation distance.

3.2 Models of Computation

The model of computation we use is a labelled (prime) event structure [32], or *event structure* for short. Event structures have been widely used and studied in the literature, and have been used to give a true-concurrent semantics to process calculi such as CCS, CSP, SCCS and ACP (e.g., [31]). The advantages of prime event structures include their underlying simplicity and how they naturally describe fundamental notions present in behavioural models and code including sequential, parallel and iterative behaviour (or the unfoldings thereof) as well as nondeterminism (cf. [6,19]), and are hence our model of choice. Event structures also have well-defined composition operators and can be used to represent unfoldings of graphs and models such as Petri nets (cf. e.g., [26]).

To use event structures as a model capturing the behaviour of a process, piece of code or component, we add labels to the events, associating the events to actions that have to be performed, conditions that have to be checked, statements that have to be executed, and so on. Further enriching an event structure with labelling functions gives us a mechanism to introduce further measures which can reflect properties of interest for our computations. However, existing composition mechanisms for event structures ignore labels and are hence inadequate for our use here. By converting our problem to an SMT problem, we circumvent this and we can search for the computations that satisfy our criteria without the need to create a composite model.

The formal definition of an event structure below is taken from [19].

Definition 1. *An* event structure *is a triple* $E = (Ev, \rightarrow^*, \#)$ *where* Ev *is a set of events and* $\rightarrow^*, \# \subseteq Ev \times Ev$ *are binary relations called* causality *and* conflict, *respectively. Causality* $\rightarrow^*$ *is a partial order. Conflict* $\#$ *is symmetric and irreflexive, and propagates over causality, i.e.,* $e\#e' \wedge e' \rightarrow^* e'' \Rightarrow e\#e''$ *for all* $e, e', e'' \in Ev$. *Two events* $e, e' \in Ev$ *are* concurrent, e *co* e' *iff* $\neg(e \rightarrow^* e' \vee e' \rightarrow^* e \vee e\#e')$. $C \subseteq Ev$ *is a* configuration *iff (1)* C *is* conflict-free*:* $\forall e, e' \in C \neg(e\#e')$ *and (2)* downward-closed*:* $e \in C$ *and* $e' \rightarrow^* e$ *implies* $e' \in C$.

An event structure consists of a set of event occurrences together with binary relations for expressing causal dependency (called *causality*) and nondeterminism (called *conflict*). The causality relation implies a (partial) order among event occurrences, while the conflict relation expresses how the occurrence of certain events excludes the occurrence of others. From the two relations defined over the set of events, a further relation is derived, namely the *concurrency* relation *co*. Two events are concurrent if and only if they are completely unrelated, i.e., neither related by causality nor by conflict. We assume a *discrete* structure which guarantees a finite model and is sufficient for our purposes, that is, there are always only a finite number of causally related predecessors to an event e. This is referred to as the *local configuration* of e and written $\downarrow e$. Discreteness is important here because computations always have a starting point. Immediate causality between two events e and e' is written $e \rightarrow e'$ and indicates that no other event can occur in between. An event can have one or more immediate successors. Finally, a configuration C as defined above (downwards-closed and conflict-free) is a *trace of execution* if and only if it is maximal.

Depending on what interpretation we want to give to an event structure, we define a set of labels, and a labelling function is a partial function that associates subsets of labels to events. We can define several labelling functions to add different measures and parameters of interest. We use LES to refer to labelled event structures in the following, and we assume that the labelling functions are defined for different concrete problems as needed.

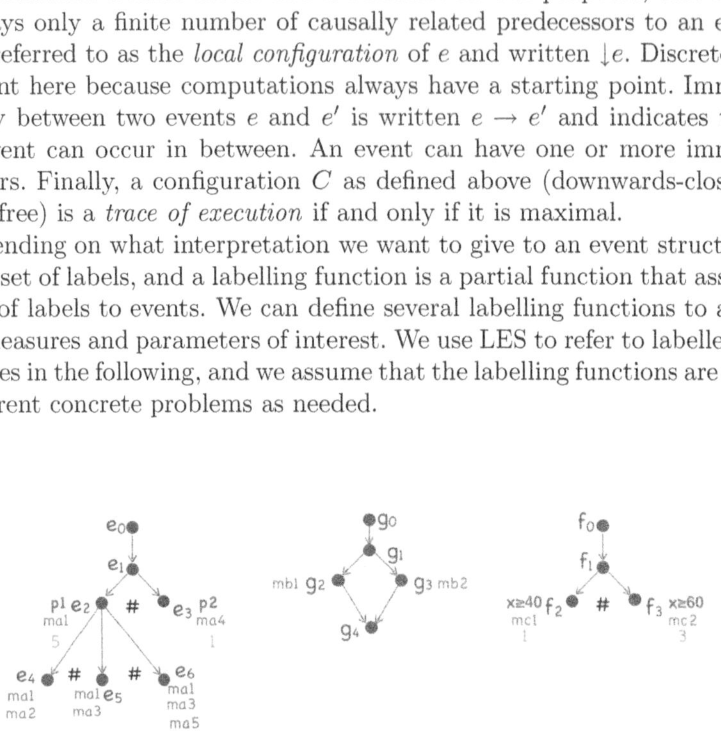

Fig. 2. Three event structures with labels shown.

Consider the three structures shown in Fig. 2 with events given as $e_0, e_1, \ldots,$ $g_0, g_1, \ldots,$ $f_0, f_1, \ldots,$ explicit immediate causality shown (e.g., $e_0 \rightarrow e_1$), direct conflict between events at the same level (e.g., $e_2 \# e_3$), and so on. In this example events g_2 and g_3 are concurrent. Additional labels (given in different colours) are shown next to the events. Let p_1 and p_2 indicate conditions associated to events e_2 and e_3 respectively, where each condition has to hold for the corresponding event to occur; priorities are given next to events as natural numbers; and additional actions (ma_1, mb_1, etc.) are shown as well. The search across these three very simple models can give us 8 possible traces of execution, but different traces may be required under different conditions. Furthermore, we may have additional information that tells us that certain actions should not be done together (e.g., ma_1 and mc_2), even though they are associated to events with higher priority.

Additional information, such as actions that should not be done together, preferences over the use of certain resources, probabilistic information contained in data, etc., can be added to the solver as well. To keep the overall formalism cohesive, we will represent this information as a LES. We will explore the models of preferences defined for CP-nets [5] for our context here, and how these can be adapted to LES. In CP-nets preferences are represented as a partial order with added priorities and optimisation criteria. Since our LES contains partial orders (in the binary relation causality), the approach taken will be a natural extension which needs to incorporate conflict and concurrency as well. The process of generating SMT encodings from our LES-preferences will hence be the same.

3.3 Computation Distance, Comparison and Evaluation

An SMT solver will generate one optimal solution with respect to the parameter we are trying to optimise. In some cases there may be more than one solution for the same optimal value. In these circumstances, it is worth to be able to characterise the *distance* between the different solutions/computations with the same optimal value, between an optimal solution and a second best, or between two solutions that optimise different parameters. In our case solutions are traces of execution across our input structures. One approach to consider for the distance between two solutions can be how many changes have to be made from one solution to reach the other. The notion of Levenshtein distance [20] for strings, which measures the number of changes between two strings required to make them equal, may be useful when comparing traces of executions. Since sequences of tasks representing a process can been seen as graphs, graph-based edit-distances-algorithms, which extend Levenshtein distance, may be more appropriate [15]. A further useful notion for our model is that of a CP-net distance as described in [21] which is based on distances between partial orders. We expect the later notion to be particularly relevant because event structure causality is a partial order. Whilst *causality* is one of the relations contained in event structures, we also need to consider conflict and concurrency as other relations that may have an impact on our possible distance metrics, as well as any information contained in the event labels (depending on which criteria is being used in the search). Indeed, several notions of computation distance may be necessary.

For instance, when observing the models in Fig. 2, the path that leads to e_5 is very similar to the path that leads to e_6, and the difference is contained in the labels: the choice of e_6 implies a further action ma_5 not taken in e_5. Further information is needed to understand and explain the difference that this additional action may entail.

We can capture the steps taken to go between solutions (traces of execution), and this will allow us to compare a given trace with an optimal solution obtained by the solver with respect to a given criteria, or for two solutions for different criteria to be compared. A further search could be used to get the sequence of steps to go between solutions, and this could be represented as a logical formula not just to formalise their distance but to explore how to justify their difference.

3.4 Explanations

In our case, the solver will return one or more possible solutions (if any exists) for different criteria we may wish to optimise. In addition to understanding why two traces may be different as given by the notion of distance, we also need to be able to explain a computation on its own which involves justifying the events in the trace as well as any inherent concurrency.

We presented an argumentation model to justify the choices on a clinical pathway, as identified by the SMT solver for multimorbid patients in [30]. While the solver only encoded drug information in the optimal path, we can consider all additional information available in our models (and formulated into our SMT encoding in step ①) to justify an event in a path. Even though our earlier work used simple *pharmaceutical graphs* in the medical context (where nodes were associated to drugs prescribed for treatment in different stages of the condition), further information can be used if available. In addition this approach can be generalised to explanations of similar structures such as our LES. To explain a given trace, we can extract from the event labels all the information that describes that trace and formulate it in first-order logic. Explanations can focus on particular parameters to keep the explanations (their associated formulae) more succinct.

We note that we also need notions of trace equivalence with respect to the arguments (parameters) used to explain different computations. In other words, two computations may be different (the events and relations are different) but their associated explanations can be reduced to the same first-order logical statement and can hence be treated as equivalent under the arguments used. We want to explore the significance of such equivalence notions in practice and we will be inspired by reflections on equivalence such as those given in [28] concerning equivalences between constraint satisfaction problems.

3.5 A Clinical Context

Clinical guidelines are evidence-based care plans which detail the essential steps to be followed when caring for patients with a specific clinical problem and play an important role in improving healthcare for people with long-term conditions. To think about guidelines from a computer science point of view, we can see them as process descriptions, behavioural models, graphs, etc. There are guidelines for managing the treatment for chronic diseases such as diabetes, cardiovascular disease, chronic kidney disease, cancer, chronic obstructive pulmonary disease, and so on. Guidelines include recommendations for the medications (or group of medications) to be given at different stages of the treatment plan as well as alternatives, and are revised regularly.

When patients have multimorbidity, they are implicitly following several clinical guidelines for their individual diseases in parallel. Clinical guidelines offer treatment recommendations for chronic conditions, but often do not take into account the possible presence of comorbidities. Concretely, for patients with multimorbidity current guideline recommendations rapidly lead to *polypharmacy* (i.e., the prescribing of 5 or more medications) without providing guidance on how best to prioritise recommendations [17]. The risk of medication harm is exacerbated, that is, it is possible for patients to take medications that lead to adverse drug reactions, or for particular combinations of drugs to be less effective if administered at the same time.

In earlier work, we explored the combination of formal verification techniques, such as constraint solvers and theorem provers, to identify steps in different guidelines that cause problems if carried out together (e.g., two drugs prescribed for different conditions may interact, food may interact with a drug, health recommendations may contradict each other) whilst at the same time find the preferred alternative according to a certain criteria (e.g., drug efficacy, prevalent disease, patient allergies, preferences, etc.). In the initial proposed approach [18], we introduced medication effectiveness (given by drug companies) as the only criteria for finding the best solution. The approach associated a positive score to each medication capturing effectiveness, and a negative score to pairs of medications with known adverse reactions. This score is used by an SMT solver [24] to find the ideal solution with the highest possible score. The approach was illustrated with an example of a patient with five comorbidities from a much cited medical paper [13], and refined in subsequent work establishing an algorithm that searches for optimal medication combinations across treatments maximising medication efficacy, minimising adverse reactions, avoiding intolerances and undesired side effects [7,8,10,12]. At present there is no attempt at deriving explanations for the solutions obtained or a justification as to how different solutions compare; patient preferences are also not modelled to a great extent; and side-effect exploration is currently restricted to a Boolean characterisation.

Recall the models shown in Fig. 2, and assume that they denote the (unfoldings of) treatments (derived from guidelines) for three conditions that a patient may be undergoing. Each circle is an event denoting the occurrence of something (an action, a clinical examination, taking a medication, etc.). The initial events (e_0, g_0 and f_0) indicate the diagnosis of the corresponding disease. At times there may be a choice between treatment options (e.g., e_2 and e_3). We indicate in red the occurrence associated to an event. Some occurrences have conditions on them, for instance `p1` has to hold for e_2 to be able to occur; $x \geq 40$ must hold at for event f_2 for medication `mc1` to be prescribed.

Assume that we know that the occurrence of `ma1` conflicts with `mc2`, and `ma2` conflicts with `mb2` (domain knowledge). In order to find our optimal paths, we need to know in addition how effective drugs are considered to be when used for a condition and reported side effects. To simplify the presentation here, assume here that a drug is only used in the context of one treatment. Drug effectiveness, side effects and likelihood of side effects are captured for our example in Table 1. In addition, drugs are known to interact with others. Sometimes additional drugs are added to compensate the interactions as shown in Table 2.

We want to combine the diagrams of Fig. 2 in a way that the known underlying conflicts are taken into account. To do so, we need to search valid paths across the three structures that avoid given drug interactions and/or side effects

Table 1. Drug Effectiveness and Side Effects.

Drug	Effectiveness	Side Effects	Likelihood
ma1	ve_1 1000	s0	rare ($\leq$ 20%)
ma4	ve_4 900	s1	common ($\geq$ 60%)
		s2	rare ($\leq$ 20%)
ma5	ve_5 600	s3	very common ($\geq$ 80%)

Table 2. Drug Interactions.

Drugs	Conflict Level	*Score*
ma1, mc2	severe	$v1$-2000
ma1, ma5, mc2	mild	$v2$-600
ma2, mb2	severe	$v3$-1800

as desired. Intuitively, an optimal solution which focuses on maximising drug effectiveness and minimising interaction score, would give us the execution path that includes events e_6 and f_2. If a patient prefers to avoid side effect s3 then the optimal solution would include event e_4 instead which excludes the medication more likely going to contribute to the side effect.

4 Concluding Remarks

We presented a vision investigating the use of logic as a unifying tool for *modelling*, *reasoning*, *searching* and *explaining* optimal traces of execution. Understanding a notion of distance between traces of execution (with the same optimal value or similar) can be important to decide what solution to choose, what trade-offs may have to be made as a consequence, and so on. We are currently working towards the formalisation of different notions of distance in order to be able to: *compare* arbitrary solutions; *evaluate* a particular execution with respect to the optimal solution; and *explain* solutions. In other words, the idea is to explore how the interplay between a distance measure and logic can be used to explain different solutions adding domain knowledge (e.g., side effects, patient preferences) to clarify them.

References

1. Avgerinos, T., Cha, S.K., Rebert, A., Schwartz, E.J., Woo, M., Brumley, D.: Automatic exploit generation. Commun. ACM **57**, 74–84 (2014)
2. Barrett, C., Sebastiani, R., Seshia, S., Tinelli, C.: Satisfiability modulo theories. In: Biere, A., Heule, M.J.H., van Maaren, H., Walsh, T. (eds.) Handbook of Satisfiability, Frontiers in Artificial Intelligence and Applications, vol. 185, chap. 26, pp. 825–885. IOS Press (2009)

3. Barrett, C., Tinelli, C.: Satisfiability modulo theories. In: Clarke, E., Henzinger, T., Veith, H., Bloem, R. (eds.) Handbook of Model Checking, chap. 11, pp. 305–344. Springer (2018). https://doi.org/10.1007/978-3-319-10575-8_11
4. Biere, A., Kröning, D.: Sat-based model checking. In: Clarke, E., Henzinger, T., Veith, H., Bloem, R. (eds.) Handbook of Model Checking, chap. 10, pp. 277–304. Springer (2018). https://doi.org/10.1007/978-3-319-10575-8_10
5. Boutilier, C., Brafman, R., Domshlak, C., Hoos, H.H., Poole, D.: CP-Nets: a tool for representing and reasoning with conditional ceteris paribus preference statements. J. Artif. Intell. Res. **21**, 135–191 (2004)
6. Bowles, J.: Decomposing Interactions. In: Johnson, M., Vene, V. (eds.) Algebraic Methodology and Software Technology: 11th International Conference, Kuressaare, Estonia, 5-8 July 2006. LNCS, vol. 4019, pp. 189–203. Springer (2006). https://doi.org/10.1007/11784180_16
7. Bowles, J., Caminati, M.: A flexible approach for finding optimal paths with minimal conflicts. In: International Conference on Formal Engineering Methods. LNCS, vol. 10610, pp. 209–225. Springer (2017). https://doi.org/10.1007/978-3-319-68690-5_13
8. Bowles, J., Caminati, M.: Balancing prescriptions with constraint solvers. In: Liò, P., Zuliani, P. (eds.) Automated Reasoning for Systems Biology and Medicine, Computational Biology, vol. 30, pp. 243–267. Springer (2019). https://doi.org/10.1007/978-3-030-17297-8_9
9. Bowles, J., Caminati, M.: An integrated approach to a combinatorial optimisation problem. In: Ahrendt, W., Tarifa, S.L.T. (eds.) Integrated Formal Methods - 15th International Conference, IFM 2019, Bergen, Norway, December 2-6, 2019, Proceedings. LNCS, vol. 11918, pp. 284–302. Springer (2019). https://doi.org/10.1007/978-3-030-34968-4_16
10. Bowles, J., Caminati, M.: Correct composition in the presence of behavioural conflicts and dephasing. Sci. Comput. Program. **185** (2020). https://doi.org/10.1016/j.scico.2019.102323
11. Bowles, J., Caminati, M.: A formally verified SMT approach to true concurrency. In: Calimeri, F., Perri, S., Zumpano, E. (eds.) Proceedings of the 35th Italian Conference on Computational Logic - CILC 2020, Rende, Italy, 13-15 October 2020. CEUR Workshop Proceedings, vol. 2710, pp. 357–371. CEUR-WS.org (2020). http://ceur-ws.org/Vol-2710/paper23.pdf
12. Bowles, J., Caminati, M., Cha, S., Mendoza, J.: A framework for automated conflict detection and resolution in medical guidelines. Sci. Comput. Program. **182**, 42–63 (2019). https://doi.org/10.1016/j.scico.2019.07.002, https://www.sciencedirect.com/science/article/pii/S0167642319300759
13. Boyd, C., Darer, J., Boult, C., Fried, L., Boult, L., Wu, A.: Clinical practice guidelines and quality of care for older patients with multiple comorbid diseases: implications for pay for performance. JAMA **294**(6), 716–24 (2005)
14. Donaldson, A., Haller, L., Kroening, D.: Strengthening induction-based race checking with lightweight static analysis. In: VMCAI. LNCS, vol. 6538, pp. 169–183. Springer (2011). https://doi.org/10.1007/978-3-642-18275-4_13
15. Gao, X., Xiao, B., Tao, D., Li, X.: A survey of graph edit distance. Pattern Anal. Appl. **13**, 113–129 (2010)
16. Gent, I., Jefferson, C., Miguel, I.: Minion: A fast scalable constraint solver. In: ECAI 2006, pp. 98–102. IOS Press (2006)
17. Hughes, L., McMurdo, M.E.T., Guthrie, B.: Guidelines for people not for diseases: the challenges of applying UK clinical guidelines to people with multimorbidity. Age Ageing **42**, 62–69 (2013)

18. Kovalov, A., Bowles, J.: Avoiding medication conflicts for patients with multimorbidities. In: 12th International Conference on Integrated Formal Methods (iFM 2016). LNCS, vol. 9681, pp. 376–392. Springer (2016). https://doi.org/10.1007/978-3-319-33693-0_24
19. Küster-Filipe, J.: Modelling concurrent interactions. Theoret. Comput. Sci. **351**, 203–220 (2006)
20. Levenshtein, V.: Binary codes capable of correcting deletions, insertions and reversals. Soviet Physics-Doklady **10**, 707–710 (1966)
21. Loreggia, A., Mattei, N., Rossi, F., Venable, K.B.: On the distance between CP-nets. In: Proceedins of the 17th International Conference on Autonomous Agents and Multiagent Systems (AAMAS 2018), pp. 955–963. ACM (2018)
22. Moura, L., Passmore, G.: The strategy challenge in SMT solving. In: Automated Reasoning and Mathematics. LNCS, vol. 7788, pp. 15–44. Springer (2013). https://doi.org/10.1007/978-3-642-36675-8_2
23. Moura, L.D., Bjørner, N.: Z3: An efficient SMT solver. In: TACAS 2008. LNCS, vol. 4963, pp. 337–340. Springer (2008). https://doi.org/10.1007/978-3-540-78800-3_24
24. Moura, L.D., Bjørner, N.: Satisfiability modulo theories: introduction and applications. Commun. ACM **54**(9), 69–77 (2011)
25. Nethercote, N., Stuckey, P., Becket, R., Brand, S., Duck, G., Tack, G.: Minizinc: towards a standard CP modelling language. In: PPCP 2007, pp. 529–543. Springer (2007). https://doi.org/10.1007/978-3-540-74970-7_38
26. Nielsen, M., Plotkin, G., Winskel, G.: Petri nets, event structures and domains, part I. TCS **13**, 85–108 (1981)
27. Nipkow, T., Paulson, L.C., Wenzel, M.: Isabelle/HOL — A Proof Assistant for Higher-Order Logic, LNCS, vol. 2283. Springer (2002). https://doi.org/10.1007/3-540-45949-9
28. Rossi, F., Petrie, C., Dhar, V.: On the equivalence of constraint satisfaction problems. Tech. Rep. ACT-AI-222-89, MCC Technical Report (1989)
29. Shaheen, Q., Toniolo, A., Bowles, J.: Dialogue games for explaining medication choices. In: Gutiérrez-Basulto, V., Kliegr, T., Soylu, A., Giese, M., Roman, D. (eds.) Rules and Reasoning - 4th International Joint Conference, RuleML+RR 2020, Oslo, Norway, June 29 - July 1, 2020, Proceedings. LNCS, vol. 12173, pp. 97–111. Springer (2020). https://doi.org/10.1007/978-3-030-57977-7_7
30. Shaheen, Q., Toniolo, A., Bowles, J.: Argumentation-based explanations of multimorbidity treatment plans. In: PRIMA 2020: Principles and Practice of Multi-Agent Systems. LNCS, vol. 12568. Springer (2021). https://doi.org/10.1007/978-3-030-69322-0_29
31. Winskel, G.: Event structure semantics for CCS and related languages. In: Nielsen, M., Schmidt, E. (eds.) Automata, Languages, and Programming. LNCS, vol. 140, pp. 561–576. Springer (1982). https://doi.org/10.1007/BFb0012800
32. Winskel, G., Nielsen, M.: Models for Concurrency. In: Abramsky, S., Gabbay, D., Maibaum, T. (eds.) Handbook of Logic in Computer Science, Vol. 4, Semantic Modelling, pp. 1–148. Oxford Science Publications (1995)

Modelling and Verification of an Application for Managing Sensitive Health Data

Almo Cuci[1], Umar Ozeer[2], and Gwen Salaün[1(✉)]

[1] University of Grenoble Alpes, CNRS, Grenoble INP, Inria, LIG, 38000 Grenoble, France
gwen.salaun@inria.fr
[2] Euris Cloud Santé, Paris, France

Abstract. The digitisation of personal health information (PHI) through electronic health record (EHR) is now widely adopted due to their efficiency in terms of cost, storage, processing, and the subsequent quality of delivering patient care. However, security concerns remain one of its major setback. In order to handle EHR, institutions need to comply with their local government security regulations. These regulations control to which extent health data can be processed, transmitted, and stored as well as define how misuses are addressed. φ-comp has been proposed as an industrial solution for monitoring, assessing, and evaluating the compliance of health applications with respect to defined security regulations. φ-comp is able to assess the level of security risk of an application at runtime and to automatically perform the required mitigation actions to recover a compliant environment. Since the risk associated to sensitive health data is critical, there is a need of guarantees in terms of correctness of the φ-comp approach. In this paper, we first present a formal specification of φ-comp representing all the components of the solution as well as their behaviour, that is, the way they all interact together to implement the whole approach from monitoring to mitigation. In a second step, some important properties of interest are formalised and analysed using model checking techniques on several realistic applications.

1 Introduction

An Electronic health record (EHR) consists of a digital version of a patient's personal health information (PHI) such as medications and laboratory test results. The digitisation of healthcare has revolutionised the efficiency of the industry in terms of storage, transmission, and processing capabilities as well as in terms of quality, cost, and time effectiveness of patient care. In order to host an environment (infrastructure, application, services, solutions) that manipulates PHI via EHR, institutions need to comply to the security regulations enforced by the local regulating authorities. These regulations control to which extent personal health information can be processed, transmitted, shared, and stored. In

G. Broccia and A. Cerone (Eds.): DataMod 2023, LNCS 14618, pp. 127–141, 2025.
https://doi.org/10.1007/978-3-031-87217-4_7

addition, control audits can take place at any given time to check whether the hosted platforms respect the high security protocols imposed. In such a context, all activities (system logs, application logs, user activities, operations performed, etc.) should be logged and stored in a secure manner.

φ-comp [15,16] is a security compliance monitoring and management solution for sensitive health data environment, which respects existing security regulations. It monitors, computes, and evaluates the security compliance of health applications and their underlying infrastructures. The monitored data are reported and classified with respect to four security areas (confidentiality, integrity, availability, traceability). These data are analysed by security area and further evaluated into three levels of risk (identified by colors), namely nominal behaviour (blue), potential threat (orange), and non-compliant behaviour (red). In the latter case, risk mitigation actions are automatically performed so as to attenuate the level of risk and restore a compliant behaviour. System administrators are also notified in case of non-compliance, so that manual interventions can be carried out if required. Monitored data as well as performed mitigation actions are logged for *a posteriori* auditing. These logs are used for generation of compliance reports for the hosting institution and for on-demand request from supervising authorities.

Since health data and associated security risks are crucial, there is a need of guarantees in terms of correctness of the φ-comp approach. In this paper, we first present a formal specification of φ-comp representing all the components of the solution's architecture as well as the behaviour of all components including the way they interact together. This specification step is achieved using the LNT process algebraic specification language [2,7]. In a second step, some important properties of interest are formalised using the MCL logic [13] and analysed using model checking techniques on several realistic applications. As far as analysis is concerned, we rely on the CADP verification toolbox [6], which provides powerful model checking tools for automating these analysis steps. The experiments we carried out on these applications confirmed that all properties were satisfied, thus convincing the protocol's designers of the correctness of the φ-comp solution.

The rest of the paper is organized as follows. Section 2 presents the φ-comp solution with more details. Section 3 describes the formal specification of the φ-comp protocol. Section 4 introduces the definition of properties and their verification using model checking techniques. Section 5 surveys related work and Sect. 6 concludes the paper.

2 Presentation of φ-Comp

φ-comp [15,16] is a security compliance monitoring and management solution, which was designed to target cloud computing environments that house sensitive health data. In the rest of this section, we successively present the application model, the architecture of the solution and we give a short description of the components involved in the φ-comp approach.

2.1 Application Model

The application model provides an abstract view of the computing environment, and consists of the infrastructure and the application.

An infrastructure consists of a set of virtual machines (VM) and the physical network connecting them. The infrastructure hosts the application. To do so, it provides the physical resources (CPU, memory, disk, bandwidth, etc.) for executing applicative entities. For illustration purposes, we give in Fig. 1 an example of application model consisting of three VMs and two physical networks (net1 and net2) connecting them.

An application consists of a set of software entities and a set of bindings implementing the communication between software entities. A binding is directed according to the functional dependency between the entities and can be optional or mandatory. A software entity is functional and compliant when all of its mandatory bindings are satisfied, that is, connected to functional entities. Consequently, when a software entity is non-compliant, this may impact other entities depending on it. The compliance of a software entity only depends on its mandatory dependencies. To ensure deployment of a compliant application, cycles of (mandatory) dependencies are forbidden.

Figure 1 shows an example of application consisting of three software entities. VM1 hosts a front-end HTTP server (e.g., Apache), VM2 hosts an application server (e.g., Tomcat), and VM3 hosts a relational database system (e.g., MariaDB). The front-end server is connected to the application server via binding b1 and the application server is connected to the database via binding b2. These bindings allow communication between these entities and give the direction of the functional dependencies.

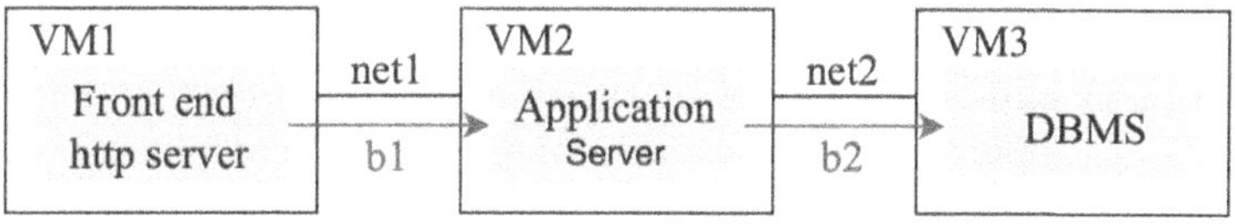

Fig. 1. An Instance of an Application Model

2.2 Compliance Management Protocol

Figure 2 gives an overview of the architecture of the φ-comp solution. The components involved in this architecture are first introduced. In a second step, we describe how they interact together in order to fulfil the compliance management's goals.

Probes and Enforcers are deployed on the environment or application to be managed whereas the other ones are part of the proposed solution and thus deployed on a dedicated infrastructure. Probes monitor the application and

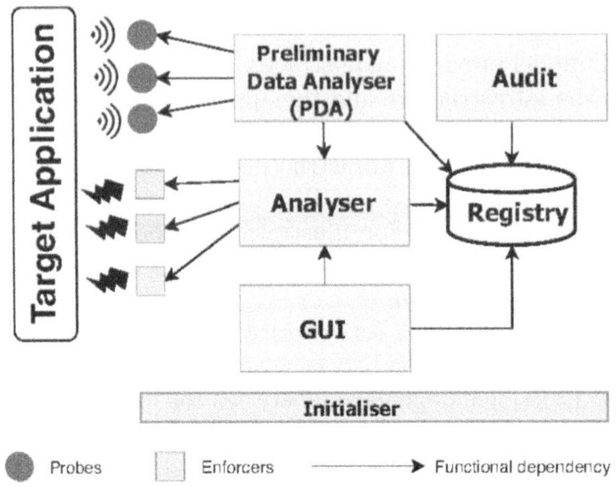

Fig. 2. Architecture of the Protocol

report observation data periodically. Enforcers perform actions on the environment when asked, in order to apply mitigation actions and attenuate the level of risk.

The Preliminary Data Analyser (PDA) receives observation data reported by Probes. The main goal of the PDA is to compute a preliminary security analysis based on these data.

The role of the Analyser is to evaluate the level of risk and to check whether all entities remain compliant. When the Analyser detects a problem or a non-compliance, it computes the required mitigation actions to be applied on the environment.

The Registry aims at storing all information received or computed by φ-comp, that is the data reported by probes, the compliant/non-compliant behaviour of the target environment and all the mitigation actions taken by the Analyser in case of non-compliance. The data stored in the registry are preserved for a determined period of time depending on the required regulations (e.g., one year for HDS regulation).

The Graphical User Interface (GUI) displays information in real time about the monitored application, particularly the current security risk and level of compliance of each entity in the target environment. The GUI allows administrators to work together for handling security issues and carrying out investigations regarding the source of these problems.

The Audit component generates periodically or on demand security reports based on the behaviour of the target application.

The Initialiser component is used for configuring φ-comp by defining the placement and deployment of probes and enforcers on the target environment. The Initialiser is also in charge of ensuring the consistent start up of the different participants of φ-comp by considering their functional dependencies.

Let us now focus on how all these components work together to monitor the application, analyse identified risks, and mitigate them in order to maintain compliance. Figure 3 describes the way these components work together using a workflow description. Probes monitor the application and report observation data to the PDA. Several levels of security risks are computed from these data and a preliminary analysis is established by the PDA for each security area. Assuming that a target environment is initially compliant, the Analyser is notified whenever there is risk identified in the preliminary analysis. The Analyser then evaluates the current security risk relative to each security area for each infrastructure and applicative entity into three levels represented as colors (blue, orange, and red). If the risk is blue, no mitigation actions is taken. If the risk is orange, there is a potential threat and mitigation actions are recommended but not mandatory. If the risk is red, the Analyser carries out a deeper analysis of the problem and its potential impact on other entities. If the risk concerns a software entity, the impact is propagated to all mandatory dependent entities. In the case of a red risk for a software entity all its dependent entities are also assigned a red risk. A red risk systematically implies the execution of mitigation actions in order to reduce the level of risk and recover a compliant environment. The precise definition of mitigation actions are decided by the Analyser. In case of changes in the compliance level, the GUI is updated and administrators are notified. Mitigation actions are submitted to Enforcers which apply them on the target environment.

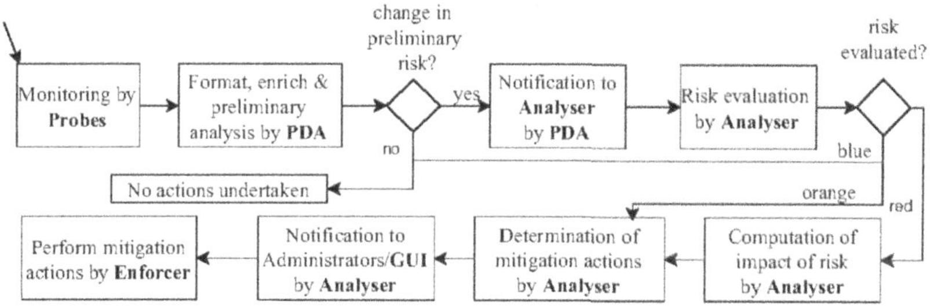

Fig. 3. Overview of Compliance Management

3 Formal Specification

In this section, we introduce the LNT specification for the φ-comp solution. We chose LNT [2,7] as specification language because it is expressive enough and adequate for formally describing communicating systems as the solution presented beforehand in this paper. Moreover, it is equipped with CADP [6], a rich toolbox for analysing LNT specifications using model checking techniques. It is worth noting that other languages (and verification tools) with similar specificities could have been used instead (e.g., Promela/Spin [8] or mCRL2 [1]).

LNT is an extension of LOTOS [9], an ISO standardised process algebra, which allows the definition of data types, functions, and processes. Processes define actions (that can come with incoming or outgoing parameters) and these actions can be organised using several operators, among which: sequential composition (;), conditional statement (**if-then-else**), hiding (**hide**) that hides some action in a behaviour, non-deterministic choice (**select**), parallel composition (**par**) where the communication between the involved processes is carried out by rendezvous on a list of synchronised actions, looping behaviours described using process calls or explicit operators (**while**, **for**, **loop**), and assignment (:=) where the variable should be defined beforehand (either in a **var** block or as a formal parameter). LNT is formally defined using operational semantics based on Labelled Transition Systems. Last but not least, it is worth saying that the default communication model in LNT is synchronous communication (handshake communication), which is fine since the implementation of φ-comp relies on TCP/IP.

In the rest of this section, we present how the different elements of the φ-comp framework are specified using LNT. The specification consists of about 2000 lines of LNT.

3.1 Application Model

First of all, a model of the application is specified in LNT. Data types are used to describe the application model, that is, VMs, software entities or components, and bindings between components. More precisely, an application consists of a set of VMs, a physical network connecting these VMs, and a set of bindings connecting the components hosted on the VMs. Each binding also has a Boolean parameter indicating whether this binding is mandatory (if not, it is optional). A VM consists of an identifier and a set of components.

Figure 4 gives an excerpt of LNT specification describing the virtual machines and bindings corresponding to the application shown in Fig. 1. One can see that each VM hosts a single component (C1, C2, and C3). This excerpt of LNT also shows there are three bindings, there is for instance a binding between C1 hosted on the front-end server and C2 hosted on the application server. The physical network is not made explicit in this example for simplification purposes. The final part of Fig. 1 shows that the application consists of three parts: an identifier, a set of VMs, and a set of bindings.

3.2 Management Protocol

This section presents successively the specification of each participant of the management protocol, and the main process describing how all participants interact together to model the whole management protocol. It is worth noting that several components (Audit, Registry, GUI and Initialiser) are left outside of the specification because their role does not impact the behaviour of the protocol. In contrast, the following entities are crucial and are made explicit in the specification: Probes, PDA, Analyser and Enforcers.

```
var C1 , C2 , C3 : COMPONENT,
    ALLVM        : VMs,
    ALLBDN       : BDNs,
    APP          : APPLICATION
in

 C1 := COMPONENT(1) ;
 C2 := COMPONENT(2) ;
 C3 := COMPONENT(3) ;

 ALLVM := VMs ( { VM( 1, "FRONT" , {C1}),
                  VM( 2, "SERVER" , {C2}),
                  VM( 3, "DBMS" , {C3}) } ) ;

 ALLBDN := BDNs (
   { BINDING( VM( 1, "FRONT" , {C1}) , VM( 2, "SERVER" , {C2}) , TRUE),
     BINDING( VM( 2, "SERVER" , {C2}) , VM( 3, "DBMS" , {C3}) , TRUE),
     BINDING( VM( 1, "FRONT" , {C1}) , VM( 3, "DBMS" , {C3}) , FALSE) } );

 APP := APPLICATION( "model-316" , ALLVM, ALLBDN ) ;

end var
```

Fig. 4. Example of Application Model in LNT

Probe processes mostly capture observation messages obtained by monitoring the application and are useful to identify problems for each security area. The Probe acts as a listener mechanism. Every probe is identified by a unique identifier and has as parameter the unique identifier of the entity being monitored. Every time a probe raises an alert, this observation comes with a timestamp and a triple (obs, val, ra) corresponding respectively to the observation made by the probe, its value, and the risk area associated with this observation.

The *PDA* process receives observation messages issued by the Probe component. Each message contains information about the security areas, the policy used to evaluate the risk (optimistic or pessimistic) and an entity weight value (low, medium, high). Based on these inputs, the PDA process computes a preliminary risk level. This risk level is specified using multiple *if-else* conditions for each parameter value observed in the respective messages. For the values out of the normal scope, a warning or critical preliminary risk score is assigned as result. More precisely, the preliminary risk has four fields to store the score for each security risk area, and three levels of criticity (information, warning, critical). Once computed, this preliminary risk level is submitted to the next component (Analyser) for a finer analysis, and this message contains the preliminary risk score type, information about the security areas, the policy used for evaluation and the entity weight.

The *Analyser* process can be seen like a decision-making mechanism. It receives a preliminary risk message from the PDA process, and goes further in its evaluation of the risk and the compliance of the entity. Based on the information received, the Analyser process can either decide to ignore the message or to trigger a mitigation action by issuing a message to the enforcers with precise countermeasures to be initiated. The mechanism of taking mitigation action relies on three inputs: the preliminary risk score of a single-dimension security area, the policy used (pessimistic, optimistic) and the entity weight. The output is a final risk label of the color blue, orange, or red. This output is computed using the table given in Fig. 5.

Prelim risk / Weight	Optimistic			Pessimistic		
	info	warning	critical	info	warning	critical
Low						
Medium						
High						

Fig. 5. Compliance Evaluation Results

If the final score is blue, the Analyser process ignores it. If the compliance score is orange, the Analyser process keeps monitoring the progress of the specific parameter in this security area. If it is red, then mitigation actions are required. For each security area parameter of the entity that is violated, a countermeasure is required in order to mitigate the risk and set the entity back to compliant behaviour.

Mitigation actions are computed via a dedicated process (called 'mitigate'). This process takes as input the decision issued by the Analyser process (with all the aforementioned parameters), and compute the corresponding mitigation action per security area. As a result, a mitigation action consists of the entity identifier and the action to be taken (e.g., restart VM, add CPU, isolate from internet, log modifications, restart probe, etc.).

These mitigation actions have as target the *enforcers*, which are in charge of actually triggering these actions. Enforcers are able to access to the source of the problem and implement the mitigation actions. Since the specification is abstract, there is no real change of the application. Therefore, the specification can issue and propose countermeasures but they are not actually exploited because the application is not a real one, but just a model of the real one. However, this is fine enough, because the main goal of the analysis steps is to show that the decision process is correct (in case of detected issue, the right decision is taken).

In our model, there is one more process called *pbinjector*. This process is used for issuing potential problems occuring on the application and thus for simulating the execution of the φ-comp solution when examples of risks occur. To do so, this process simulates different states of the software entities and particularly abnormal values are of interest to us. The states of the entity represent the compliance of the security areas. This process is very useful to simulate many scenarios, that turn out to be interesting in terms of exhaustive verification as we will see in Sect. 4.

Finally, the main process represents all processes (probes, PDA, analyser, enforcers, and problem injector) in parallel as shown in Fig. 6. Beyond putting all processes in parallel, the main process also makes explicit how these processes interact together, thus making explicit the architecture given in Fig. 2. In the parallel composition, we can see the names of the processes (e.g., 'probe' or 'pda'). Before these names, there is an arrow preceded by a list of actions. These actions correspond to the actions on which a process has to synchronize with the other processes. As an example, one can see that the action ANALYSISEVENT appears before the 'pda' process and before the 'analyser' process, meaning that both processes synchronize on this action and by doing so exchange information of interest with respect to the analysis of the detected problem.

```
process MAIN [ PROBEVENT: any, ANALYSISEVENT: any, DECISION: any,
    COUNTERMEASURE: any] is
 var app: APPLICATION in
    app:= application() ; use app;
 par
    PROBEVENT -> pbinjector [PROBEVENT]
 ||
    PROBEVENT -> probe [PROBEVENT]
 ||
    PROBEVENT, ANALYSISEVENT -> pda [PROBEVENT , ANALYSISEVENT]
 ||
    ANALYSISEVENT , DECISION -> analyser [ANALYSISEVENT , DECISION]
 ||
    DECISION , COUNTERMEASURE -> mitigate [DECISION , COUNTERMEASURE]
 end par
 end var
end process
```

Fig. 6. Main Process in LNT

4 Verification

In this section, we first explain how properties are verified. Then, we present the list of properties to be ensured. Finally, we comment on the results of analysis of these properties on realistic scenarios.

4.1 Model Checking

In this section, in a first step, we introduce the properties that must be preserved by the health management solution. These properties are then formally specified using the MCL language and automatically analysed using the CADP model checker. MCL [13] is an extension of the alternation-free μ-calculus with regular expressions, data-based constructs, and fairness operators. CADP [6] is a rich verification toolbox that implements the results of concurrency theory and is used for the design of asynchronous concurrent systems, such as communication protocols, distributed systems, asynchronous circuits, multiprocessor architectures or web services. It provides a wide set of functionalities, ranging from step-by-step simulation to massively parallel model-checking. The toolbox offers a compiler for several input formalisms, one of which is LNT. In this work, we particularly rely on the Evaluator model checker, which takes as input an LNT specification and an MCL formula, and returns a Boolean verdict and a counterexample if the property is violated.

4.2 Properties

The main goal of the analysis steps is to ensure that the decision process is performed correctly when a problem is detected, resulting at the end by the right decision taken by the φ-comp solution for mitigating this problem. Keeping this idea in mind, let us now introduce the properties, which were identified as important for the approach, and are listed below:

- The solution systematically detects and handles every raised problem (probe).
- Every problem corresponding to a non compliance is followed by a mitigation action.
- A specific non-compliance problem of one entity should not affect the other entities connected to that entity.
- Entities subject to mitigation actions can keep communicating normally with the other connected entities.
- Mitigation actions are only performed when there is a non-compliance.
- The correct mitigation action is performed when there is a non-compliance.
- When a mitigation action is performed on an entity, the latter becomes compliant.

In the rest of this section, we present with more details the two first properties, which are the most important ones.

The first property (Fig. 7) is specified as a liveness property (inevitable property), and checks whether every probe raised by the environment is systematically detected. This is written in MCL as follows using the inevitable pattern and indicating (using "?any") that any parameter can come with the PROBEVENT action:

```
"MODEL-316.bcg" |= with evaluator4
      INEVITABLE ({ PROBEVENT ?any ... });
expected TRUE;
```

Fig. 7. MCL Property for Probe Detection

The second property (Fig. 8) states that every time an action is raised by a probe indicating a non-compliant behaviour for a specific software entity, there must be a reaction from φ-comp in the form of a mitigation action. This reaction is actually justified only if the risk is assessed as critical (red) by the analysis process.

The MCL property formalising this requirement relies on regular expressions. These expressions are required to match the parameters coming with the actions used in the LNT specification. As an example, PRELIMINARY_RISK is accompanied with several numbers (between 0 and 4) giving information about potential risks, and this is expressed using the regular expressions appearing in Fig. 8. Moreover, we use exclamation marks followed by a number to indicate repetition of a same parameter. The number is used like an identifier (exclamation marks with the same number indicate the same parameter).

More technically speaking now, the MCL property given in Fig. 8 for illustration purposes consists of two parts. The first part shows that a traceability problem is detected (MESSAGE2_TRACEABILITY) and the decision is taken of restarting the corresponding service (DECISION !RESTART_SERVICE). The second part of the property aims at checking whether the response to mitigate the risk is the correct one. To do so, we check that the parameters appearing in the ANALYSISEVENT action are the same as in the DECISION action. In particular, the Probe identifier is extracted from the observation message and we compare if it has the same value as the identifier issued with the mitigation action. If this is the case, it means that every non-compliant behaviour is mitigated by the correct action.

```
"MODEL-316.bcg" = total rename
  "ANALYSISEVENT !PRELIMINARY_RISK (\([0-4]\), \([0-4]\), \([0-4]\),
      \([0-4]\))
                 !MESSAGE2_TRACEABILITY (\([0-4]\), \([0-4]\), .*) .*"
                 -> "ANALYSISEVENT !\1 !\2 !\3 !\4 !\5 !\6",
  "DECISION !RESTART_SERVICE (\([A-Z]*\), .*)
            !MESSAGE2_TRACEABILITY (\([0-4]\), \([0-4]\), .*), .*"
            -> "DECISION !\1 !\2 !\3"
in generation of "INSTANCE4.lnt";

"MODEL-316.bcg" |= with evaluator4 [ true* . { ANALYSISEVENT !3 !3 !3
     !4 !1 !1 } ]
        < (not 'PROBEVENT !.*')* . { DECISION !TRUE !1 !1 } > true;
     expected TRUE;
```

Fig. 8. MCL Property for Systematic Mitigation Action

4.3 Results

In this section, we comment on the analysis of realistic scenarios using the CADP model checker. The properties were analysed on a set of realistic applications where we vary the number of virtual machines, software entities, and bindings. In order to simulate real scenarios, we added a new process (pbinjector, see Sect. 3) whose role is to inject problems of any kind to the application (confidentiality, integrity, availability, traceability). In its current version, the φ-comp approach can support several problems but not at the same time, it handles them one after the other. Therefore, in our verification scenarios, we respected this specific assumption as well.

As a result, all the properties were analysed and turn out to be satisfied on the aforementioned concrete applications (with 4–5 virtual machines, which is usually the number of machines handled by the φ-comp framework). Moreover, it is worth noting that this is not necessary to use large applications for verification purposes, because most problems are usually found on small yet pathological applications. It takes up to a few minutes to verify all properties on a realistic application, which is reasonable because the model checking of the φ-comp solution is executed off-line.

5 Related Work

In this section, we first present several works dedicated to the specification and verification of management applications in cloud computing or Fog computing/IoT. At the end of the section, we compare our work with respect to these related works.

In [4,5,18], the authors present a self-deployment protocol that was designed to automatically configure cloud applications consisting of a set of software elements to be deployed on different virtual machines. This protocol starts the software elements in a certain order, using a decentralised algorithm. It works in a decentralised way, i.e., there is no need for a centralised server. It also starts the software elements in a certain order, respecting important architectural invariants. This protocol supports virtual machine and network failures, and always succeeds in deploying an application when faced with a finite number of failures. A formal specification of the protocol allowed the successful verification of important properties to be preserved.

[11,12] propose verification of IoT applications before deployment using model checking techniques. [3] applies infinite-state model checking to formally verify IoT protocols such as the Pub/Sub consistency protocol adopted by the REDIS distributed file system. The verification method is based on a combination of SMT solvers and overapproximations as those implemented in the Cubicle verification tool. This work focuses on the verification of the communication techniques used in IoT systems. Since these protocols involve infinite data structures, the authors chose to use analysis techniques capable of reasoning on infinite state spaces.

[14] focuses on large applications relying on widely distributed and replicated storage of data for scalability, availability, and disaster tolerance. Maintaining high degrees of data consistency requires costly communication across distant sites, applications over such distributed and partially replicated data is complex. This paper proposes to use rewriting logic and its associated Maude tool environment to formally model and analyze both the correctness and the performance of state-of-the-art distributed transaction systems designs, as well as on how to automatically obtain a correct-by-construction distributed implementation of a promising design.

[10] proposes BiiMED, which is a Blockchain framework for Enhancing Data Interoperability and Integrity regarding EHR-sharing. This solution consists of an access management system allowing the exchange of EHRs between different medical providers and a decentralized Trusted Third Party Auditor for ensuring

data integrity. This work also introduces two validation techniques for enhancing the quality and correctness of the proposed solution: Formal verification checks the correctness of a mathematical model describing the behaviour of the system whereas model-based testing derives test suites from the model and executes them to validate its correctness.

[17] focus on a failure management protocol, which allows the supervision of IoT applications and the management of failures. This protocol targets stateful IoT applications in the sense that those applications handle and store data during their execution. When a failure occurs, the protocol detects the failure and restores a consistent pre-failure state of the application to make it functional again. Since designing such distributed protocol is error-prone, it was specified and analysed using formal specification techniques and model checking tools in order to ensure that the protocol respects some important properties. These analysis steps helped to detect several issues and clarify some subtle parts of the protocol.

In this paper, we decided to rely on model checking techniques, as it was the case in [5,17], because these techniques turn out to be effective in order to validate the correctness of important properties on representative applications. It is worth noting that this work was achieved in collaboration with a company (Euris), and that formal verification techniques were applied on a software solution used in an industrial context. Last but not least, to the best of our knowledge, this is the first time formal verification techniques are used for cloud platforms dealing with healthcare.

6 Concluding Remarks

In this paper, we have focused on a health management framework, which allows the storage, monitoring and supervision of health cloud applications. When a problem is detected, it is analysed and, if necessary, a decision is taken to apply a mitigation action. Since this solution targets health data and applications, it makes it critical and it is therefore crucial that specific properties of correctness are preserved by the solution. It was decided to rely on formal specification techniques and verification tools in order to ensure that the solution respects some important properties. In particular, we used a process algebraic specification language and model checking techniques for verifying these properties. The analysis of several applications and scenarios show that the aforementioned properties were satisfied, thus showing that the approach works as expected.

The main perspective of this work is to improve the current management protocol by making use of blockchains in order to store the health data in a secure way while providing traceability and transparency of the approach. Developing such a solution consists first in designing a new solution for the distributed storage of health data in the cloud by using blockchain technologies. Similarly to what we have done in this paper, we will also make use of model checking techniques for validating the solution. Beyond analysis and certification, we finally plan to implement the proposal using cloud and blockchain technologies.

Acknowledgements. The authors would like to thank Frédéric Lang for his help in the specification and verification of the φ-comp solution.

References

1. Atif, M., Groote, J.F.: Understanding behaviour of distributed systems using mCRL2, 1, vol. 458. Springer (2023). https://doi.org/10.1007/978-3-031-23008-0
2. Champelovier, D., et al.: Reference manual of the LNT to LOTOS translator (Version 6.7). INRIA/VASY and INRIA/CONVECS, pp. 153 (2018)
3. Delzanno, G.: Formal verification of internet of things protocols. In: Proceedings of FRIDA 2018 (2018)
4. Etchevers, X., Salaün, G., Boyer, F., Coupaye, T., Palma, N.D.: Reliable self-deployment of cloud applications. In: Proceedings of SAC 2014, pp. 1331–1338. ACM (2014)
5. Etchevers, X., Salaün, G., Boyer, F., Coupaye, T., Palma, N.D.: Reliable self-deployment of distributed cloud applications. Softw. Pract. Exper. **47**(1), 3–20 (2017)
6. Garavel, H., Lang, F., Mateescu, R., Serwe, W.: CADP 2011: a toolbox for the construction and analysis of distributed processes. STTT **15**(2), 89–107 (2013)
7. Garavel, H., Lang, F., Serwe, W.: From LOTOS to LNT. In: Katoen, J.-P., Langerak, R., Rensink, A. (eds.) ModelEd, TestEd, TrustEd – Essays Dedicated to Ed Brinksma on the Occasion of His 60th Birthday, vol. 10500, pp. 3–26 (2017)
8. Holzmann, G.J.: The SPIN Model Checker - Primer and Reference Manual. Addison-Wesley (2004)
9. ISO: LOTOS — A Formal Description Technique Based on the Temporal Ordering of Observational Behaviour. Technical Report 8807, ISO (1989)
10. Jabbar, R., Krichen, M., Fetais, N., Barkaoui, K.: Adopting formal verification and model-based testing techniques for validating a blockchain-based healthcare records sharing system. In: Proceedings of ICEIS 2020, pp. 261–268. SCITEPRESS (2020)
11. Krishna, A., Pallec, M.L., Mateescu, R., Noirie, L., Salaün, G.: IoT composer: composition and deployment of IoT applications. In: Proceedings of ICSE 2019, pp. 19–22. IEEE / ACM (2019)
12. Krishna, A., Pallec, M.L., Mateescu, R., Noirie, L., Salaün, G.: Rigorous design and deployment of IoT applications. In: Proceedings of FormaliSE 2019, pp. 21–30 (2019)
13. Mateescu, R., Thivolle, D.: A model checking language for concurrent value-passing systems. In: Cuellar, J., Maibaum, T., Sere, K. (eds.) FM 2008. LNCS, vol. 5014, pp. 148–164. Springer, Heidelberg (2008). https://doi.org/10.1007/978-3-540-68237-0_12
14. Ölveczky, P.C.: Design and validation of cloud storage systems using rewriting logic. In: Proceedings of SYNASC 2019, pp. 17–21. IEEE (2019)
15. Ozeer, U.: φ comp: An architecture for monitoring and enforcing security compliance in sensitive health data environment. In: Proceedings of ICSA 2021, pp. 70–77. IEEE (2021)
16. Ozeer, U., Pouye, B.: Risk analysis based security compliance assessment and management for sensitive health data environment. In: Proceedings of HealthCom 2020, pp. 1–7. IEEE (2020)

17. Ozeer, U., Salaün, G., Letondeur, L., Ottogalli, F.-G., Vincent, J.-M.: Verification of a failure management protocol for stateful IoT applications. In: ter Beek, M.H., Ničković, D. (eds.) FMICS 2020. LNCS, vol. 12327, pp. 272–287. Springer, Cham (2020). https://doi.org/10.1007/978-3-030-58298-2_12
18. Salaün, G., Etchevers, X., De Palma, N., Boyer, F., Coupaye, T.: Verification of a self-configuration protocol for distributed applications in the cloud. In: Cámara, J., de Lemos, R., Ghezzi, C., Lopes, A. (eds.) Assurances for Self-Adaptive Systems. LNCS, vol. 7740, pp. 60–79. Springer, Heidelberg (2013). https://doi.org/10.1007/978-3-642-36249-1_3

Natural Language Processing

Evaluating Large Language Models and Prompt Variants on the Task of Detecting Cease and Desist Violations in German Online Product Descriptions

Marian Lambert[1(✉)], Nico Döring[1], Thomas Schuster[2], and Norbert Schmitz[2]

[1] XPACE GmbH, Blücherstr. 32, 75177 Pforzheim, Germany
marian.lambert@xpace.de
[2] Pforzheim University, Tiefenbronner Street 65, 75175 Pforzheim, Germany

Abstract. This paper compares different large language models (LLMs) on the task of detecting violations of cease and desist declarations in German online product descriptions as part of the KIVEDU project. We evaluate two proprietary LLMs by OpenAI (`gpt-3.5-turbo-0301` and `gpt-3.5-turbo-0613`) and three open source LLMs by various organizations (`LLaMA2`, `StableBeluga2`, and `Platypus2`) using different variations in text input (prompt) on a dataset of 116 manually labeled pairs of cease and desist declarations and product descriptions. The evaluation aims to explore two research questions: 1) Which LLM is most adept at identifying violations? and 2) How do prompt variations impact model performance? The results show that `StableBeluga2` performed best, achieving the highest accuracy and micro F1 score. It was also the most reliable model with minimal deviations in performance across prompt variants. The `Platypus2` and `gpt-3.5-turbo-0301` models also achieved good results though they displayed greater variability in their performance. The worst-performing model was `LLaMA2`. The results further show that prompting had a significant impact on model performance, with the presence of a step-by-step instruction generally decreasing performance and a "yes"/"no" output format leading to higher performance. However, this was highly dependent on the specific model. Role prompting and providing a longer vs. shorter instruction had a minimal impact on performance across models. Overall, the study demonstrates the potential of LLMs in automating the detection of cease and desist violations in online product descriptions. Further research is needed to evaluate other LLM models and prompt variations, as well as to explore approaches like LLM fine-tuning on domain-specific data to further improve performance.

Keywords: NLP · Large Language Model · Consumer Protection · Consumer Rights Enforcement · Prompt Engineering · LegalTech

G. Broccia and A. Cerone (Eds.): DataMod 2023, LNCS 14618, pp. 145–163, 2025.
https://doi.org/10.1007/978-3-031-87217-4_8

1 Introduction

The rapid digitization of commerce has led to an increase in the number of products and services available online. As consumers increasingly shift to e-commerce platforms for their purchasing needs, the volume of online offerings also continues to rise. However, rising alongside the digital growth is the incidence of consumer-rights infringing behaviors, notably in the form of misleading or false product descriptions and deceptive advertising claims.

A study conducted in 2014 emphasized this concern [8]: approximately 37% of the European Union's e-commerce activities were found non-compliant with the Union consumer law. This deviation from legal standards has wrought an estimated annual financial detriment of €770 million upon consumers. While this poses evident financial ramifications, it further exacerbates the competitive market dynamics, putting compliant businesses at an unfair disadvantage.

To counteract these activities in Germany, consumer protection agencies (and other entitled organizations) can request infringing companies to sign a *cease and desist declaration*. This legal document binds the signing company to abstain from involving in similar unfair practices in the future. Nonetheless, ensuring compliance with these declarations, i.e. verifying that the company does not participate in similar infringing behavior, remains a significant challenge. Consumer protection agencies, grappling with constraints in resources, find it burdensome to conduct routine checks for adherence. The manual nature of these verification processes renders them not only time-intensive but also financially costly.

This difficulty in monitoring compliance often provides companies with an opportunity to persist in their unfair practices, infringing upon consumer rights without significant checks. Such unchecked behavior not only endangers consumers but also undermines fair competition in the market, creating an unfavorable environment for competitors who operate ethically.

Recent strides in the realm of natural language processing (NLP), particularly the advent of large language models (LLMs), offer a promising avenue to address this challenge. The capabilities exhibited by these models pave the way for automating the otherwise manual processes, thus offering support in consumer rights enforcement. In a recent publication, we introduced the KIVEDU project which aspires to revolutionize the enforcement of consumer rights in Germany through the use of LLMs and other AI technologies [24].[1] In its current, initial phase, the project focuses on automating the identification of cease and desist violations in German product descriptions.

This technical research paper delves into our preliminary assessment of implementing various LLMs, encompassing both proprietary and open source models, in conjunction with multiple text input (prompt) variations on a manually curated test dataset. At its core, our exploration is guided by two central research questions:

RQ1: Which of the tested LLMs emerges as the most adept for the specific task of identifying cease and desist violations in German product descriptions?

[1] Project website can be found online at https://www.kivedu-projekt.de.

RQ2: How do variations in the provided prompt influence the overall performance of the LLMs on this task?

The remaining document is structured as follows: In Sect. 2, we present a short review of related works. This will be followed by a section introducing the theoretical underpinnings, primarily introducing LLMs and their application potential for the challenge at hand. Section 4 outlines our methodology using a zero-shot prompting approach. Further, the experimental framework is presented in Sect. 5, including details of the tested models, dataset and prompt variations. We then present and discuss our results in Sect. 6. Lastly, Sect. 7 gives a conclusive summary and projections for future avenues of research.

2 Related Works

In this section, we present related publications and projects that use AI and Machine Learning (ML) in the area of consumer protection. We conclude this section with a short paragraph on how our problem description differs from the ones presented here.

For years, researchers have studied ML applications in consumer protection law, initially focusing on Terms of Service (ToS) and privacy contracts. A pivotal study by Lippi et al. used ML techniques like support vector machines (SVM) and tree kernels to identify unfair clauses in online contracts, setting a new standard in performance beyond random guessing [12].

Braun and his team (2019) described the potential of legal tech in strengthening consumer rights, showcasing two models that interpret, assess, and summarize the terms of service of German online retailers [3]. They also delved into automated recognition of unlawful sections within German terms and conditions (TaC) [2]. Utilizing a pre-trained German BERT language model [7], they were able to pinpoint illegal content with high accuracy. Based on these results, the CLAUDETTE tool was created. This tool not only enlarges the base dataset to cover 50 ToS, but also employs various ML techniques, including Deep Learning, for a detailed categorization into specific classes of unfairness [13]. This tool has also been used to identify confusing or unfair privacy terms related to the European General Data Protection Regulation [6].

Besides identifying biased or illicit terms in online default agreements, ML has also been utilized by Trappey et al. to analyze and pinpoint judgment documents from US trademark dispute precedent cases [22]. Furthermore, in the realm of patent law, ML has been employed to forecast legal conflicts [10, 14].

Moreover, in 2018, Chakrabarti and colleagues designed an ML-driven system to detect and extract high-risk sections within contracts and then categorize them into different risk levels [4]. They utilized paragraph vectors for training and applied classification methods encompassing multiple versions of SVM and Naive Bayes models, attaining high accuracy rates.

Generally, it can be observed that there is limited research on applications of LLMs towards tasks in the legal domain. To the best of our knowledge, no published work exists for a use case similar to that presented in this paper. Therefore, our project distinguishes itself from the publications presented above in various ways. Firstly, we don't address typical contracts like ToS or privacy policies. Our focus is on cease and desist declarations, which are civil law agreements between businesses and consumer protection agencies or other qualified organizations. These declarations often have unique and highly specific characteristics, presenting obstacles for machine learning training and analysis. Moreover, determining a legal violation is not just dependent on the wording of the cease and desist declaration, but also on the related online product description that may contain the infringement. As a result, we can't label whole sections as unjust, in contrast to the methods used in the cited publications. A comprehensive individual review of the cease and desist declaration, considering both its specific wording and the surrounding context, is essential. For these reasons, and contrary to the cited literature, we are utilising current state-of-the-art LLMs for our specific use case.

3 Theoretical Background

In this section, we introduce the most important theoretical concepts of our research. We begin by explaining the purpose of cease and desist declarations in Germany and the mechanisms for their verification. Subsequently, we explore the challenges of automating the detection of violations in these declarations and discuss the limitations of conventional ML models for this task. We then introduce LLMs, explain how they are trained and emphasize their suitability for addressing this challenge. Finally, we show how LLMs can be applied to our specific problem.

3.1 Cease and Desist Declarations in Germany

Consumer protection organizations (as well as business associations, competitors and the chamber of industry and commerce) in Germany can issue a cease and desist declaration to offending companies when they violate consumer rights by advertising with inaccurate or misleading online product descriptions. This statement, which identifies the precise infringement (for instance, claiming that a food supplement can treat cancer), acts as a legally binding commitment of the company to refrain from similar conduct in the future. If it signs the declaration, the corporation may be subject to fines for repeated infractions. To make sure a company is adhering, consumer protection organizations must continuously check public product descriptions to make sure they don't violate any agreements the company has signed. AI can be used to speed up this time-consuming task, which frequently entails reading through thousands of product descriptions and hundreds of cease and desist declarations. Monitoring can be automated by an AI model that assesses if a violation is present.

Yet, automatically detecting violations is a nuanced task demanding intricate language understanding and good reasoning capabilities. Slight variations in the phrasing or semantic meaning of the declaration or the product description can be pivotal in determining a potential violation. For instance, a firm might be prohibited from promoting a banking account as "the *first* CO2 neutral account", but a statement like "open *your first* CO2 neutral account" might be compliant. Thus, the ability to distinguish subtle differences in linguistic constructions and semantics is highly important.

3.2 Challenges

Traditional machine learning techniques, which were successful in many of the examples we discussed above, face difficulties with this task. They have trouble understanding language and place an excessive reliance on large amounts of training data.

Data Dependency. The vast majority of machine learning approaches are heavily reliant on extensive datasets to train effectively. In the context of cease and desist declaration violations, obtaining a vast number of relevant and varied examples is inherently challenging given the specificity and infrequency of such cases, particularly in our situation where we focused on a specific area (online product descriptions) and language (German).

Nuanced Language Understanding. Existing models may struggle with comprehending the nuanced differences in terms and phrases, leading to potential oversight in intricate cases. This is due to the fact that they do not have a deeper understanding of the (German) language and thus will fail to identify words or phrases which are semantically similar but did not occur in the training data.

3.3 Large Language Models

Given these limitations of traditional ML approaches, large language models present a promising innovation in the realm of Deep Learning. Large language models refers to a family of neural network models (often based on the *transformer* architecture [23]) which are designed for processing and generating human language. LLMs are pre-trained on massive text data from the internet [26]. Given a text input (prompt), these models generate text as output based on which words are most probable and helpful (text generation). LLMs are characterized by a large number of model parameters, reaching hundreds of billions. Due to their size, LLMs exhibit exceptional understanding of human language and can reliably solve a variety of downstream tasks without any specific training data, such as question answering, translating between multiple languages, classifying sentiments in a text, and summarizing long passages [26].

Large language models are typically trained following a two-tiered process (see [26]). In the initial stage, known as *pre-training*, the model processes expansive text datasets (often sourced from the internet) with the task of learning to predict subsequent words in sentences. Through this, it familiarizes itself with grammatical structures, real-world facts, and even reasoning skills. The all-rounded model resulting from this stage is often referred to as a *base LLM*. This type of model can reliably predict the next word in a sentence and be used on a variety of tasks. However, for more complex tasks, their usability is limited as they tend to not follow instructions provided in the prompt.

To solve this limitation, the base model can further be refined in a process called *fine-tuning*, where it's trained to follow provided instructions. This often includes an approach called reinforcement learning through human feedback (RLHF) [27]. Essentially, a reward model is trained on human-provided data to determine the usefulness of input-output pairs of the base model. The base model is then fine-tuned through reinforcement learning utilizing the reward model. The result of this process is an *instruction-tuned* LLM, which can reliably follow provided instructions and provide helpful outputs.

3.4 Detecting Cease and Desist Violations with LLMs

The capabilities of LLMs are exceptional. In particular, their ability to solve multiple tasks without requiring unique model architectures and training data for each sets them apart. The concept of transfer learning, where knowledge from one domain can be repurposed for another, negates the necessity for vast labeled datasets across all applications. Given these benefits, this paper presents an evaluation of applying different LLMs on the task of identifying cease and desist violations in German product descriptions. For this use case, LLMs can be applied in two ways.

Prompting. This approach hinges on text generation. The fine-tuned LLM is provided with a text input (prompt) encompassing an instruction of what to do, i.e. decide whether a violation is present or not, and the cease and desist declaration as well as product description. It then generates an output, indicating whether a violation is present or not. In the standard case of *zero-shot prompting*, the model is not provided with any specific examples of how a correct input-output pair should look like; it generates its output only from the provided instruction. In the case of *one-* or *few-shot prompting*, the model is additionally provided with one or multiple correct input-output pairs in the prompt, thus giving the model the opportunity to learn from examples.

Classification Head Fine-Tuning. In this approach, a classification head is trained on the intermediate outputs of the fine-tuned LLM. This essentially constructs a specialized classification model that is fine-tuned for the specific task at hand. At the same time, it retains the extensive language understanding capabilities inherent in the LLM. While this strategy aims to yield more consistent outputs, it comes with a limitation: it requires a large set of labeled data for training. Such extensive labeled data is often scarce in specialized fields like ours, making this approach less feasible for our particular context. Therefore, our paper chooses to focus on the first strategy, namely the prompting approach, and more specifically on zero-shot prompting.

4 Methodology

Following the zero-shot prompting approach, we developed a process of deciding whether a product description violates a cease and desist declaration which consists of *prompt construction*, *inference* and *output parsing*.

Prompt Construction. In this step, we construct the text input which will be passed to the model. This input encompasses a *main prompt* consisting of multiple variable components (role, instruction, step-by-step instruction and output format) and the *target* which contains the relevant passage of the cease and desist declaration and the product description (see Fig. 1 for the generic prompt structure and an example prompt). The components of the main prompt are based on general prompt engineering guidelines and have been shown to improve LLM performance. In particular, the *role* component assigns a role to the LLM with the aim of inducing behavior that is more suited for solving the task at hand [19]. The *instruction* component provides the general instruction for the task. The *step-by-step instruction* provides a detailed iterative instruction for solving the task (chain of thought prompting). This has been shown to help LLMs solve more complex tasks [25]. Lastly, the *output format* component provides guidance on how the output of the LLM should look like (e.g. JSON or "yes"/"no"). The specific values we used for each component will be introduced in the next section.

Inference. We pass the prompt constructed in the previous step to the LLM and capture the generated output. Depending on the expected output (provided in the output format component), we might limit the number of tokens generated by the LLM to save on inference time and cost.

Output Parsing. We parse the generated output to receive a binary decision on whether a violation is present or not. This step also depends on the expected output format.

5 Experimental Setup

We evaluated five LLMs using different prompt variations on a manually curated test dataset to provide answers to the question of which LLM is best suited for identifying cease and desist violations in product descriptions (**RQ1**) and how different prompt variants impact model performance (**RQ2**). Our experimental setup consists of *five parts*: the dataset, tested LLMs, prompt variants, evaluation metrics, and evaluation process. We will now introduce each component in detail and explain our evaluation process.

5.1 Dataset

Our dataset consists of 116 manually labeled pairs of cease and desist declarations (81 unique) and product descriptions (106 unique) in German language. In 84 cases, the product description contains a violation of the corresponding

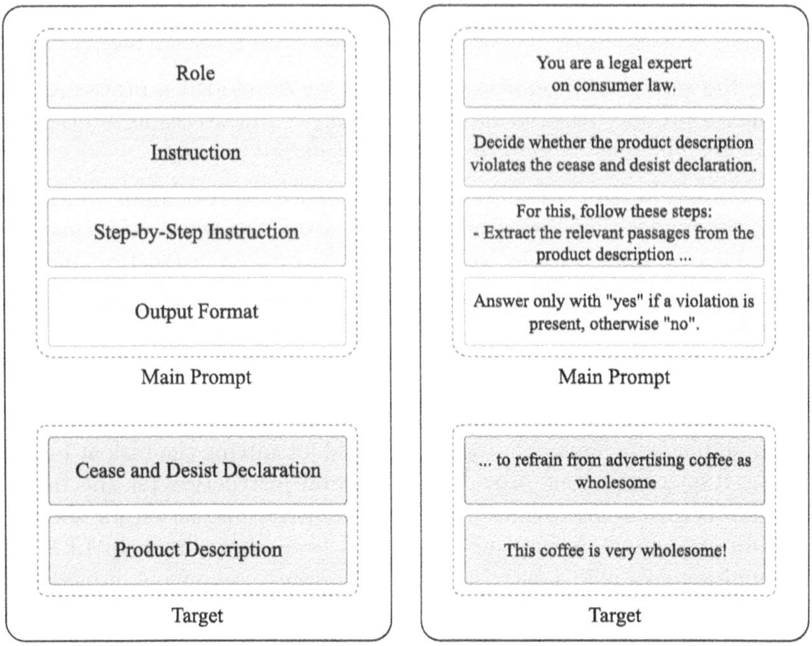

Fig. 1. Prompt Structure (left) and Example Prompt (right)

declaration. The remaining 32 cases contain no violation. The dataset spans a wide range of product types, including supplements, medication, books, food, financial services, beverages and more. All pairs are based on real-world examples, but some were modified to specifically include or not include a violation. The dataset was created and labeled by studied experts in the field of consumer law and e-commerce. Unfortunately, due to data privacy limitations, we cannot publish the dataset.

5.2 Tested LLMs

In our experiments, we evaluated two proprietary and three open source LLMs (see Table 1). They are all instruction-tuned LLMs and were released or last updated within the last six months at the time of writing. Both `gpt-3.5-turbo` models are different versions of the same underlying model (from March 1st 2023 and June 13th 2023 respectively). `StableBeluga2` and `Platypus2` are both either directly or indirectly based on `LLaMA2`. They are ranking in the top ten on the Huggingface Open LLM Leaderboard at the time of writing [1]. We chose these LLMs as they are known to perform very well, have a large enough context size of around 4000 tokens, were also trained on German text and were fairly easy and cheap to use. Other suitable, proprietary LLMs like `Claude2`, `PaLM2` or `GPT-4` were either not available to us or too expensive to evaluate systematically.

Table 1. Overview of the tested LLMs

Model	Organization	Context Size	# Parameters	License
`gpt-3.5-turbo-0301` [18]	OpenAI	4096	175B	Proprietary
`gpt-3.5-turbo-0613` [18]	OpenAI	4096	175B	Proprietary
`LLaMA2` [21]	Meta	4096	70B	Open Source
`StableBeluga2` [15,17,21]	StabilityAi	4096	70B	Open Source
`Platypus2` [9,11,21]	garage-bAInd	4096	70B	Open Source

5.3 Tested Prompt Variants

As explained in the last section, the main prompt we used consisted of different variable components (see Fig. 1). To evaluate the impact of different prompt variations, we came up with different values for each component and evaluated all LLMs with each combination of components on the entire dataset (72 prompts in total). The values we used for each component are presented in Table 2, translated to English. For our experiments, we used the original German variants. The structure of the *target* part of the prompt remained constant except for the actual values of the cease and desist declaration and product description which were added based on the current case from the test dataset.

5.4 Evaluation Metrics

By comparing the parsed outputs from the model with the true labels from our dataset, we can calculate different classification metrics. On top of the traditional metrics like accuracy, F1 scores (both macro, i.e. unweighted mean of the F1 scores for each class, and micro, i.e. taking total true positives, false negatives and false positives across classes into account), precision and recall, we also calculate the *total accuracy* which counts cases where the parsing failed as incorrectly classified examples. Total accuracy is the most important metric to evaluate for us as many LLMs generated invalid outputs which can lead to misleading accuracy and F1 scores. In particular, we give special attention to accuracy and micro F1 scores. This is due to the fact that our dataset is imbalanced, and these metrics combined provide a more comprehensive perspective, ensuring that the model performs well across all classes, not just the majority ones.

5.5 Evaluation Process

We implemented all LLMs using the Python library `langchain` which provides us with a common interface to use for our evaluation process. For parameters, we adhered to each model's default settings as per its documentation. However, we minimized the temperature and limited token generation to 16 for faster inference. We designed prompt variants by computing the cartesian product of each prompt component. Each prompt variant was then systematically run through the dataset for each model. Certain models necessitated slight prompt modifications to align with their specific prompting formats.

Table 2. Prompt Components

ID	Content (translated to English from German)
	Role
none	-
expert	You are an expert for consumer protection and competition law
	Instruction
default	Your task is to find out whether the product description in the triple quotes violates the cease and desist letter in the triple quotes.
short	Check whether the product description contains a violation of the cease and desist letter.
verbose	Your task is to find out whether the product description in the triple quotes violates the cease-and-desist declaration in the triple quotes. A violation occurs if the product description contains formulations or statements that were prohibited in the cease-and-desist declaration. You must decide for yourself whether the exact wording must be present, or whether wording in the spirit is already sufficient.
default_verbose	You will receive a cease-and-desist letter that describes what action is to be refrained from and a description with which a product is advertised online. Check whether the product description contains a violation of the cease-and-desist declaration.
	Step-by-Step
none	-
default	To solve the task, perform the following steps: Step 1: Read the cease and desist letter carefully. The cease-and-desist declaration describes what behavior is to be refrained from. Step 2: Read the product description carefully and look for phrases that could constitute a violation of the cease-and-desist letter. Step 3: Extract the maximum of three most important passages from the product description and the cease-and-desist declaration. If there are no relevant passages, leave the corresponding fields blank. Step 4: Compare the extracted passages from the product description with the extracted passages from the cease and desist letter. Step 5: Write a reason why the product description does or does not violate the cease and desist letter. Step 6: Decide whether or not the product description violates the cease and desist letter.
exact_loose_match_hint	*Similar to default, but contains a hint for handling edge cases*
	Output Format
binary_numeric	Answer "1" if there is a violation of the cease and desist letter in the product description. Otherwise, answer with "0". Do not write any other text, answer only with "1" or "0".
binary_yes_no	Answer "Yes" if there is a violation of the cease and desist letter in the product description. Otherwise, answer "No." Do not write any other text, answer only with "Yes" or "No".
binary_semantic	Answer "Violation" if there is a violation of the cease and desist letter in the product description. Otherwise, respond with "No violation." Do not write any other text, answer only with "Infringement" or "No Infringement".

We send every generated output to a parser that trims any leading or trailing whitespace and attempts to match it to either "1" or "0", "yes" or "no", and "violation" or "no violation". If a match is identified, the model's prediction is recorded as a binary value. If no match is found, the example is labeled incorrect, affecting only the total accuracy of the classification metrics.

The experiments were run over the course of five days on an `NVIDIA DGX A100` instance utilizing six `NVIDIA A100` GPUs with 80 GB of VRAM each. The results were saved to an MLflow tracking server and evaluated using the `pandas` and `matplotlib` Python libraries.

6 Results and Discussion

We present a statistical evaluation of model performance as measured by total accuracy, accuracy and micro F1 across all prompt variants in Table 3. The data shows that `StableBeluga2` was the best performing model with a total accuracy of 84.5% on the best prompt variant, meaning it generated a valid and correct prediction for 84.5% of test cases. It is closely followed by `Platypus2` (81.9%) and `gpt-3.5-turbo-0301` (80.17%). The newer `gpt-3.5-turbo-0613` performed significantly worse and `LLaMA2` achieved the lowest performance. Looking at the mean total accuracy over all variants, `StableBeluga2` again seemed to provide the most reliable performance while the other models showed a fairly low average performance. This can also be seen by looking at the *Min* and *Std* (standard deviation) columns. Except for `StableBeluga2`, all models had some variants with a total accuracy of or close to 0% and also fairly high standard deviation. This can be attributed to a large portion of prompt variants for which the models did not generate any or few valid parseable outputs. Interestingly, while `LlaMA2` generally performed worst, its performance appears to be more stable across prompt variants than the other models (excluding `StableBeluga2` which performed exceptionally well on all prompt variants).

Even when only considering the valid outputs of each model using the accuracy metric, we can see that `StableBeluga2` was the most reliable with an average 80% of valid outputs being correct though `gpt-3.5-turbo-0301` was not far behind. Also, `gpt-3.5-turbo-0301` seemed to perform much more reliably with a significantly reduced standard deviation. `LLaMA2`, on the other hand, appeared to have a much higher variance across variants. This does not change significantly when looking at the micro F1 scores which means that all models performed similarly on both classes. For clarity, we omit the *Max* and *Min* values for accuracy and micro F1. Displaying them could be misleading, as certain prompt variants may result in a limited number of valid outputs. If these outputs happen to be correct, it could artificially inflate performance metrics.

To conclude, our evaluation shows that `StableBeluga2` was by far the best performing and most reliable model across all prompt variants, classes and metrics. In second place, we see `gpt-3.5-turbo-0301`, closely followed by `Platypus2`. The newer `gpt-3.5-turbo-0613` exhibited significantly lower performance and higher variance across prompt variants compared to its predecessor. This observation is not surprising as changes in model performance over time have also been reported by other researchers for this model though performance of `gpt-3.5-turbo` generally improved over time in their experiments [5]. `LLaMA2` performed worst overall.

Table 3. Performance of tested LLMs across all variants

	Total Accuracy				Accuracy		Micro F1	
Model	Mean	Max	Min	Std	Mean	Std	Mean	Std
gpt-3.5-turbo-0301	50.34%	80.17%	3.45%	18.77%	72.50%	7.76%	67.22%	10.13%
gpt-3.5-turbo-0613	33.37%	75.86%	0.00%	31.29%	59.76%	33.96%	56.52%	32.56%
llama2	9.90%	61.21%	0.00%	14.13%	42.66%	44.97%	40.11%	43.17%
platypus2	49.55%	81.90%	0.00%	35.33%	49.55%	35.33%	50.42%	35.95%
stablebeluga2	**79.55%**	**84.48%**	**70.69%**	**3.33%**	**80.00%**	**3.52%**	**80.26%**	**2.85%**

Regarding the performance of individual prompt components, we present a statistical evaluation of total accuracy, accuracy and micro F1 for each component value across all models in Table 4. For the *role* component, using the values with id `expert` or `none` did not lead to a significant difference in performance. This is in-line with recent, anecdotal observations that role prompting is less effective or not effective at all for newer models. However, it might also be attributed to the fact that role prompting often impacts the style of the generated text which is not of importance in cases where binary outputs are generated.

Table 4. Performance for each prompt component across all models

	Total Accuracy		Accuracy		Micro F1	
ID	Mean	Std	Mean	Std	Mean	Std
			Role			
expert	44.27%	32.47%	60.43%	32.86%	58.22%	32.24%
none	44.81%	33.19%	61.36%	33.03%	59.59%	32.56%
			Instruction			
default	42.86%	33.30%	61.11%	32.95%	58.97%	32.54%
def_verb	44.62%	33.30%	61.82%	33.19%	59.31%	32.76%
short	47.01%	32.09%	61.47%	32.79%	59.74%	32.38%
verbose	43.67%	32.86%	59.17%	33.15%	57.60%	32.28%
			Step-by-Step			
default	36.14%	33.51%	56.49%	36.64%	55.31%	36.26%
elmh	41.40%	32.81%	58.19%	34.88%	56.42%	34.15%
none	56.08%	28.78%	67.99%	25.06%	64.99%	24.95%
			Output Format			
binary_numeric	35.27%	35.85%	46.53%	38.51%	45.98%	38.06%
binary_semantic	43.89%	34.25%	58.24%	34.70%	56.10%	34.25%
binary_yes_no	54.46%	24.47%	77.92%	8.39%	74.64%	10.63%

For the *instruction* component, the value with id `short` appeared to perform slightly better than other values. This is a surprising observation as it is typically recommended to provide the model with detailed and comprehensive instructions to achieve better performance. That being said, when only considering the successfully parsed examples, all values of the *instruction* component appeared to perform similarly. In other words, the `short` instruction seems to lead to a slightly higher rate of correctly formatted outputs but does not improve performance itself.

For the *step-by-step* component, we see that best performance (both total accuracy as well as raw performance) is achieved using no value at all. This stands in contrast to reports that framing instructions in an itemized manner or allowing for a chain-of-thought improves performance [16,25]. However, the results presented here might be explained by the fact that these strategies are only effective when the model is allowed to output its thoughts which was not the case here. In all other cases, the model might be misled or distracted when providing these instructions.

Lastly, for the *output format* component, best performance was achieved using a "yes" / "no" format. Interestingly, this not only improved the models' ability to generate valid outputs but also their ability to correctly identify violations. Even more, variance in accuracy and micro F1 also appears to be significantly reduced across models when using the "yes" / "no" format.

To summarize, across all models, only the selection of the *step-by-step* and *output format* components appeared to make a significant difference for model performance. In particular, leaving out the step-by-step instruction and requesting a simple "yes" / "no" format had the highest positive impact on performance. This finding is consistent with the fact that irrelevant text input can potentially distract LLMs from the core information and consequently decrease performance [20].

Regarding individual combinations of components (i.e. individual prompts) across models, we display the top-3 prompts (ranked by total accuracy, accuracy and micro F1) in Table 5. We can see that best performance (both total accuracy, accuracy and micro F1) was achieved using a combination of `none` for the *role* component and `binary_yes_no` for *output format*. While the result for the output format is not surprising, the clear result for the role component is slightly unexpected as there was no clear difference looking at the components individually. However, even a small performance boost for one value (which can indeed be seen in Table 4 when comparing `expert` vs `none`) can lead to it dominating the best instances due to tail dependence.

Interestingly, leaving out the *step-by-step* component was only optimal in terms of total accuracy. This suggests that not providing a step-by-step instruction generally helped the model generate more valid outputs, but adding it *can* significantly improve raw model performance. That being said, standard deviation was exceptionally high for values other than `none` (see Table 4).

With respect to the *instruction* component, no clear effect can be seen as all component values are present in the top-3 runs (see Table 5).

Table 5. Performance for individual Prompts across all models

Component IDs				Total Accuracy		Accuracy		Micro F1	
Role	Instr.	St.-St.	Output Form.	Mean	Std	Mean	Std	Mean	Std
Top-3 by Total Accuracy									
none	default	none	binary_y_n	69.66%	7.01%	73.52%	2.44%	69.35%	6.99%
none	verbose	none	binary_y_n	68.97%	8.18%	74.48%	1.54%	70.81%	6.71%
none	short	none	binary_y_n	68.28%	22.50%	77.94%	3.31%	73.91%	8.64%
Top-3 by Accuracy									
none	short	default	binary_y_n	50.52%	29.53%	83.10%	11.40%	82.17%	10.53%
none	def_verb	default	binary_y_n	44.31%	31.30%	82.89%	8.61%	80.30%	10.67%
none	short	elmh	binary_y_n	52.41%	25.64%	80.78%	12.04%	78.28%	13.89%
Top-3 by Micro F1									
none	short	default	binary_y_n	50.52%	29.53%	83.10%	11.40%	82.17%	10.53%
none	def_verb	default	binary_y_n	44.31%	31.30%	82.89%	8.61%	80.30%	10.67%
none	short	elmh	binary_y_n	52.41%	25.64%	80.78%	12.04%	78.28%	13.89%

For performance of individual prompts per model, we display the top-3 prompts by total accuracy, accuracy and micro F1 per model (excluding the worst performing models `LLaMA2` and `gpt-3.5-turbo-0613`) in Table 6. These results are generally consistent with our previous findings. One thing to note is that only the `Platypus2` model seemed to perform best using a "yes"/"no" output format. All other models performed better using a numeric or semantic format. Manual inspection showed that this is due to the fact that `Platypus2` mostly outputs decimal numbers instead of integers resulting in invalid outputs for a numeric output format.

Also, only `Platypus2` consistently performed best without a step-by-step instruction. The other models benefited from a more detailed guidance when looking at accuracy and micro F1 (both `StableBeluga2` and `gpt-3.5-turbo-0301`) or even total accuracy (only `StableBeluga2`).

An important observation from Table 6 is that while `gpt-3.5-turbo-0301` achieved exceptionally high accuracy and micro F1 scores (100%) with some prompt variants, its low total accuracy ($< 10\%$) suggests that the model produced a small number of valid outputs in these cases. Of the valid outputs, all were correct. It's crucial to understand that these metrics, in isolation, do not capture the model's overall performance.

Finally, for the best model (`StableBeluga2`), we present the performance (total accuracy) of each prompt variant in a grid of heatmaps in Fig. 2.[2] The figure clearly shows that performance was lowest for the "yes"/"no" output format (middle column) and best for the numeric format (left column). Also, there does not seem to be a significant difference between the `none` (top row) and

[2] Heatmap visualizations are available for all models in our project GitHub repository: https://github.com/ecapx/kivedu-public.

Table 6. Performance for individual Prompts per Model

Model	Role	Instr.	St.-St.	Output Form.	Total Acc.	Accuracy	Micro F1
Top-3 by Total Accuracy per Model							
gpt-3.5-turbo-0301	none	short	none	binary_num	80.17%	80.17%	79.86%
	none	short	none	binary_y_n	80.17%	80.17%	78.72%
	expert	def_verb	elmh	binary_num	74.14%	74.78%	68.87%
platypus2	none	short	none	binary_y_n	81.90%	81.90%	82.67%
	none	def_verb	none	binary_y_n	78.45%	78.45%	78.90%
	none	default	none	binary_sem	77.59%	77.59%	78.74%
stablebeluga2	none	def_verb	default	binary_sem	84.48%	85.22%	84.57%
	none	verbose	elmh	binary_num	83.62%	84.35%	83.28%
	none	def_verb	elmh	binary_num	83.62%	84.35%	82.67%
Top-3 by Accuracy per Model							
gpt-3.5-turbo-0301	none	default	default	binary_num	6.03%	100.00%	100.00%
	none	default	default	binary_sem	3.45%	100.00%	100.00%
	none	def_verb	default	binary_num	15.52%	94.74%	93.93%
platypus2	none	short	none	binary_y_n	81.90%	81.90%	82.67%
	none	def_verb	none	binary_y_n	78.45%	78.45%	78.90%
	none	default	none	binary_sem	77.59%	77.59%	78.74%
stablebeluga2	none	def_verb	default	binary_sem	84.48%	85.22%	84.57%
	none	verbose	elmh	binary_num	83.62%	84.35%	83.28%
	none	def_verb	elmh	binary_num	83.62%	84.35%	82.67%
Top-3 by Micro F1 per Model							
gpt-3.5-turbo-0301	none	default	default	binary_num	6.03%	100.00%	100.00%
	none	default	default	binary_sem	3.45%	100.00%	100.00%
	none	def_verb	default	binary_num	15.52%	94.74%	93.93%
platypus2	none	short	none	binary_y_n	81.90%	81.90%	82.67%
	none	def_verb	none	binary_y_n	78.45%	78.45%	78.90%
	none	default	none	binary_sem	77.59%	77.59%	78.74%
stablebeluga2	none	def_verb	default	binary_sem	84.48%	85.22%	84.57%
	expert	def_verb	default	binary_sem	83.62%	84.35%	84.35%
	none	default	elmh	binary_sem	82.76%	83.48%	83.71%

`expert` (bottom row) values for the *role* component which is consistent with our previous findings. While generally, there was not a big performance difference between the *step-by-step* component values, removing that component led to a significant performance drop when using the `binary_semantic` output format (heatmaps in right column). We are not sure why this is the case, it might be that a numeric or "yes"/"no" output is less ambiguous and less context-dependent than a semantic output format, enabling the model to perform well even when no explicit guidance is provided.

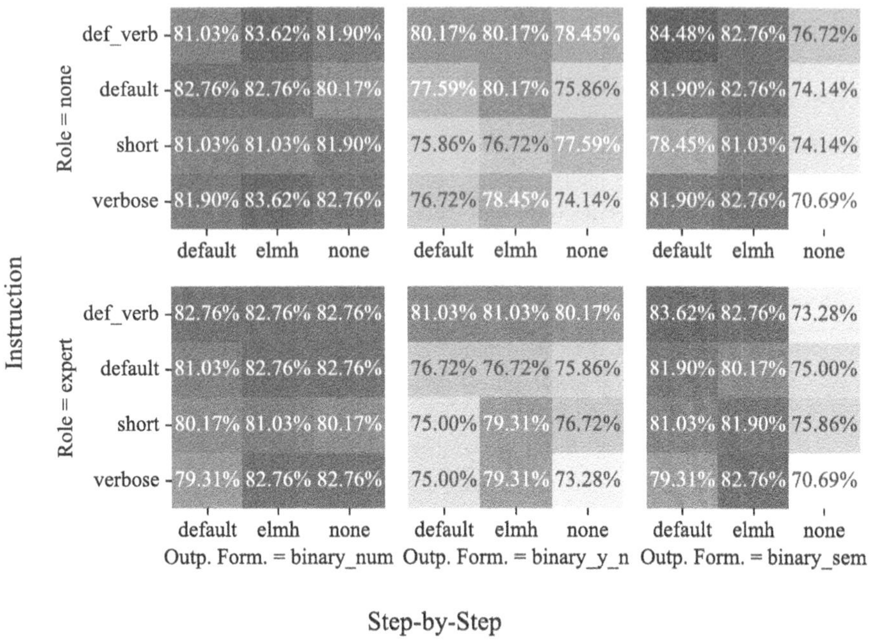

Fig. 2. Total Accuracy of StableBeluga2 for each prompt variant

7 Conclusion

In this paper, we evaluated multiple state-of-the-art LLMs using different prompt variants on the task of identifying cease and desist violations in German product descriptions. We ran evaluations for 5 LLMs (2 proprietary, 3 open source) with 72 prompt variants (consisting of 4 different components) each on a manually curated dataset of 116 examples. Our objective was to determine the superior model for this particular task (**RQ1**) and to understand the influence of prompt variations on model performance (**RQ2**).

For **RQ1**, our evaluation reveals that `StableBeluga2` outperformed the other models, achieving the highest metrics in both accuracy and micro F1 score. Additionally, `StableBeluga2` proved to be the most reliable, consistently delivering high performance with minimal variance across prompts. Following closely behind were `Platypus2` and `gpt-3.5-turbo-0301`, which also exhibited high performance for the most effective prompt variants but showed significant variations depending on the specific prompt. Although `gpt-3.5-turbo-0613` demonstrated good performance in optimal conditions, it was highly sensitive to the choice of prompt and ultimately yielded a low average performance. `LLaMA2` was the worst-performing model, scoring lowest in both average and peak performance.

Regarding **RQ2**, our experiments demonstrate that the choice of prompt can have a significant impact on model performance. This variation can be attributed to the difficulty some prompts introduce in task comprehension for the model. Additionally, some prompts lead to an increased number of invalid outputs, consequently lowering the overall performance. We found that there was no significant difference between including a role in the prompt versus omitting it. Similarly, providing the model with a detailed versus a short instruction only had a low impact on performance. However, generally speaking, providing a step-by-step instruction decreased model performance significantly compared to not providing one - both in terms of total accuracy, taking invalid outputs into account, as well as accuracy, leaving out invalid outputs. Moreover, the performance was highest when using a "yes"/"no" output format, compared to semantic or numeric output formats.

We also observed that several of these results were highly dependent on the particular model. For example, the highest performance for `gpt-3.5-turbo-0301` and `StableBeluga2` were achieved with a numeric or semantic output format, not a "yes"/"no" format. Similarly, when a step-by-step instruction was present, these models appeared to perform better on raw identification but worse on total accuracy. Thus, the optimal prompt is highly dependent on the employed LLM and only few general recommendations can be made independent of models.

As part of the KIVEDU project, this evaluation provides a promising assessment of the application of LLMs for the detection of cease and desist violations in German product descriptions. It demonstrates that AI can support and automate the current process to ensure consumer rights and foster fair competition. In future work, we aim to conduct a more comprehensive evaluation that encompasses additional LLMs, a broader range of prompt variants, including one-shot and few-shot prompting, as well as multiple languages and an expanded dataset. In addition, we plan to fine-tune the tested LLMs with domain-specific data to further improve performance.

References

1. Beeching, E., et al.: Open LLM Leaderboard (2023). https://huggingface.co/spaces/HuggingFaceH4/open_llm_leaderboard
2. Braun, D., Matthes, F.: NLP for consumer protection: battling illegal clauses in german terms and conditions in online shopping. In: Proceedings of the 1st Workshop on NLP for Positive Impact, pp. 93–99. Association for Computational Linguistics, Online (2021). https://doi.org/10.18653/v1/2021.nlp4posimpact-1.10
3. Braun, D., Scepankova, E., Holl, P., Matthes, F.: Consumer protection in the digital era: the potential of customer-centered LegalTech. In: David, K., Geihs, K., Lange, M., Stumme, G. (eds.) INFORMATIK 2019: 50 Jahre Gesellschaft für Informatik - Informatik für Gesellschaft, pp. 407–420. Gesellschaft für Informatik e.V., Bonn (2019). https://doi.org/10.18420/inf2019_58
4. Chakrabarti, D., et al.: Use of artificial intelligence to analyse risk in legal documents for a better decision support. In: TENCON 2018 - 2018 IEEE Region 10 Conference, pp. 0683–0688. IEEE, Jeju, Korea (South) (2018). https://doi.org/10.1109/TENCON.2018.8650382

5. Chen, L., Zaharia, M., Zou, J.: How is ChatGPT's behavior changing over time? (2023). https://doi.org/10.48550/arXiv.2307.09009, http://arxiv.org/abs/2307.09009, arXiv:2307.09009
6. Contissa, G., et al.: Claudette meets GDPR: automating the evaluation of privacy policies using. Artif. Intell. (2018). https://doi.org/10.2139/ssrn.3208596
7. Devlin, J., Chang, M.W., Lee, K., Toutanova, K.: BERT: pre-training of deep bidirectional transformers for language understanding (2019). https://doi.org/10.48550/arXiv.1810.04805
8. European Commission: 2016/0148 (COD) Cooperation between national authorities responsible for the enforcement of consumer protection laws (2016). https://eur-lex.europa.eu/legal-content/EN/TXT/?uri=celex:52016PC0283
9. Hu, E.J., et al.: LoRA: Low-rank adaptation of large language models (2021). https://doi.org/10.48550/arXiv.2106.09685, http://arxiv.org/abs/2106.09685, arXiv:2106.09685
10. Juranek, S., Otneim, H.: Using machine learning to predict patent lawsuits (2021). https://doi.org/10.2139/ssrn.3871701
11. Lee, A.N., Hunter, C.J., Ruiz, N.: Platypus: quick, cheap, and powerful refinement of LLMs. arXiv preprint arxiv:2308.07317 (2023)
12. Lippi, M., et al.: Automated detection of unfair clauses in online consumer contracts. In: Legal Knowledge and Information Systems, pp. 145–154. IOS Press (2017). https://doi.org/10.3233/978-1-61499-838-9-145
13. Lippi, M., et al.: CLAUDETTE: an automated detector of potentially unfair clauses in online terms of service. Artif. Intell. Law **27**(2), 117–139 (2019). https://doi.org/10.1007/s10506-019-09243-2
14. Liu, Q., Wu, H., Ye, Y., Zhao, H., Liu, C., Du, D.: Patent litigation prediction: a convolutional tensor factorization approach. In: International Joint Conference on Artificial Intelligence (2018). https://doi.org/10.24963/ijcai.2018/701
15. Mahan, D., Carlow, R., Castricato, L., Cooper, N., Laforte, C.: Stable beluga models. https://huggingface.co/stabilityai/StableBeluga2
16. Mishra, S., Khashabi, D., Baral, C., Choi, Y., Hajishirzi, H.: Reframing instructional prompts to GPTk's language. In: Findings of the Association for Computational Linguistics: ACL 2022, pp. 589–612. Association for Computational Linguistics, Dublin, Ireland (2022). https://doi.org/10.18653/v1/2022.findings-acl.50, https://aclanthology.org/2022.findings-acl.50
17. Mukherjee, S., Mitra, A., Jawahar, G., Agarwal, S., Palangi, H., Awadallah, A.: Orca: progressive learning from complex explanation traces of GPT-4 (2023). https://doi.org/10.48550/arXiv.2306.02707, http://arxiv.org/abs/2306.02707, arXiv:2306.02707
18. OpenAI: Introducing ChatGPT (2022). https://openai.com/blog/chatgpt
19. Shanahan, M., McDonell, K., Reynolds, L.: Role-play with large language models (2023). https://doi.org/10.48550/arXiv.2305.16367, http://arxiv.org/abs/2305.16367, arXiv:2305.16367
20. Shi, F., et al.: Large language models can be easily distracted by irrelevant context (2023). https://doi.org/10.48550/arXiv.2302.00093, http://arxiv.org/abs/2302.00093, arXiv:2302.00093
21. Touvron, H., et al.: Llama 2: open foundation and fine-tuned chat models (2023). https://doi.org/10.48550/arXiv.2307.09288, http://arxiv.org/abs/2307.09288, arXiv:2307.09288
22. Trappey, C.V., Trappey, A.J.C., Liu, B.H.: Identify trademark legal case precedents - Using machine learning to enable semantic analysis of judgments. World Patent Inf. **62**, 101980 (2020). https://doi.org/10.1016/j.wpi.2020.101980

23. Vaswani, A., et al.: Attention is all you need. In: Advances in Neural Information Processing Systems, vol. 30. Curran Associates, Inc. (2017)
24. Waidelich, L., Lambert, M., Al-Washash, Z., Kroschwald, S., Schuster, T., Döring, N.: Using Large Language Models for the Enforcement of Consumer Rights in Germany. In: Maślankowski, J., Marcinkowski, B., Rupino da Cunha, P. (eds.) Digital Transformation, pp. 1–15. LNBIP, Springer Nature Switzerland, Cham (2023). https://doi.org/10.1007/978-3-031-43590-4_1
25. Wei, J., et al.: Chain-of-Thought prompting elicits reasoning in large language models (2023). https://doi.org/10.48550/arXiv.2201.11903, http://arxiv.org/abs/2201.11903, arXiv:2201.11903
26. Zhao, W.X., et al.: A survey of large language models (2023). http://arxiv.org/abs/2303.18223, arXiv:2303.18223
27. Ziegler, D.M., et al.: Fine-Tuning language models from human preferences (2020). https://doi.org/10.48550/arXiv.1909.08593, http://arxiv.org/abs/1909.08593, arXiv:1909.08593

Author Index

G. Broccia and A. Cerone (Eds.): DataMod 2023, LNCS 14618, p. 165, 2025.
https://doi.org/10.1007/978-3-031-87217-4

The manufacturer's authorised representative in the EU is Springer Nature Customer Service Centre GmbH, Europaplatz 3, 69115 Heidelberg, Germany. If you have any concerns regarding our products, please contact ProductSafety@springernature.com

Printed and bound by CPI Group (UK) Ltd, Croydon, CR0 4YY
30/09/2026
02225576-0013